A LITTLE LEARNING

Libby Purves is one of the best known educational journalists in the UK. Her name is instantly recognised not only by education professionals but by the public at large through her broadcasting on the BBC, whether as host of the talk show *Midweek* or as presenter of the weekly Radio 4 education programme *The Learning Curve*.

This collection of the best of her writing in *The Times Educational Supplement* covers everything from issues of policy to touching tales of real life in school. Her writing is at times political, at others witty and uplifting, but it will repay reading and re-reading for both entertainment and information. She manages to write in a style that is both erudite and approachable.

Grouped into bite-size sections looking at key topics for teachers, the topics range from 'Ministerial madness' to 'What's it all really for?'. This book is a refreshing and uplifting information source for all those interested and involved in the education sector.

Libby Purves is a broadcaster and journalist, based in the UK.

A LITTLE LEARNING

Broodings from the Back of the Class

Libby Purves

Routledge
Taylor & Francis Group

LONDON AND NEW YORK

the TES

First published 2007
by Routledge
2 Park Square, Milton Park, Abingdon, Oxon, OX14 4RN

Simultaneously published in the USA and Canada
by Routledge
270 Madison Avenue, New York, NY 10016

Routledge is an imprint of the Taylor & Francis Group, an informa business

© 2007 Libby Purves
Illustrations © Bill Stott

Typeset in Galliard by
RefineCatch Limited, Bungay, Suffolk
Printed and bound in Great Britain by
Cromwell Press, Trowbridge, Wiltshire

British Library Cataloguing in Publication Data
A catalogue record for this book is available from the British Library

Library of Congress Cataloging in Publication Data
A catalog record for this book has been applied for

ISBN10: 0–415–41708–2 (hbk)
ISBN10: 0–415–41709–0 (pbk)
ISBN10: 0–203–96780–1 (ebk)

ISBN13: 978–0–415–41708–2 (hbk)
ISBN13: 978–0–415–41709–9 (pbk)
ISBN13: 978–0–203–96780–5 (ebk)

Contents

Introduction

As the 20th century limped towards its close, I found myself invited to occupy a space once a fortnight on the back page of *The Times Education Supplement*. I am not sure why. It is a serious and distinguished journal, and my broodings, musings and ravings were alternating with those of the late Professor Ted Wragg of Exeter University, who knew the educational field backwards and had long fought his corner for humane and sane education and the status of the front-line teacher. I, on the other hand, am neither teacher, educationalist, nor even a dinner lady. I did think of teaching, but bottled out in 1968. I am an outsider.

Perhaps they wanted a parent; perhaps just a nosy parker with an incurable taste for hanging around schools: the sort of mother who keeps volunteering as a classroom assistant and has to be beaten off with a stick. Or perhaps they had somehow heard about my own education, conducted as a travelling diplo-brat in Israel, Bangkok, Walberswick, Lille, Krugersdorp and Tunbridge Wells. They may have thought I could provide exotic cultural contrast. Or maybe it was just that spurious sheen of knowledge which you get from presenting an education programme on Radio 4, surrounded by ferociously bright specialist producers who download their brains into yours for short periods, thus creating the illusion that you actually understand such arcana as YELLIS and MIDYIS and national admissions policy (oh, come on, not even the Minister understands that). Perhaps they heard about our own family travails, how we started our children off in a wonderful village primary, fully intending to stay with the state till 18, and how through many vicissitudes, upsets and governmental acts of sabotage we ended up with two teenagers boarding at a socially mixed but traditionally run naval-charity school in Suffolk. Educating a child today is an education in itself.

However it came about, with some trepidation I took *The TES* space and enjoyed it immoderately. Nothing, after all, is more central and vital to civilization than education. No memories raise more weird emotional responses in adults than the ghosts of their own schooldays; no prospect makes parents more nervous than the thought of entrusting their young to a strange building smelling of chalk, trainers and disinfectant (unless, of course, it is the prospect that the young will emerge 13 years later unemployable). Moreover, few political topics in the UK today are hotter than education; and because children are messy and diverse, few workplaces generate as many laughs as schools do. Importance, emotion, comedy, even a dash of romance – what more can you want in a subject?

So here are some of the columns again. They crop up in no chronological order, so you will find yourself wafted back to forgotten scares, lost policies, bygone heroes and villains. Ah, memory lane! Remember Tessa Jowell's 'Toolkit' for non-competitive sports days? Chris Woodhead's resignation as Chief Inspector? The Millennium, the Jubilee, the debates about Middle Schools and top-up fees and girls in trousers? Remember the teacher who let her towel drop provocatively on Big Brother, the brouhaha about mini-scooters, Lenny Henry playing a superhead in *Hope and Glory*? It all flooded back. Various loopy preoccupations of my own came with it: the foundation of CARRUT – the Campaign for the Respect of Real University Teaching, the Voldemort City Academy, the usefulness of chair-stacking, the inestimable value of a School Dog, the theory that citizenship can be taught almost entirely through singing ... they're here, too. And so are some of Bill Stott's cartoons, which have often been a lot funnier and more to the point than what I wrote in the first place. Nobody draws a 14-year-old minx or a decrepit geography teacher with more loving hilarity than Bill.

Looking back, though, over six years' worth of columns, my main reaction was to wonder how I ever had the nerve. Pulling the cuttings out of the folder, I kept noticing trailers on the side of them for the proper content of *The TES*: school budgets, the struggles of teachers in Uganda, anorexia in boys, the shameful educational neglect of children in care, exam standards, the language teaching crisis, maths for engineering students. Proper topics, properly tackled, while on the back page I just tap-danced around with my comedy hat over my eyes, indulging in mad blue-sky thinking and happy reminiscence.

It was even more unnerving when I was being serious, and inadvertently tapped into the occasional vein of pure boiling hatred. Strewth, education does raise the passions! The letters column and *The TES* website were bad enough at times, but the magisterial tone of letters that thudded onto my own breakfast-table was plain terrifying. I have always thought of myself as a bit of an old fuddy-duddy in my approach to parenthood and education, but when in spring 2000 I had the nerve to applaud the courtroom victory of Summerhill 'free' School over a particularly hateful and bullying OFSTED, someone purporting to be a former head wrote:

'I can just guess what sort of home you run, you with your ultra-liberal trendy views. Let me guess. In your no doubt Islington circle, the children are ungoverned, spoilt, foul-mouthed, idle and intransigent, a prey to drugs, incapable of learning anything by heart, sloppily dressed and engaged in premature relationships which you, with your lip-service to freedom, will encourage them to pursue under your own roof. Such children grow up with no understanding of discipline, tradition, culture or patriotism.'

Gulp. I looked around wildly, with that fatal assumption we all tend to make that a Headmaster must somehow know best. But that very week one of my children (in rural Suffolk, not Islington) was playing Lady Bracknell, word-perfect and deploying an accent of such dowagerish authority that it clearly came from years of careful observation of the Pony Club instructresses under whom she had toiled, rising at dawn in the holidays to polish her hairy little mount. Her brother, meanwhile, was busy drilling a squad of 20 younger boys, in bell-bottoms and naval kerchiefs, for a ceremonial parade in front of the Second Sea Lord with a band playing 'Heart of Oak'. For a trendy ultraliberal, I plainly wasn't trying hard enough to persuade them into sex 'n' drugs and rock 'n' roll. Poor demented old Head, though: you have to feel sorry for anyone with blood pressure like that.

Still, I don't know how I had the nerve. Teachers still inspire me with the awe they always did: magical beings, performing daily miracles like getting a whole roomful of lairy five-year-olds singing 'The Wheels of the Bus', understanding physics, and confronting huge knuckle-dragging boys with quiet aplomb. How dare I write of their world? I feel my courage failing again, even now. If it wasn't for the chance to show off Bill's cartoons one more time, I wouldn't be doing this at all.

Libby Purves 2007

Apple for the teacher, bananas for the head

Like a red rag

A Hampshire headmaster, I hear to my joy, is planning to change school uniform because part of it is red. He has heard that red encourages aggression, tension and behaviour problems, and wants a colour more conducive to peaceful concentration. Pastel blue, perhaps, or Hare Krishna yellow. Or perhaps good old bottle-green or battleship grey, as worn with loathing by generations of grammar-school swots. At the moment, he says darkly, the children en masse are 'a sea of red' which his consultant psychologist says may accentuate aggression.

Well, this is why one loves headmasters so much. At their best, they relieve their solid humdrum virtues with a rich vein of lunacy rarely achieved by headmistresses. But this particular example struck a chord with me, since the school where I spent four years just happened to have a uniform whose brown skirt was jazzed up by a a bright red cardigan, bright red sweater and – to top it off – a bright red cloak with a hood, of the kind worn by little girls tripping through the forest with basketfuls of goodies for bedridden transvestite wolves.

The learned nuns liked the red. Never having done a course in colour psychology as part of their novitiate, they merely thought it 'cheerful', and the older ones would sometimes observe senti-mentally that we looked like little robin redbreasts hopping around. Local youths in the park also failed to recognise our dangerousness, and shouted 'Santa Claus!' at us as we slouched by on Sunday walks.

I have been cudgelling my brains to remember any occasion when the redness made us aggressive. A control is available: in the summer we slopped around in cotton print shifts which looked like some-thing run up for a wartime orphanage, I remember feeling quite aggressive about those, with no red in sight.

I do not recall hair-pulling or pinching breaking out in the winter terms when the whole school was muffled up in garish scarlet, although I do remember tying up a small friend in a large cloak and rolling her downhill like a ball (at her own request, I hasten to say.

In those days one made one's own fun). I also remember that there were brown reefer jackets as an alternative to cloaks, but that they were generally regarded as inferior, possibly because they made it harder to smuggle in bottles of Merrydown cider and unauthorised rabbits.

But science marches on, and it would be impolite to question the 'academic research' on which the Hampshire school bases its fears.

Possibly we need even more rigorous research on the effect of uniforms on school ambience. Red is the least of their problems. There are far more urgent issues.

Take pleats. Pleated skirts, say my research sources, are a root cause of depression in older schoolgirls. You sit down a lot, at school.

The rooms are warm, the seats hard wood. Your pleats, one by one, give up the unequal struggle with your backside. You stand up. You smooth your skirt; and you know without looking that there is a depressing flat bit forming, in which your bum definitely does look big. You are going to have to iron this skirt with as much care as if you loved it.

Suddenly life seems pointless.

The A-line skirt, beloved of the bog-standard British school, is not a lot better. There are very good reasons why fashion gave up the A-line in 1969. A sort of dreary, tubal pointlessness infuses it; again the risk of depression looms large. As for the boys, what does it do to a lad to wear grey socks which wrinkle down? Or shorts beyond the age of four?

And blazers! You could make a worryingly good case for the theory that blazers make children more right-wing. For all the attempts of fashion to vary them, there is something about putting on a double-breasted blazer which causes an invisible Jimmy Edwards moustache to sprout on your upper lip, a Leslie Phillips leer to twist beneath it, and your hand to start groping for a gin-and-pink and a golf club. When some schools are out, the whole town seems infested with miniature Terry-Thomas clones from 1955.

When the blazers are striped, you add the extra risk of fixating the children, to the point that they can only ever be happy in a career as a deckchair attendant or city trader. I have no time to share my research on the peril of badges (how do you suppose the head prefect and captain of games cope at university stripped of insignia? Their whole life post-school must be like one long military disgrace).

But the question of ties must be faced. The morality watchdogs must speak out. Pop psychology has known for years that a woman adjusting a man's tie symbolises something saucily different. Are schoolchildren old enough for this blatant suggestiveness? We need a national debate. It is never too late to panic.

MARCH 12 2004

In praise of *The Beano*

A spell of looking after my brother's house and two fine nephews brings an unexpected literary bonus. Technically, I am spending the school day beavering away at the next novel, with cultural interludes at the local museums; but given the younger lad's matchless collection of old Beanos. I have to admit that a considerable amount of time has been spent lying on the sofa reacquainting myself with the noble and timeless canon of DC Thomson's masterwork.

The Beano is just as I remember it. Incredibly, children in this knowing, neurotic, stress-obsessed, streetwise age are still offered the carefree macho mischief of Dennis the Menace and the low cunning of Roger the Dodger.

The couch potato generation is taken back to an era of homemade go-karts and grubby knees. Little girls, normally enjoined by every shopping mall and horrid moppet-magazine to dress like miniature hookers and bat their eyes at boy bands, are still supplied with the alternative robustness of Minnie the Minx and Ivy the Terrible. The sons and daughters of the empathetic, child-centred education age are still buying and reading The Bash Street Kids, and entering their world of authority-baiting, atavistically braving the swishing of canes and the thundering of headmaster. I find this all strangely reassuring. Psychologists could explain it: even the most pampered child suffers a sense of powerlessness, and the Beano gang offer a brief blessed escape into a parallel world of bouncy revolt.

I have to admit, though, that I had my own spell of revolt against the Beano in my children's first years at primary school. They read it, but I was uneasy. The Bash Street Kids quite seriously upset me then: what I saw were gentle loving children in a gentle loving village school, where the teachers were not mortarboarded foes from Planet 1950 but just another set of caring friendly adults, aunts and uncles and mentors. When a French primary class was held hostage by a gunman, and it was on the news that the teacher had chosen heroically to stay with her charges, my eldest (aged about seven) said with scorn 'Of course she stayed, she was the *teacher*'.

Teachers to him were good: they led and protected you. So the Beano vision of ragging and raging seemed to me, for that brief idyllic period, a downright insult.

Now I look afresh, and understand the need for caricature and rebellion. But there is something else there too which I had never noticed. The Bash Street Kids and their longsuffering 'Teecher' are bound together in a way that is not entirely negative. The real enemy, frankly, is the Headmaster, before whom Teecher has to grovel; often his rampaging kids actually step in to save his face.

In one episode, the scene opens on a normal day when the Kids have hung Teecher up from the ceiling by his ankles and are bouncing footballs off his head and fighting on the desks, with Smiffy bashing Plug's nose (Ouch! Ooof! Splat!). A lawyer comes in and informs Teecher that he has inherited a castle in Scotland, whereon he resigns joyfully; but the Kids – desperate to see it – start dusting him off and buffing his moustache with a clothesbrush and pleading to be taken there. And they are: the whole mob of them, although it turns out to be only a bouncy castle.

In another story he wins the lottery, slaps a note on the Headmaster's nose saying 'I quit! YAHOO!' and drives off in a gold-plated car to fly to the sun. Inevitably, the Kids have stowed away in the overhead luggage lockers – they cannot conceive of life without him. After a lot of fighting and chaos (Thud! Boot! Biff! Swoosh! Wahey!) the whole lot of them are strapped together and thrown out of the plane on to a desert island. Here, resourceful as ever, they catch fish and make a fire and build a shelter.

Teecher, as a matter of course, shares the tent they make out of Fatty's shirt, says 'Well done!' when they get the campfire going, and relishes the fish dinner (Guzzle! Slurp!). Unfortunately, it turns out that Smiffy lit the fire with the million pounds in bank-notes, so they send a message in a bottle and poor old Teecher has to go back and grovel to the Head yet again, to get his tough old job back.

But you see what I mean? Teecher and the Kids are bound together, they belong together, they are a tribe. There is loyalty there, a devil-you-know attachment, a sort of love. They are in competition but not in mutual contempt. It's not such a bad picture, really. Splat! Oof!

OCTOBER 26 2000

Lessons for leaders

Hooray! Into our parched lives drop the healing words of the National College of School Leadership. From this week, you can build your own head-teacher in five easy-to-follow key stages.

We are offered a 'leadership development framework' which will 'ensure' ongoing development throughout a head's career. So if any of you lot are skulking in your offices muttering 'Psha, I finished developing 10 years ago, bog off', you can forget it. I am particularly intrigued by the idea of the 'five stages of leadership' and have prepared some helpful worksheets which go something like this:

Stage 1: say boo! to goose.

Stage 2 (still easy): deny day off to NQT who might cry.

Stage 3: (tougher) tell hulking, crew-cut, ex-territorial head of D & T department that no, there is absolutely no question of replacing the lathe before 2004.

Stage 4: inform mass meeting of parents that 200 completed GCSE papers got inadvertently posted into the wheelie-bin by a member of staff who cannot now be traced.

Stage 5: Tell Miss Mountshaft (estd. 1963 in the music department) that no, this is not a very tactful year to put on her cherished production of *The Desert Song*.

There may be fabulous, inspired, life-enhancing stuff in the real guidelines, but my instinctive nervousness comes from having watched the world change through my own working life. It is apparent to the idlest eye that the notion of 'management training' has somehow crept out of its natural home in the jampot of industry, dripped off the spoon and spread like a sweet viscous stain across the national tablecloth. This managerialist ethic says that if you can run a ginger-biscuit factory then you can run the BBC; and that a school or college presents challenges no different from a chain of theme pubs.

The result is a generation of bright-eyed, well-groomed, smiling clones with a penchant for going on about 'the three Cs' or 'the two big Hs'. They love flip-charts and consultants and stupid gimmicks such as having no desk, or writing the days of the week on the doormat. They refer to people as 'human resources' and draw complicated diagrams on the tablecloth. They are quite seductive, actually, flickering with a sort of chilly-blue electricity. Unfortunately, they often have little grasp of what the organisation actually does, and after a while flounce back to the biscuit factory muttering about defeat at the hands of an 'entrenched culture'.

This is a risk in every profession, but particularly in schools. I once went to a conference of middle-school headteachers, and discovered that they had spent the morning schmoozing around local factories. 'Oh,' I said, 'to see what sort of employers waiting for your kids? Good idea.'

'No,' said the organisers, scandalised, 'to learn about line-management techniques.' Whereon I got stroppy and harangued them with my heartfelt belief that schools have little to learn from commerce and industry. This is not least because the first thing a management guru would say on contemplating some of our schools would be: 'Sack your suppliers, they're giving you rubbish kids to work with, order in some better ones.' This would not, even today, go down terribly well with the clientèle. So let us hope that the leadership college accepts the uniqueness of schools and the batty diversity of good heads. I have known jolly ones, jokey ones and painfully shy ones who can't handle parents but are adored by children. I have known meeters-and-greeters, smarmballs and ascetics, remote scholarly figures who impress from afar and hearty ones who gallop onto the football pitch. All have their good points; including the former head who, when asked by the school newspaper: 'Sir, what do you do all day?' replied grandly: 'I sit in my office, and I Care.'

The chief thing, the unteachable thing, is to lead from the front and be fearless. Think of Mayor Giuliani amid the rubble, scolding and encouraging and keeping the show on the road. Opening his own post in the anthrax panic, he reminds me of my first BBC boss, a sweetly vague old boy who, during the IRA letter-bomb campaign, trundled in early every morning to defuse the post so the receptionist wouldn't have to. Lead from the front, keep your nerve, care. Maybe five key stages will help. But I'm not sure.

JUNE 4 2004

Shocked by staff rooms

This is a bit embarrassing. I am always aware, when sprawling around in this space, that I am not a teacher. Quite wanted to be, eyed up a couple of postgraduate certificate in education courses – but bottled out. So I exist here only as parent, journalist, school governor, intrusive novelist and general hanger-on to the coat-tails of education. If you mighty teachers are rugby legend Jonah Lomu, hammering up and down the pedagogical field against all odds, I am the spotty fan with a rattle in the back row of the stands. It is not my place to tell you what to think.

But someone must be frank. You must control yourselves, you really must. When you feel that hand itching for the mouse, when the shimmering screen lures you and the warm, welcoming arms of *The TES* website enfold you at the end of a bruising day, you mustn't give in. You are still on display.

This cyber staffroom has got a large picture window, and all the rest of us – parents, governors, journalists – are out there pressing our greasy noses to that window and gasping. You are shocking us. We get upset easily.

It began a few months ago when the savvy education correspondent of the *Telegraph*, John Clare, was answering a question about sarky teachers and quoted some of the put-downs suggested by contributors to *The TES* online forum.

They were breathtakingly nasty: 'I bet your village is missing its idiot' and 'I hope you look forward to life on the dole' were among the pleasanter ones; others were targeted mercilessly at the insecurities and unhappinesses of adolescence. These were mean bastards, and proud of it. We gulped, and hoped that they were a minority.

From then on I got interested in the forum, and have to say that by and large it reflects well on the profession and its attitudes, with most of the jokes well within the bounds of acceptability. As one said, think of it as Primal Scream therapy. I liked the dilemma of the teacher facing parents' evening and wondering whether 'to give

it to 'em both barrels about what arseholes their kids really are. Should I?'

One could sympathise. I also liked the sociological observations about whether you can tell how tough a class will be by the names in the register: Liam and Kyle are trouble, but interestingly so is Jessica (though Sophie is a goody-goody, obviously). The cowboy names, says one sage, are always the ones to watch: Dwayne, Wayne, Ryan, Lee. Girls beginning with 'Ch' are dodgy, especially Chantelle.

Well, fine. It's interesting. It's shop-talk. It's fun to press your nose to the staffroom window and make a mental note that your little Dwayne and Charmaine may be up against prejudice when they hit Reception.

But then suddenly a harmless observation by David Waugh on the boredom of exam invigilation loosed another flood of evil teachers onto the website, and the watchful journalists spotted it again and revealed you in all your splendid nastiness. Playing 'chicken' with the other invigilator is fine, and we can put up with squeaky-shoe concerts, but do we anxious parents, with chicks going through public exams, really want to know that some of you are playing 'Ugly', by trying to stare out the ugliest kid in the room? Or competing as to who can hand out most unwanted fresh paper to bewildered brats who didn't want it? Or playing 'Good kid, bad kid' quizzes with the other teacher?

Look, as I said, this is embarrassing. We should know really that you're only human, and need to blow off steam. We shouldn't be surprised if you express the odd cynical view, find some children nicer to look at than others, or yawn at the tedium of watching young minds grappling with the most important hours of their fledgling careers. But we really don't want to know, OK?

We want to imagine that each of you is Mr Chips, and that as you stride the aisles of the exam hall you are looking down benevolently on the efforts of anxious youth, wishing them well, exuding affectionate hope for their futures.

It would be nice if a few of you were praying; nuns at my school used to invigilate while saying their Rosary. A lot of you, no doubt, are indeed doing something along those lines, either sacred or secular.

But it would be a real favour to us outsiders if the rest of you – Mr Nasty, Miss Cynical, Dr Pissedoff – would just keep off the public websites and confine your primal screaming to the saloon bar of the Pedagogue's Arms after hours. We're easily shocked. We need to believe that you're better than us: more patient, more dedicated, cleverer.

I'm off for the smelling-salts now, and an hour in a darkened room.

Correction!

I am walking-wounded, definitely bruised. Always am, at this time of year: it's when the typescript of the latest novel comes back from the copy-editor. And believe me, this particular juncture of an author's life takes you straight back to the school experience, complete with tantrums, tears, and plummeting self-esteem.

Copy editors are ruthless people. Their chief function is to make sure that the text is clearly prepared for the printer, with house styles observed regarding single and double quote marks, etc. They are not there as literary critics, and must patiently plough through any amount of sentimental rubbish without wincing, turning a blind eye to cliché, weak characterization and barking-mad improbability, provided the chronology works and the heroine's hair doesn't keep changing colour.

But there is other territory too, a literary no-man's land where correctness is a matter of taste. Roaming this territory, swishing their pencils like Malacca canes, they display scornful views about commas and deadhead my flowering semi-colons. They draw wiggly lines under repetitions, sometimes intentional ones. They beg to differ about the way people talk: you may have heard your characters speaking in your head, but if the copy-editor prefers all characters to speak in correct grammar, or doesn't accept that the spelling 'yeh' correctly renders a particular kind of 'yes' – in goes their version and you furiously rub it out. They are ruthless about metaphors, too – 'Can an office be described as "worried?" ' they ask, with barely veiled contempt.

But then, just as you are about to drive round and kill them with your bare hands, they suddenly save your bacon by writing some essential, worried correction: 'Given that the boy is only 2 months old on p.154, how come it is sitting up?' or 'His car was dark blue on p.23'. Oh yes, we need them, as we need newspaper subs: but some copy editors have such an idiosyncratic approach that it is unwise for the sensitive author even to look at their strictures without a large indiarubber in the fist.

Such people – indispensible to quality and dangerous to self-esteem – are at their most infuriating when they are right. That is why they waft you back to your school years. Sometimes, coming to the end of a laboriously edited chapter, I have found myself looking round in a puzzled fashion for the mark. 8/10, surely? Or an alpha minus? Or maybe a sarcastic little comment like 'You would do better if you spent more time with the sources before you start' or 'A little too fond of your own theories, Elizabeth'.

Children care about their work as much as adults do; and I have always been fascinated, as a parent, by the different approaches teachers take to this very personal business of writing all over people's work with angry red pens. Comparing notes with friends, it would seem that in the primary sector there was a long period when it was unfashionable to red-pen every spelling mistake. 'It's all smiley faces' grumbled one parent, who kept his own green pen to do the corrective job. Only twice have I personally encountered the literate parent's nightmare: the situation where Teacher has flamboyantly corrected the child's spelling when the child was actually right. A friend had this happen so often to her bright 7-year-old that she remonstrated; the frost lasted all the way to Year 6.

More interesting is the text that sixth-form teachers deliver in the margin of essays in History and English. This I love: there can be a real sense of intellectual excitement in that ribbon of tiny writing, snaking up the side with 'Charles the Bold said something very similar, I can lend you the book' or 'cf Shelley, Alastor, II 12–128' or 'The point is that Garibaldi WOULD have known . . .'. Sometimes – as with a sympathetic fiction editor – marginalia are good company, part of shared enjoyment. Sometimes they are unsympathetic or malevolent. But you'd miss them if they weren't there.

I have a friend – a writer of argumentative history books – who delights in hauling out his own works in university libraries in the hope of finding marginal notes. He once found 'Wrong, wrong, wrong, you stupid git', but usually has to content himself with underlinings and exclamation marks. He has yet to share the experience related by Alan Bennett, who found a passage in a book marked by a long, wavering pencil line in the margin. He read it several times very attentively to try and see what had so moved the previous reader. After a while the line blew away: it was a hair.

Teachers are tribes too

Just at the start of the school year, it was dead thoughtful of the Government's FRANK drug service to supply a guide to teenage 'tribes'. Teachers, after all, grew up when it was only Mods and Rockers, or Punks and New Romantics. A few, nearing retirement, may possibly have been Teddy-boys. But a worrying number of us are probably old enough to remember a time when it was OK just to be an individual – albeit an unpolished one – and adults did not yet cower in respectful awe at the 'culture' of yoof. Some may even naïvely feel that it is possible for a 16-year-old to like several different kinds of music, and even clothing.

Anybody with such a laughably straightforward mind-set could get dangerously muddled trying to distinguish between Indies and Trendies, Gangstas and Skaters, Goths and Moshers. God forbid that a teacher should use the wrong word or fail to realise that 'minging' is not only the opposite of 'ba-aaad' (meaning 'good'), but belongs to a different tribe altogether. No: let the staffroom pin up the guide, remember never to say 'bling' to a Mosher, praise Travis to a Goth or confuse the gold hoop earrings of a female Scally with the i-Pod leads of a Trendy. Let them remember that a Gangsta will not thank you for asking whether the O'Neill hoodie left in the corner is his (only skaters wear O'Neill). Above all, let teachers try not to notice that only two categories – 'Geeks' and 'Sporties' – represent what they think of as a normal pleasant pupil.

However, it is clear that in this democratic age the pupils have equal rights to a guide to teachers' tribes. The Government is no doubt working on it. Secret leaks so far reveal the following categories: *Coolcats, Misfits, Tolerators, Understanders, Martinets, Timeservers, Artistes,* and *Prims.* Pay attention, kids: careful study of clothing, language and behaviour will reveal where your teacher is (as we yoof commentators say) coming from.

Coolcats are obvious. They took up teaching because they liked being leader of the pack at school and don't want to lose touch with teenage life. Usually male, they dress sharply, hate discipline, and secretly want to be Robin Williams. *Misfits* only took up teaching because a PGCE year was preferable to looking for a job. They hate it, and only carry on in the feeble hope of getting onto *That'll Teach 'Em* and kick-starting a media career.

Tolerators are gentle souls, in loose clothing, who believe that idleness or rudeness can be understood in terms of faulty upbringing. Their classes are chaos, and you need never hand in any homework. However, you can learn a surprising amount from them and they do at least like you. *Understanders* look similar on the surface, but in fact are failed therapists who have a toxic obsession with getting to the bottom of pupils' problems, even when pupils resist analysis and find their probings embarrassing.

Martinets are the strict ones: when they watch *That'll Teach 'Em* it is with wistful longing for the days when you could insult and hit pupils whenever you felt like it. They wear terrible string ties, and scowl a lot. *Timeservers* are often *Martinets* who have got weary, and bored with the modern inability to punish children savagely, so they are only staying on to bump up the pension a bit. You can identify them by the gardening catalogue they read during invigilations.

Which leaves the *Artistes* and the *Prims*. *Artistes* are more often male than female; they went into teaching because it provided a captive audience for their repertoire of jokes, funny accents, weirdly inventive classroom games and bursts of theatrically-enhanced rage. Bold boys love them. Timid ones and self-conscious girls are less keen, and prefer the final category: the *Prims*.

Prims are an ever-growing tribe. Often female, always tidy, they have thoroughly embraced the modern culture of safety, political correctness, written risk assessments, coursework and Sats. They find the literacy hour prescription reassuring, rather than insulting. They do things by the book, never lose books or turn up late, and mark all homework in small precise writing. Ofsted inspectors nod approvingly as they 'deliver' their lessons with monotone efficiency.

The trouble is that everyone else in the staffroom hates them, and would like to put nasty things into their neat little salad lunchboxes. But they don't dare. The *Prims* will all be deputy heads soon.

MAY 7 2004

Homework fails the test

Hoorah for headmaster Mr Elder, I say, even if he is one of those uppity prep school heads who frighten us all so much. He has drawn mainstream newspaper attention to himself by abolishing homework at his Scottish school, and he gives two reasons.

First, he says, parents help their children, and their meddling confuses them. Second, says this robust chap, home is for home life; children should learn to make their own judgements about things they want to study further when the long school day is done.

The first argument is one which only a smoothly confident head would dare to make, since while it is true that maths and science help from parents can be toxic, there are other areas in which educated parents quite often get seriously irritated by young teachers' errors – notably bad spelling and erroneous claims like 'Oval means eggshaped' (that one sent a friend of mine roaring down to his daughter's school, steam hissing out of his ears, crying 'Ovoid, Ovoid!').

But his second argument is bang on. Homework, certainly for the under-12s, is a sacred cow which is way overdue for the slaughterhouse. We have allowed it to creep downward through the age range until it now afflicts even children of six and seven.

Government prodnoses are forever preaching the importance of homework and setting silly targets about how many minutes per day each age should do; because they do not understand children and wish to appear to be 'driving up standards' without actually spending money.

Meanwhile, self-advertising schools make much of their homework demands because they want to give the impression that they are highly academic places full of aspiring, focused, middle-class children from homes full of books. And pushy, silly parents brag over coffee that their little Demetrius has 'at least an hour every night', to make other parents feel inferior and panicky.

But, from my observation, what really happens is that, more often than not, teachers set homework, not to improve children's learning, but because the school policy says they have to. Young children bring home dreary, repetitive, joyless tasks which teach them nothing new. The process often involves either a great deal of colouring-in, or thoroughly upsetting everybody as rows break out over the bizarre demands of New Maths.

And that is before all the other rows: the one about having the telly on while you work, the one about getting down to it before *The Simpsons*, or (with the more anxious child) the row over bedtime getting later and later because he is sitting up weeping over the infernal homework.

The result is that learning becomes associated with oppression, tension, misery and excuses. Conscientious little children struggle often for two hours after a long school day; feckless ones finish their homework on the bus. Parents get home from their own stressful days and are unable to enjoy their children's company because of the need to nag them. Children, desperate for a break, habitually tell lies about having no homework.

Different teachers get their wires crossed, so some nights there is hardly any whereas the next night there is three hours' worth. Heavy bagsful of books are carried to and from schools on young shoulders, foreshadowing a future epidemic of bad backs.

And when the stuff is actually handed in, are the teachers happy? No. They groan. Marking is just more work for them to do, and the three-way relationship between teacher, child and subject has been poisoned by resentment.

Of course there has to be some homework later on, at secondary school. Of course children gradually have to learn to do things alone, without someone standing over them. But primary school homework is not the way to do it.

In my ideal world a primary teacher would simply ask for a little bit of reading with parents in the first years, and thereafter set nothing compulsory for the hours after school. Children would be encouraged to explore ideas and subjects independently, as their own interest or sense of need dictated; books would be freely lent by the school for private reading, and anything brought in voluntarily by an enterprising child would be welcomed, praised and discussed.

And when the time came for formal homework, at 12 or so, the children would swell with pride at this badge of adulthood and positively enjoy bringing it home.

Oh, the dream!

APRIL 13 2001

Freddie hates nice Miss Horrid

It was mid-November and she was in a bit of a state.

Fretting, stalking up and down the kitchen, spilling her coffee, talking fast and nervously, unable to take a healthy interest in the latest spicy gossip of the school-gate set. Clearly a family crisis.

No – worse – a school crisis. After a smooth and cheerful introduction to the reception class and a starry first year ('Excellent progress in reading and number work, confident with others') the education process had hit its first terrible stumbling-block, the Nemesis that they never warn you about in the antenatal ward. The worst has happened. Her son hates his teacher.

Schoolteachers, worn smooth by living among the rough-and-tumble of mutually abrasive personalities year in, year out, probably don't understand how much a family frets over such matters. Staggering into the staffroom with a skirtful of poster-paints and alien snot, the front-line guerilla swigs back her coffee, raids the school secretary's Jaffa Cakes, tips a pile of DFEE leaflets off the comfy chair, and reflects that phew, so far all seems to be going OK with the 30 new moppets inherited from Year 1.

For her – or him – school is just a familiar working environment, safe and colourful and under control. Those children who remain enigmas after the first few weeks of the new year will, the teacher knows, be most likely to yield up the key to their personality in due course, and everyone will be friends. It'll all come out in the wash, it always has before. It's just school, that's all.

In the home, however, emotion seethes. New parents retain from early schooldays a set of flashing neon memories, and emotions which are suddenly raw all over again. Daddy remembers Mr Snogbin, who hit him with a ruler in 1963 for tipping back his chair. Mummy snivels at the long-buried memory of wetting herself in mixed infants and being issued with spare knickers by an unsympathetic Miss Pigwhistle in front of everybody. They quell their panic with difficulty, but empathy throbs within them every

time small Freddie announces that Miss Horrid hates him, that it is mutual, and that she is a bad witch.

Each morning, Freddie announces that he has a tummy ache. Everyone knows why. Mother and father are in despair: last year he loved Mrs Darling's class, the school has a shining reputation, and Miss Horrid was delightful on parents' evening. None of the other mothers has a child who hates her. And yet their life is blighted, day after day, by Freddie's insistence that she is Cruella deVil.

Apart from anything else, a hideous social dilemma confronts the parents. Six is too young to sort out your own incompatibilities, but what exactly is the etiquette for informing a cheerful, hard-working, kind teacher that your child can't stand her? How do you tell a transparently nice woman that she's an ogre? Mother snivels. Bravely, Father volunteers to have a word, but when Miss Horrid flashes him her saintly, teacherly smile he ends up muttering a few platitudes about reading schemes and fleeing back to the Volvo. Eventually Mother takes the initiative and asks for A Private Word.

'The thing is,' she pipes 'Freddie's terribly nervous, though he doesn't look it . . . and he's getting a bit stressed in the new class . . . and . . .' Miss Horrid reassures her. She'll give Freddie lots of individual attention. Mother panics, remembering the morning's scene ('She stares at me! She picks on me! She hates me! I hate her!') Mum starts to backtrack – 'Better to ignore him, perhaps? Let him find his own level?' She fiddles with her scarf and patient Miss Horrid eventually, gently brings the interview to a close because three other mothers are glaring balefully througt the glass door, waiting to bend her ear about dyslexia and missing inhalers.

Stalemate. Personally, I favour the direct approach.

'Look, there's something we have to work out, as a parent-teacher team. I have great respect for you as a professional and as it happens I really like you as a person, but we have to face the fact that for some weird reason Freddie hates you. We're going to have to work out a strategy for winning him round.' A more cowardly version substitutes the words 'is a bit scared of you' for 'hates you'.

But I would be fascinated to hear the teacher's side. How does it feel to be informed that a small child, who liked his last teacher, harbours a passionate burning dislike for you?

It must be even worse than those very personal bad reviews which set us novelists and broadcasters snivelling and brooding for days on end. What is the professional response? Do you want us to be honest with you, or would you rather not?

JUNE 22 2001

Sitting at the back, with raffia

I WAS going to make some jokes about exams, but facts beat me to it, wilder and more improbable. There was the girl who sat eight hours of exams in one day, the accidentally pre-marketed pure maths paper costing £400 a peep, and then the famous Impossible Physics Question about the moon from the Assessment and Qualification Alliance. Top marks to the school whose pupils were visibly 'distressed' by it; most of those canvassed didn't actually notice anything wrong.

That's physics A-level for you. My husband, reminiscing happily about his, has warned the new generation that physics practical is always a joy, involving grandiose yet cheeseparing questions along the lines of: 'Given that the speed of light is constant, use the beaker and string provided to prove the second law of thermodynamics.'

But, since exams this year come into the couldn't-make-it-up category, I shan't. Rather, let teachers note a small report in *The Times* about a psychologist employed by Odeon cinemas (I know, I know), Donna Dawson. She has been identifying personality types according to where people sit in the cinema. There are four types, which you may recognise from the classroom scuffle.

Those who make for the front row, she says, are 'extrovert, self-confident and assertive', bore easily, like action films and gangs of friends. This may be baffling for teachers, in whose experience the front row is monopolised by keen swots, while the easily bored extroverts make straight for the back row, to avoid close supervision and to have a wide range of necks at which to aim spitballs.

Those who head for the middle of a row in a cinema, says Ms Dawson, are 'flexible, adaptable and easy-going'. They head off aggression with humour. That might apply to classrooms, where humorists are certainly happier right in the middle so that as many people as possible can hear their jokes, and so that they have four directions in which to pass witty drawings.

Next, she tells us that those who go for the end of the row and bag aisle seats are 'detached observers, loners and eccentrics', who want more personal space and a quick escape. Now this might well apply to cinemas, with exits on both sides; but in classrooms we have a distinction to make.

Those who choose the aisle seats near the door plainly want to bolt for freedom. But a different, more mental form of escape is sought by those who go for the other end of the row, the window seats. They want to stare out at the sunshine and fantasise about flying out of the window like Batman. They also like the physical release of being asked to work the window-opening pole.

Ms Dawson's fourth type of cinemagoer is the kind found in the back row, who have 'trouble opening up to others'. Where they would sit in a classroom is problematical. They might indeed join the rioters in the back, but equally they might opt for the front row to fix the teacher with an insolent, borderline-psychotic stare in the hope of freaking her out.

When it comes to academic conferences, there is another research project waiting for the Odeon's in-house psychologist. Speaking as a seasoned chairperson of such conferences (they like an amateur in the hot-seat), I can tell you that the journalists always go for the second row, as near the exits as they can; that the front row is full of caring-professions who have sunny natures and nothing to hide; that headteachers like to be surrounded by other headteachers like wilde-beeste huddling for safety at a watering-hole; that the intent women in the middle whose hands shoot up simultaneously like synchron-ised swimmers are school nurses; that the man who ignores the flat writing-surface on the arm of his chair to scribble secretively on his knee is from the Office for Standards in Education; and that if you take a question from the back, it almost always turns out to be a really, really angry Scot who begins 'I've been teaching for 20 years . . .'

There should be more research like this. What can you learn about a teacher by whether he/she prefers to perch on the edge of the desk? Is it true that higher grades are generally achieved by pupils who tilt their chairs backwards, showing extrovert enjoyment of the subject? Would it be better if everyone sat in a circle on the floor for caring subjects such as PSE and poetry?

And was a whole generation blighted by being seated in form order, back in the days when – as the line in Victoria Wood's play has it – 'There was no such thing as dyslexia, you were sat at the back, with raffia'?

SEPTEMBER 14 2001

Thoughts for worms on the turn

THE worm is turning. Teachers are fed up with being insulted and regimented and made to do government paperwork. But teachers are a scarce commodity. We hear daily wither-wringing tales about schools fighting over the precious few pedagogues left, with the losers unwillingly forced to settle for knuckle-dragging, inadequates fresh from the hulks and sewers.

In Britain today, properly-qualified teachers are gold-dust. Everyone wants them. The laws of the market, therefore dictate that teachers have the upper hand. They are the better mousetrap, and the world is beating a path to their door. Only it doesn't feel that way, does it? Teachers feel just as fed up and put-upon as they always have done, and are hell-bent on making themselves even rarer by taking early retirement at, say, 33.

This is the situation, as laid out by our diligent media, and there has to be a solution. With the market-forces argument in view, a bracing headmistress and former OFSTED inspector wrote to the *Independent* this week. Resign, she said. Resign en masse, and then band together in regional associations and offer your services, under contract, to local authorities. Don't let them own you. Have clients, not bosses; be a contractor, not a serf. You may end up in exactly the same job in the same school, but it will feel different. You can lay down your conditions of work, demand extra money for bureaucratic chores and use that money to pay an assistant if you want. Your scarcity will make the paymasters meek and compliant. You will at last be free to do the job you trained for.

It is a wonderfully persuasive argument. All the forecasters say that the world is moving away from an employee-culture and towards a contract-culture. Free-lancing and contracting are the future. There will not be careers, set pay-scales, drearily slow upward slopes to retirement. Instead there will be clients and service providers and deals between them based on merit and availability. Why shouldn't this apply to teaching? In a small way it already does: the exodus from school jobs is eased by agency teachers, just as agency nurses staff the hospitals if and when it suits them. The boss, the generalissimo with guaranteed troop numbers to deploy, is the truly endangered species.

But beware. I am a freelance and I know the pitfalls. I became one in the late 1970s when although I dearly loved my radio work, I could no longer bear the repressive, clodhopping, patronising staff culture of the BBC. The straw that broke my back was its hideous habit of having your annual report read to you by some boss-class idiot who couldn't do your job to save his life. Assessments, personnel officers, attachments, civil service pay grades – pah, who needed that stuff? I walked down the road on my last day saying 'I am Libby Purves Limited, as good as my last gig!', spent my pension fund on loose living, and thereafter have been self-employed. Freelancing is not a life for the faint-hearted, nor for the disorganised. Since those who are rebellious enough to walk out of steady jobs are rarely very organised by nature, this presents problems. The contractor lives in a different world from the staffer. He or she must learn when to say yes or no to jobs, be endlessly pleasant and always on top form. Paperwork increases, only this time at home: you have to keep books, put away the tax money in a separate account, know whether you are VAT-able and pay money into a boring old pension run by some dodgy operator, because nobody else will care what happens to you when you are old. If you are a freelance contractor you can't throw sickies without losing money, and you certainly can't afford to stop delivering at full throttle and wreck your reputation just because you've got a new baby at home keeping you awake. Worst of all, you can't blame anybody but yourself when the work dries up. It is, however, a grand life if you don't weaken. You earn more, and make your own decisions about how long your holidays will be. Employers are more polite. The relationship of need and supply is clearer, and you never again get that glum feeling that you ought to be grateful to the kind people for giving you a job. You work because your work is needed and the proof is that your invoices get paid. You have a certain pride, which at times outweighs your terror. But before you hurl yourselves on the fire, think about it quietly for a bit with your head resting on a nice cool changing-room locker.

It's a big step.

Oh Sir, you are a card

My favourite toy right now is a pack of cards, produced by the Young Enterprise group at my children's old school. It is a variant on 'Top Trumps' entitled 'Teacher Trumps', in which 30 of the hapless staff of Royal Hospital school are photographed and allocated points according to years in post (the longest is 34), strictness, coolness, and hierarchy (though I notice that no one gets lower than five out of 10, which is prudent. It would be very wounding to a sensitive newly qualified teacher to score only one for hierarchy).

On the coolness scale, the top scorers are the deputy head, who is leaving – clearly a very cool thing to do – and one member of the craft and design technology department. The least cool is Mr Simmons, which is pretty ungrateful of the little beasts since he is the teacher in charge of the whole project. Mind you, he deserves it, since in the 'Did you know . . .?' box at the bottom of each card, the interesting fact he offers is: 'My favourite song is *Always look on the bright side of life.*'

This box at the bottom of each card has proved the most riveting insight into the staffroom that I have yet had, and that is after eight years as a governor, parent and aunt.

Some of the so-called 'Interesting Facts' offered by the staffroom are sporty CV stuff: being in lacrosse team, coaching for Zimbabwe, etc. Many are sedate in the extreme: they admit to being beekeepers, model railway enthusiasts, archaeologists, Carol Vorderman fans, listeners to *The Archers* – all that sort of teacherly thing.

One or two are sweetly personal – 'When I met my wife on a beach in Aberystwyth I was wearing big glasses and a duffel coat'. One is a bit unnerving, and will not be quoted because I do not want reprisals (you know who you are, Sir, and frankly, you should move on. Queen Victoria is dead.) The head plays safe with 'I have a passion for limestone landscapes', though I frankly fail to see how that deserves a seven for coolness. Though I suppose ogling headlands is a lot cooler than having a passion for Carol Vorderman. This coolness quotient at least has nothing to do with age: one veteran of 25 years at the school offers the fact that he was actually at the first-ever punk concert, the Sex Pistols' gig in Manchester.

But the joy of it is that when you offer teachers a chance to give you one interesting fact, you also get some splendidly wild insights into the early lives and skills of the modern pedagogue. You get a former professional jewellery designer, a chap who worked in the fingerprinting department at New Scotland Yard, and one who says darkly, without further explanation, 'I have appeared in *Byker Grove*. Twice'. Quiet, dignified Miss B 'used to ride horses bareback in a circus'. Gentle, pastoral Mrs F was 'once a bouncer in a London nightclub'. Dr S once spent a weekend at Balmoral (spookily, this seems to make him three points cooler than the Sex Pistols man). And so on.

This idea should spread. The cards are selling like hot cakes and have had to be reprinted. You don't need to get the copyright on Top Trumps: why not Happy Families, with teachers and support staff grouped by department? 'Have you got Miss Miles, the head of English? Thank you, and have you got Mr Miggins, the deputy? Thank you . . . and Ellen, the learning support assistant? Look, you must have – you're cheating . . .' Or perhaps you could have a version of Animal Snap, in which instead of making the noise each animal produces, you have to shout the catchphrase of each staff member ('Now do be quiet!' or 'If I have to say it once more!'). Or you could adapt that childhood favourite Old Maid, though that might be taken the wrong way.

Maybe you could move on and design a Monopoly board of school life with 'Go straight to detention, do not collect GCSE' and an opportunity to build coursework points if you land sufficiently often on the geography teacher. Or – if your school has sufficient superannuated punks, bouncers, bareback riders and limestone fanatics – it shouldn't take long to devise a riveting school version of Trivial Pursuit. 'Which member of the science department once owned a pair of attack Dobermanns called Pinky and Perky?' 'Whose PHSE lesson ended up being condemned in the *Daily Mail*?' 'How many of the history department can juggle?' 'Which female member of staff dated the schoolboy Hugh Grant when he still had spots?'

Everyone would buy a set. You'd coin it.

JUNE 27 2003

Unforgettable

I met Don Black the other day – East End boy turned global lyricist, the man who, more than 35 years, wrote the words of those songs you croon to yourself in the bath – 'Born Free', 'Diamonds are Forever', 'Love Changes Everything'. It led me to look over the words of 'To Sir with Love', as rendered somewhat brassily by Lulu and rather more soulfully by Vonda Shepherd on the Ally McBeal soundtrack.

I had forgotten what a startling, rare love song it is: a love song to a teacher, a guide and mentor and most beloved Sir. 'How do you thank someone' sings the chanteuse 'who has taken you from crayons to perfume?' This teacher is not the victim of Pink-Floydian cries of 'We don't need no education! . . . No dark sarcasm in the classroom! . . . Teacher! Leave those kids alone!' but 'a friend who taught me right from wrong, and weak from strong . . .'

Well, wow. What a great anthem for the end of another term, the sticky exhausted exam-soaked farewell to another school year. So prurient are we these days, so riveted by the possibility of head girls running off with maths masters and unbalanced supply teachers getting it on with priapic Year 11s, that we concentrate on preventing congress and elopement, and forget the pure and gentle old relationship, the platonic, grateful, sentimental affections that can arise in school life. To Sir, with Love. To Miss, in grateful memory. To the Best Head Ever. Sniff. Tears in the eyes.

Some friendships last forever: Tony Blair and Eric Anderson, or indeed my friend Emily and the history teacher of 1965 who was the first adult to give her intellectual confidence, and who she still visits monthly in his nursing home – 'Not for his sake, either. For mine'. Mostly, though, I think that for my generation it has been rare to forge a post-school, equal-terms friendship with a former teacher. In the 1960s the glass walls still stretched from floor to ceiling, the generation gap seemed unbridgeable even between 18 and 25, the decorum of school life hung between us as a great mournful gulf. Perhaps that's why there's such sentiment in 'To Sir with Love' –

because in that era, in Don Black's era and mine, it wasn't really likely to be a lifetime friendship, even if you lived within the same neighbourhood. It's always the impossible relationships which shine the brightest on the misty horizon: just as it is always the remote, half-remembered awful teachers who become sacred monsters in the distorting glass of the Friends Reunited website.

I think, though, that things have changed. I suspect that the present generation of school-leavers will be more likely to extend a school friendship with a teacher into the rest of life, with ease. And not in an erotic way either – wash your mouth out you dirty beasts! I mean that real friendship can flower more readily in this more informal age, particularly when education extends into the sixth form. My children's generation seem more natural, more joshing, more jokey with their teachers as they reach the end of school life.

University students go back and have a drink with the former Sir or Miss, pass on the gossip and the handy hints for getting the next generation onto the right course. Gap year postcards arrive not only for parents but for favoured teachers, and are pinned up in the staffroom. Teachers climb down more readily from their professional dignity, and go to the pub with former pupils, and gradually the sense of daring in the pupil and of awkward patronage in the teacher can subside, and staffroom gossip can even be shared on an adult-to-adult basis, and guffaws exchanged over bygone detentions and sparring-matches. 'Remember that school trip when we couldn't find Kevin anywhere and he was asleep on the bog in the National Theatre? Remember prize day when the Lord Lieutenant was so boring Miss Runcible fell off her chair because she'd been up all night doing reports?'

I hope it is getting easier. I hope the Sirs and Misses of today, who are after all only human beings needing affection as much as any of us, are becoming friends with ex-pupils. It would be a nice reflection on which to end the school year.

Have a good summer. Be sure to take an ex-pupil to the pub. Some of them can even drive you home, these days. Perhaps there'll be karaoke. Perhaps he, or she, will sing 'To Sir, with Love'. One can dream.

NOVEMBER 10 2000

Just another page in the cat-tray

Once he was a demigod, and now he's one of us. The chief inspector of schools is taking the well-worn road from public service to media. He is going to work for the *Daily Telegraph*. It will, he informed John Humphries, be nice to be able to speak out frankly on education issues, for a change. The resultant snort of incredulous mirth from the *Today* presenter ('You haven't exactly held back so far . . .') set up echoes nationwide.

But in households of hacks and opinion mongers, we furrowed our brows and wondered what would be the kindest way to break to poor Chris Woodhead the awful reality of the life he is about to embrace. From now on – after a brief compulsory quarantine – he can indeed be forthright. That's the good news.

And the bad news? The bad news, mate, is that nobody has to listen any more. You are no longer Il Dottore, Mister Inspector, the Big Chief, He Who Must be Obeyed. The Education Secretary is no longer compelled to defend you at every turn.

You are just another voice in a very large cacophony. From now on, what you say may be read with pleasure (you do have a nice turn of phrase) but it will often be met with words which no Big Cheese ever normally hears. Words like 'so what?' and 'sez you'.

Apart from a few deeply sad individuals suffering from personal confusion, no columnist really has the slightest illusion about their importance. We are readers too, so we know how readers operate. They pick up the paper, tickle the cat's ear, glance at the news, let their eye slide to the opinion, and read the first couple of lines and whatever inflammatory title has been slapped on by a sub-editor. If it grabs them, they read on; if they get to the end, you are flattered.

But even then, they may just be using you as an irritant, their 'two minutes hate' for the day. On laying you aside, very possibly in the cat-tray, they snort and say 'God, where do these people *live*?' or 'Right/left-wing pillock'. If you are particularly sapient, they will agree with half your points, while dismissing the rest as just the sort of hooey you'd expect from a convent girl/failed politician. Readers are not respectful.

Mr Woodhead is a clever chap and probably knows this already, but even so it may come as a shock when it actually happens. After all, it happens regularly to other eminences.

I am told (mainly by the spouses, I must admit) that nothing is tougher than the first year after a headteacher goes cold turkey and has nowhere to be head of any more. They find it a relief to get rid of the paperwork and the aggravation, but are caught on the back foot by the cruel loss of gravitas.

Imagine: you have years of striding on to a podium in an awed hush, and being permitted to deliver any old cliché without catcalls or insurrection. You are accustomed to having your jokes laughed at even when they are terrible, and to express hurtful and insulting personal assessments of quite tall human beings, who instead of promptly telling you your own deficiencies, just say 'Thank you, sir' as they leave. You have a secretary who is good at stopping people getting in and boring you.

And then you are out, and nobody's future depends on you. Total strangers with studs in their noses call you 'grandad' and advise you to get out of the way of their micro-scooters.

You think of a nice ironic little joke, and realise that you have no audience beyond the wife and dog, and the features editor of the local paper who has offered you a column says he doesn't find it particularly funny, actually. You end up writing letters to the papers beginning with the announcement that you were a headteacher for 26 years, which unaccountably causes the letters editor to put it on a pile marked 'Fillers'.

And, because you are a decent type with a sense of humour, you accept all this powerlessness and get on with the rest of your life. It is a common experience. I am sure that Mr Woodhead is entirely prepared for the fact that from now on, none of the teachers, heads, inspectors or parents who once stood in awe of him has to listen to a word he says.

Unless the words themselves, unbacked by position or politics, truly strike home to the heart.

NOVEMBER 4 2005

A new regime

In the United States last week Wal-Mart, parent company of Asda, was leaked as hatching a diabolically cunning scheme. It is, the reports said, trying to dissuade far employees from applying to the chain by ensuring that every job contains some physical aspects. For example, 'all cashiers to do some trolley stacking'.

There was an implication that employers are fed up with handing out sick pay for the myriad ailments which we are always being told will fell the obese. The suggestion is that this is a mere commercial decision, and will prevent anyone large from applying to the store.

But the more I thought about the idea, the more strangely attractive it was. It may well backfire on the firm, with increasingly long (and wide) queues forming as those who feel the need for a bit more exercise in their life apply to work for Wal-Mart.

Think about it. Rather than being stuck for eight hours on a till, sitting on your ever-spreading bum, swiping barcodes and pushing the conveyor-belt control, life would become varied. From time to time you would be made to stand up, walk around, put stuff on shelves or push trolleys into lines of other trolleys (which is not, if truth be told, all that strenuous. Indeed your impressive bulk might come in handy for the bit where you lean on the line of 40 trolleys and crash them into the parking pen. Ker-ching!)

It could be tremendous fun. Get the body moving, blood circularing, see new views, avoid the damn customers for an hour, escape the neon flicker and get a bit of fresh car-park air in your lungs. It would be a more-than-welcome respite from watching an endless procession of stressed shoppers, ready-meals and bagged salads rolling past your checkout.

I couldn't think what it reminded me of, and why the pleasure seemed so vivid and immediately imaginable. Then I remembered. School! It brought back those wonderful moments back at the dear old convent when a lesson got cut short and volunteers were hiked out of class because it was nearly Christmas, or Easter, or summer fête time, and the muscle-power of the upper-fifth was required to put out chairs or carry trestle tables for the bazaar.

Sometimes it was even better because prize day or the school play was looming, and we had to build a massive, wobbly, lethal arena of wooden steps and benches to accommodate the whole school in an impossibly small hall. I went back to Tunbridge Wells a while ago and was thrilled to see that the hollow wooden step things are still there, battered but unbowed, still accommodating rows of small brown-skirted backsides. No doubt the new generation of little girls is practising for pop-concert life by learning how to sit with other people's knees sticking into the back of your neck.

But it was the moving, the setting up that was the real fun. Oh, the crashing and the banging, the scraping and bustling, the heaving and giggling and grunting, the cacophony of metal chair-frames being stacked or unstacked! Oh, the sheer physical relief of hauling and pushing and playing at removal-men, rather than preparing for O-level stress by flattening out a pleated skirt on a hard chair with your tired back bent over ring-binders full of annoying stuff about the lower intestine!

It was, in a curious way, better than games. Games involved losing, and being shouted at by hearty people and given mysterious rebukes such as 'Sticks!', while dangerously hard hockey balls flew past your ear. Shoving furniture around was co-operative and larky, and no one got school-colours medals for it or picked you last for their team.

Sedentary workers, unless they are actually disabled rather than just stout, always love a bit of manual labour. Shifting filing cabinets and rolling chairs around is welcome relief from hunched brain-work. Why wait for gym-time or official sport to get your circulation going? Why not acknowledge your animal, hunter-gatherer, fight-and-flight instincts as well as your higher centres?

I reckon Wal-Mart is on the right track here. Perhaps all teachers should have a bit of gardening or DIY written into their contracts, and all children be expected to lend a hand with mortar and trowel for half an hour a day to build the new classroom block. Everyone would end up much more cheerful. What was that? Dignity? Health and safety regulations? Oh, come on! What's so healthy, or safe, or dignified, about sitting down for hours on end peering at paper?

JUNE 8 2001

Big Brother Miss

Of all the grave issues facing education today, let us turn to the most torrid. Should English and drama teachers be encouraged to drop their towels on TV? How much flesh is it suitable for a pedagogue to show on E4 digital *Big Brother*? Is it a sacking offence to kiss a housemate and threaten onscreen sex, or is it worse to be seen on primetime Channel 4 discussing the teaching profession in a glottal-stopped voice, telling a sullen youth with nose hair '*To Kill a Mockingbird*, yuh, thassa classic'?

Some time ago, during the equally torrid affair of the drama teacher who skinny-dipped with teenage boys on a school trip and got so rat-stinking drunk that she had to be put to bed by a colleague, I wrote a column here with a sad, hard moral. It pointed out, regretfully, that of all professions in an increasingly infantilised and petulant world, teaching remains one of the few in which it is necessary to be a grown-up.

However wild a party animal you may be at heart, howeverfull of 'needs' and 'issues', however loose and carefree and multi-coloured your natural personality, if you're a teacher you have to can it. You have to dress in respectable clothes, keep order, count heads, moderate your language, and watch your behaviour – as they say in business – 24-seven. On the face of it, the affair of *Big Brother* contestant Penny – otherwise known as Lisa Ellis – of the Sarah Bonnell community school is just another example of this harsh rule. Her headteacher has glumly said: 'I put it in writing to her that she would have to adhere to the code of conduct in her contract . . . I have to ensure the pupils have excellent role models'. She has also observed that she believes that the teacher may have 'decided to go down the road of enhancing her career in other directions', to wit, showbiz. Ms Ellis herself has indicated as much on screen, making it pretty clear that like most other contestants in this hideous programme she is out for instant celebrity and whatever it can bring her. So good luck to her, and may her slipping towel bring her all that she desires.

But it brings up the eternal, vexed question of the Showbiz

Teacher. The trouble with schoolteaching is that it is part scholarship, part showbiz; it always was and always will be. Given that even in the most selective of schools some 50 per cent of any set is not sincerely interested in your subject, you gotta sell your pitch. You need presence, you need originality, you need communicable energy, you need rhetoric and verbal power – you need a lot of the same things, frankly, that Denise van Outen uses to sell a song in *Chicago*. Admittedly razzle-dazzle alone doesn't get people through physics GCSE, but a bit of fairy-dust doesn't hurt. The teacher we remember forever is not the dull, strict, mumbling pedant, but the ranter, the performer. Everyone benefits from the apparent nutter who makes you stand on the table and shout Latin words, the history teacher who careers round the room throwing things and then makes you each write a brief account of what he just did, in order to demonstrate the flawed reliability of eyewitnesses. It is, perhaps, generally better if most teachers refrain from actually singing or performing the can-can, but a bit of razzmatazz goes a long way.

Therefore, in any feisty staffroom, there are at least one or two members who have yearnings to take it further: who carry in their teacherly knapsacks not a headmaster's baton but the tatty tickling-stick of a Ken Dodd, the microphone of a crooner, the sheer black tights of a soubrette.

To hell with Lord Puttnam's teaching. Oscars, they mutter; what about the real thing? And some of these frustrated performers (not only English and drama staff either) are likely to be very good teachers. So what is a head to do, in an era of staff shortage, when one of them announces that he or she wants to go on *Big Brother*, or take a sabbatical Christmas term for a panto engagement, or host a saucy local radio phone-in slot of an evening, or spend the summer holiday in seaside rep? Thwart them and they'll build up a steaming head of frustration and eventually make a run for it. Give them their way for a while, and they might just realise the desperate, miserable precariousness of the true showbiz life and return to entertaining an audience which can be put in detention for heckling.

It's a tough call. I watch, fascinated, to see whether a season in the sun has Penny limping back to the classroom, strangely grateful.

MAY 11 2001

Bring in the handymen

On a boat, if you are miles from shore and a bit of gear breaks, there is one golden rule. You don't waste time mourning over the fact that you don't have a spare. You bend your mind to the more subtle question, 'What did it do?'

Instead of focusing in horror on the lack of a proper lavatory valve or fuel-filter, you deconstruct the job that it formerly did. You don't say, 'Oh, if only we had another length of 5 mm copper pipe with a micromesh adaptor nozzle!'. You say 'What is the job it did?' and then rummage around in your box of oddments and cut up the tongues of people's deck-shoes to make gaskets. And, as often as not, it turns out that some tinfoil, the handle of a shrimping-net and a twisted pair of underpants will get you home. Sometimes, these jury-rigs are so effective you find them still in place years later. So, as we appear to have a schools emergency on our hands, let us dismantle teachers and consider what they do.

What sort of lash-up might keep the educational ship afloat? As good *TES* readers, we all agree that the long-term solution is for teaching to become a proud and envied profession. However, if high-quality repair to the vessel is not instantly available, and fresh waves of children keep battering it, we clearly must cut up a few shoes and cannibalise some old gadgets.

David Blunkett's current solution is thousands of classroom assistants. Fine. But surely there is something else lying around in the national oddments box, full of potential to help? I was brooding on this the other week when my eye fell on the story that Portsmouth and West Sussex schools are recruiting ex-servicemen and women as 'study supervisors'.

Everyone had a good giggle, imagining the army drafted into double physics in between shovelling dead sheep and having breast-enhancement surgery. And the National Union of Teachers said in its usual huffy manner that the idea is 'misguided'.

But I dunno. Deconstruct a teacher, and what do you find? There is a specialist professional, capable of planning lessons and understanding the psychology of learning; a bureaucrat who keeps immaculate records and can understand the weird language talked by exam boards (a bit like being a Parselmouth in Harry Potter, able to talk to snakes and slightly feared for it).

Within the same teacher there is a supervisor of unpredictable youth who can exert authority and organise a rabble, and a motivator whose manner and enthusiasm persuades the said rabble that it is better to co-operate than to wander off down to the chippie. And then there is a friend and counsellor of children.

Look at the functions, divide them up and consider replacing some of them with a juryrig, looking different but doing the same job. It already happens where schools have counsellors and classroom assistants, but it could be extended. Maybe those schools were barking up the right tree by touting for ex-service personnel. Soldiers, after all, know about chains of command, take orders intelligently, and tend to be optimistic, crunchy, can-do personalities. A few could liven up the atmosphere of the average knackered school: boys in particular might be edified to see tough chaps with broken noses seeming to care about whether they do their history essay.

Maybe we should go much wider. Let teachers teach, but also command an assortment of high-quality volunteers, seconded for one or two days a week. Maybe it should be routine for a local surveyor to offer six hours with geography sets, under orders from the head of department; for a publisher or journalist to take responsibility for an aspect of the English curriculum, a banker to play classroom assistant to the maths teacher, a practising engineer to join the CDT team.

It would blow a breeze in from the outer world, and put schools back at the heart of communities. We volunteers would love it, too. The world is full of people who haven't quite got the bottle to be full-time teachers, but who are energised by contact with the fizzing qualities of youth (even if we do need the rest of the week to recover). Perhaps there should be a way to let that good-will penetrate to the heart of education, not just raise funds for computers. Huh, say the teachers. 'We'd have to organise them all, more trouble than it's worth . . .' But if I were a head, I'd try it.

And if there were shy volunteers, with clerical ability, I'd bloody well work out a way to get them to do the paperwork.

Ahead by a sweaty foot

As we creak back into gear after Christmas excesses, eyeing the gym card with shuddering disfavour, it is a moment to look around at those weird people who never fall out of training and ask the eternal question: Why do headmasters run marathons?

You could put it in one of those lists of scientific puzzlers like 'Do penguins have knees?' or 'Where do flies go in the winter?'. Certainly, by note and anecdote, it is ever more apparent that something about school headship causes a man (rarely a woman) to pull on nylon shorts and pound 26 miles across London, just when any normal teacher is stretched out on the sofa eating the children's chocolate Easter eggs and watching re-runs of *I'm A Celebrity Ballroom Dancer, Please Drench Me Iin Maggots.*

Our children's first head, at the village primary, alerted us to this symbiosis of school headship and sore feet when he suddenly announced that he was doing it. He was a fit chap, keen on PE and all that; but for those of us bred to a tradition of round-shouldered and bespectacled scholars, this sudden outbreak of physical bravado was a surprise. Especially when he finished.

Within a few years the children had moved on, and the boy's next head revealed that he, too, was in strict training for the marathon. Knees bent, arms swinging, off he went in turn. Even faster. The school didn't suit, though, so next there was another head to size up. He looked suspiciously fit: before I even dared ask, he was indeed off on a half-marathon, streaking past his sixth-formers. Now, newly retired, he is going for the full 26 miles.

It is a trend, almost a plague; a mania like the ergot-fuelled dancing crazes of the middle ages. Google the words 'headmaster runs marathon' on the web, and herds of them thunder towards you, puffing and groaning towards the finishing-tape. Primary heads, secondary heads, old and young, deputies and veterans – they're all at it.

Sometimes it is gung-ho CV stuff: 'Dear boys, parents, and Old Bastardians, I would like to introduce myself as your new headmaster . . . my wife and I are looking forward to the move . . . blah,

blah . . . something about me . . . Cambridge boxing blue . . . MA . . . PGCE . . . oh yes, and I have run the London Marathon twice in under 4 hours . . .'

Or: 'Following teaching posts at Bogstandard Comprehensive, voted most improved school in its LEA, he headed the liberal studies department . . . a trained counsellor, Mr Fitball has completed the London Marathon six times . . .'

You just look, if you don't believe me. There are hundreds of them. As I write, I gather that Sir Dexter Hutt, executive head of the Ninestiles federation of secondary schools in Birmingham, is planning to run in his third (the last being seven years ago) and has set himself a target of doing it in under 3 hours 45 minutes.

So why this weird correlation of academic leadership and sweaty trainers? A brainstorming session with teacher-moles came up with several suggestions. The first, obviously, is showing off. Your pupils, especially big frightening boys, will surely revere a head who runs a marathon. As for the girls, they will see you on TV and think, 'Woooah! More than just an assembly pin-up!'.

They'll admire you . . . won't they? Well, yes. On the other hand, given the nature of running, students are just as likely to see their headmaster sitting on the pavement with his head in his hands like Paula Radcliffe, while he is insouciantly overtaken by men in flippers, girls in bunny-ears, and comedy waitress outfits carrying trays of fake champagne. So perhaps it isn't exhibitionism.

Another explanation is purely chemical: testosterone, endorphins, all that. These are alpha males. Heads are statistically more likely to be tall than short; it may yet turn out that they are left-handed as well, since research now claims that left-handers survived by being better warriors. In the jungle that is modern education, a man must hone his abilities in both fight and flight. Hence the marathons?

No: still not convinced. We scratched our heads. And at last, we came to the likeliest explanation. A former deputy head put his finger on why headmasters run marathons. 'It's desperate hunger for achievement,' he said. 'In education you're always running to stand still, putting your heart into hopeless causes, or getting a job three-quarters done and then being foiled by bureaucracy or budget shortfalls'.

He sighed, wistfully. 'In a marathon, all you have to do is keep putting one foot in front of the other and endure the pain, and you've achieved something. No LEA to trip you up.' We were silent, stunned by the brilliance of this insight. Then someone said: 'Why don't female headteachers do it much, then?'

'Easy,' said the genius. 'Women rather like failing. It makes them feel feminine.'

The conclave broke up in disarray.

Do ya think I'm sexy?

Get dressed for battle

Some conflicts are eternal, archetypal: fire and water, light and darkness, Gandalf and Saruman. Among these battles, fiercer and more implacable with every passing year, is the timeless struggle between headteachers and exhibitionist schoolgirls.

Whole careers have worn out in the desperate battle to get the blasted females to cover up. Stratagems have been tried and failed: wheedling and force and blackmail and expulsion have been deployed to little avail. Parents have been enlisted on both sides, and done precious little good to either. And still, year after year, in all but the most draconian schools, the girls strut and bare their flesh, undo buttons, thrust out cleavages, roll up waistbands and jut their defiant bellybutton-rings at weary members of staff who eventually grow too fed up and bored with the matter even to croak, 'Oh, put it away, Chantelle!'

One day the history of this war will be written (probably with a few despairing footnotes about the corresponding war with the occasional ultra-devout Muslim girl who demands her human right to peer at the world through a narrow slit even during PE and science lessons). But when the final chronicle of heads-versus-female-flesh is written, there will certainly be a chapter devoted to the épatant Kesgrave affair which hit the press last week.

Kesgrave high school, a fine institution in my own home county of Suffolk, has become the first school to give up on trying to stop girls wearing indecent miniskirts, and insist that they all wear trousers instead. Since Kesgrave has a particularly fine record of having pupils walk and bike to school, it is a particularly pressing matter for them. Frankly, as someone who drives past their cycle lane once or twice a week, I can see why. Sometimes, indeed, I can see everything. And so can the guy in the BMW in front of me, judging by the way he is weaving dazedly across the road as the Kesgrave Lolitas wiggle by.

Anyway, head and governors got so fed up with the pelmetskirts and with the tedious and time-wasting task of nagging girls and parents about them, that they have called the little minxes' bluff.

They have decreed universal trousers. Shock, horror! There was wild talk of a legal challenge, of girls having their human rights infringed; but lawyers' opinion so far is that the school is probably within its rights. After all, even the Equal Opportunities Commission has previously upheld the right of schools to stop girls wearing trousers, which I suppose implies that schools can drape children in any style of cloth they choose.

Nor do I hold out much legal hope for the doughty campaign being fought by that lad in Kent who goes to school in a skirt in order to prove some point I cannot quite put my finger on. I think he was beefing about the fact that girls could choose skirts or trousers at his school, but boys could only choose trousers. His parents, canny beings, merely say demurely that they are proud of the school for educating him to the point when he can think such philosophical issues through for himself.

Anyway, good for Kesgrave. It was time somebody introduced a new stratagem into the eternal conflict. Their cunning is admirable. The message is clear: if you girls can't be trusted with skirts, you can damn well wear trousers.

Schools have to be cunning, because they have had a lot of weapons taken out of their hands in recent decades: not only the cane and the ruler and the 'humiliating' punishment and the snap expulsion, but even the right to utter the sort of politically incorrect rebukes we used to get, along the lines of 'Cover yourself up, girl, you look like a common tart'. Enforced trousers are a useful new ploy. Well done.

It won't work, of course. In a war like this every new weapon provokes a new defence. Some girls will wear the trousers buttock-huggingly tight, so that nervous young teachers will never dare ask them to wipe the whiteboard in mixed company. Others will buy them two sizes too big and drape them from their hipbones just skimming the pubes, with sweaters stopping above the navel and puce thongs peeping out the back. Others will compensate for the cruel obscuring of their legs by unbuttoning still more of the front of their blouses or shrinking their school sweaters till they look like Jayne Mansfield.

The war goes on between girls heroically determined to look as porny as possible and teachers who would very much rather that they didn't. Nobody will ever win.

Odes to chalk and chickens

I have to admit that I have never knowingly smouldered during the course of a parents' evening. I once nearly threw my arms round Mr French, but that was pure gratitude for his being the only teacher that term not to diss my younger child for idleness. After staggering from table to table having scrappy, doodle-strewn exercise books brandished at you by stern people in cardigans, you're tearfully grateful when a teacher says: 'She's great'.

However, it would seem that parents' evenings have more sizzling potential than that, and my eyes are open now to all those missed opportunities. Thank Alan Friswell, one of the three winners of the Not in Term Time competition for teachers' love stories. There he is, glumly sitting through a grim evening session with annoying parents, and a mother turns up and grins at him. Whereon 'My heart cracks. I fall in love. Instantly and totally'. Woooarr!

It was *The TES* which started this competition, by publicising online the plaint of teachers with no time or energy to fall in love. *The Learning Curve* producers on BBC Radio 4, strangely excited by the thought of all these lonely yet patently eligible pedagogues, offered a prize for the best three stories, in 300 words, about love in the educational world. It seemed a cruelly short word-count to stipulate.

But, as it turns out, teachers are brilliant at condensing fact and emotion into few words, presumably due to years of writing report cards with teeny spaces to sum up complicated children.

The winners were Alan, the one who fell in love over the report-sheets; Angela Horne, with a poignant tribute to a late husband; and Liz Eckstein, with a beautifully telescoped story of a marriage's decay, and the wonderful final paragraph: 'You go on. You have no choice. One foot goes in front of the other. The kids make you smile and being back in school is the best, and the worst, and the best that life has. They save you. You are grateful. You go on. You plant a rosebush for the generation to come.'

But some of the near-misses stay in my head just as insistently. It is hard to forget the lesbian eye-meet between the brisk new head and the crop-haired music student with CND earrings, a *coup de foudre* while the school orchestra limps through 'Yesterday' with tambourines and recorders. Our stipulation that it should be based on real life becomes worrying when you contemplate the tale of a head and a teacher caught in flagrante by the governors ('When the meeting reconvened, the agenda had changed').

There was a worryingly erotic encounter in the stationery cupboard between a bearded geography teacher and an object of desire who turns out to be a new box of chalk: 'Silently, carefully her top is undone . . . she starts to crumble'. There are plenty of weepies: near-misses, chaps who seem all vulnerable then marry someone else, French teachers no one can ever forget, romances which begin, when someone uses someone else's special mug in the staffroom, and of course the perennial fascination of PE teachers, male and female. I suppose they are literally the fittest in the school.

A few were memories of schooldays: the worshipped Miss White of Birmingham remembered by the boy who polished her shoes daily with his best hanky – he threw it in the canal in bitterness when she married Mr Brown. There was a cracking story from Belfast about a school trip to Paris and that heady sense of growing up, gazing at the eggshell dome of Sacre Coeur and being sent by the blushing young French teacher to buy *rouge à lèvres.* Disappointed then, the girls nonetheless 'knew our time would come'. There was one poem creatively rhyming 'erotic intention' with 'detention', which may be a first in the history of the English love lyric.

And there is a secret favourite of mine from Staffordshire: an old memory of a soft, cooing voice, dark eyes, a proud carriage, a beguiling warm body and a fluttering heartbeat which transformed classroom life. The beloved in this case turns out to be a chicken called Pancake, which inhabited a primary school classroom in a free-range manner ever since the day she was hatched from the incubator on a snowy Shrove Tuesday.

Now that one really did bring a tear to the eye. Was there really a time, in vivid living memory, when you were allowed by health and safety regulators and salmonella-dreaders to have a chicken roaming free, pecking children's feet, being stroked and fluttering on to desks? Was life really so sweet and simple then, or has time rewritten every line? Ah, the way we were . . .

NOVEMBER 24 2000

Everybody's doing it except us

Now here's a question. Estimate, to within the nearest wink and nudge, the degree of prudishness that is required in a headteacher. Include in your answer a commentary on the following: clockwork willies, topless photography, Folies Bergère posters, that chap you rather wish you hadn't appointed in the art department, liqueur chocolates shaped like breasts, and the Alan Clark diaries.

I somehow don't think I shall get this debated in any dignified forum. But teachers – especially headteachers – are in a curious position. They occupy one of the few remaining pedestals in society – being expected to maintain the highest standards of personal behaviour, ideals, integrity etc, as part of the job description.

On the other hand, the society in which they operate has become breathtakingly indifferent to public display and chatter of an explicitly sexual nature.

Some of it is caused by serious news items: the campaigns against Aids meant that for the first time bodily fluids became part of common discourse, and the House of Lords argument over gay sex at 16 has enabled large numbers of once decorous journalists to fulfil a life's ambition by typing out the word buggery, not to mention quoting that weird aside by some Lord about having eaten 'the private parts of a green monkey' (though presumably not at Simpsons on the Strand).

The details of the Starr report on Clinton and Lewinsky were spread over every medium. Elderly *Telegraph* readers were forced to come to terms with concepts they last heard of from the regimental MO when the troopship left for Singapore.

At the same time, frivolity about sex has become epidemic. Fluffy teen programmes like *Friends* and films with a 12 certificate like *Bedazzled* have not the slightest hesitation about references to male size and performance. High street shops no longer bother to put their hopping clockwork penises on a high shelf, and nor do bookshops selling *Wicked Willie* and the like.

June Whitfield serenely shares a platform with Julian Clary,

Nigella Lawson saucily waves her patisserie-tongs with the observation 'I like some tong action', and minister Mowlam makes dirty
jokes on chat shows. Even the Aldeburgh Festival this year had a
fringe event involving a nude tattooed woman, a python, a drag
artiste and a sword-swallower in suspenders (they were great).

Alone in this Rabelaisian stew, headteachers forlornly clutch the
banner of decorum. Take two heartbreaking little stories: one true,
one illustrative. The true one is about Dr Stuart Newton of Selsdon
high school in Croydon, reported in *The TES* as being horrified by a
fax advertising the notorious new show Puppetry of the Penis, in
which two men manipulate their genitals into likenesses of ham-
burgers, windsurfers and the Eiffel Tower.

Dr Newton asks us to imagine the disaster if a pupil had seen the
poster and told parents. 'Schools are held responsible', he said, 'for
the morality of the nation.' In an aside so plaintive that it ought to
be set to music, he concluded: 'Fortunately, it came through to the
bursar's office.' Quite. Best place for genital origami.

The second story was fictional, but telling. On Radio 4's *Law in
Action*, a simulated panel on exclusion considered the case of a head
who excludes a top GCSE student, 16-year-old Lauren, for having
'brought the school into disrepute' by appearing topless in a men's
magazine.

The panel thought that he was wrong to put the school's fair
name above a child's future, given that she was 16 and had broken
no law. But you could see the poor head's position. Feeling responsible for the 'morality of the nation', he was trapped into taking up
the stance of the most hypothetically shockable parent.

He probably would have preferred to get Lauren in and tell her
not to be such a silly little slapper, and to keep her damn blouse on
until she's sat the last GCSE paper and can depart to the licentious
surroundings of a sixthform college. But on looking into his heart
and consulting the atavistic gods of headteacherhood, this archetypal character realised that he was going to have to be much more
shocked than that. So he excluded her, and made even more of a
fool of himself.

In both these cases the issue is not even sexual activity, but mere
modesty. And it does seem unfair that heads are expected to uphold
the sweet old virtue all unaided, and be laughed at for their pains.

NOVEMBER 5 2004

Grown-ups' rules . . . ok!

From time to time in this confusing age, one feels one's inner Victorian nonconformist rising up. He roars against immodesty and prescribes the birch, the alienist, and a generally brusque line with moral imbeciles.

Obviously, as a non-judgmental 21st century liberal, one slaps down this hellfire zealot in one's head and returns hastily to a milky modern consensus in which provocative, priapic, promiscuous and generally trollopy carryings-on are tolerated with a smile.

Live and let live, eh? Watch another episode of *Sex And The City*, refrain from speculating on how often the characters in *Friends* would have had chlamydia, and forbid yourself from putting a brick through the TV when Trinny and Susannah nag another harmless frump into wearing tight clothes on the grounds that it is everybody's duty to be a walking sexual self-advertisement.

But sometimes the demented puritan breaks out and will not be denied. It happened to me last week, reading Kate Myers' remarks about her new book *Teachers Behaving Badly?*, on the problem of predatory students who use sexuality against teachers. It is, she says, increasingly common for staff to be intimidated with obscene phone calls and text messages, propositions, assaults, sneery flirtation and generally sexualised aggression.

The old problem of a pupil falling romantically in love with a teacher is also considered, but that is – though embarrassing or tempting – at least part of the normal bumpy course of human romance. What made the blood run cold were the stories of children, encouraged to think of themselves as sexual players from an increasingly early age, using that ancient power to score off the poor devils at the chalkface.

It need not be a proposition: one boy cited 'displayed a calculating hardness . . . he was particularly stylish in his public chivalry; he could open a door for a (woman) teacher with a flourish that was at once courteous and threatening'. Little bastard! Can't you just see him – burly for his age, rejoicing in his manhood, bragging to

his mates about what he could do to Miss X if he got her up a dark alley?

Perdition seize, too, the false accusers who bring allegations as revenge; woe betide the nasty little girls who use biology to unnerve male teachers, the breast-thrusters and hip-swayers and smart-ass little madams who use their alleged time-of-the-month to embarrass poor sweating lads fresh out of PGCE.

And a pox on those born gorgeous, who use their unearned pulling-power to fuel triumphalist jeers at short, fat or bald pedagogues. Undermining and humiliating teachers is not a new sport, but according to Myers and NASUWT officers this newly sophisticated sexual edge is an underrated problem. Ultra-wets will say that the children are 'troubled' and must be gently taught not be 'inappropriate'. Tough nuts will say that teachers should cope. Naive optimists will imagine that juvenile sexual aggression is too jejune to bother with.

But all, I think, are wrong. Certainly a physically attractive, domestically secure teacher will find it easier to handle; but if you suffer the slightest private unease, disappointment or insecurity the effect of suggestive harassment from nasty teenagers must be devastating: a source of real unhappiness, if not professional disaster.

The consensus seems to be that special teacher 'training' is needed. But this particular nastiness might equally be tackled with more teacher power. In adult workplaces, the slightest suspicion of sexual harassment is now met with frightening rigour: a wrong hand on a shoulder, a joke in a pub or a clumsy compliment can land you a suspension or an industrial tribunal, cut off your salary or cost your company tens of thousands.

If a teacher sexually harasses a pupil, the pit of hell beckons. So, if kids want to be sexual players – OK, let them fall under the same yoke. Let it be known that this is a grown-up game, and sex such a powerful thing that using it as a weapon is like pulling a knife. When a brat makes suggestive remarks about a teacher being 'fit' or a minger, or sneers about their sex life, let there be shock and awe. Roll on the humiliating punishments, wash mouths out with carbolic soap. If their parents protest, tell them that they have reared disgusting little degenerates and will be hearing shortly from the social services. Let us relearn how to be shocked.

Good grief, sorry, the inner Victorian broke out just then and started laying about him like a godly Godzilla. Down, Reverend! Back in your box!

But think about it. After all, the little swines are going to be in the workplace soon, and they'll get a terrible shock when they find you can't treat real people the way they treated teachers.

Farewell, my innocent love

SPRINGTIME, hey ding-a-ding, and thoughts of love. Actually, schools and colleges are so naturally conducive to adoration, obsession, crushes and pashes that you need not wait until spring. Many a heart has yearned through long dark classroom winters, many a bum leaned on a gym radiator while its owner nursed a hopeless devotion to the biology master, the head girl, the captain of Pop, or even Reverend Mother.

Proximity does it; that and power, and the charge which comes off good teachers, mentors and local heroes. Schools are electric: even sensible mothers cast dewy looks at headteachers, and fathers adjust their ties with all the self-consciousness of calf-love before meeting the crisp, yet caring headmistress.

Do not get me wrong: the love we speak of is blamelessly Platonic. A few unscrupulous teachers may parlay it into a sexual relationship and end up in the *News of the World*, but that is not really in its nature. The moment you get someone's clothes off, the mystical adoration of the true crush dissipates into mere ordinary romance, not the same thing at all.

Your proper in-school crush is a subtle, gossamer glory; the victim is raised to ecstasy by an encouraging word, a laugh, a clap on the shoulder. The best pashes thrive in decent secrecy, letting concealment feed on their damask cheeks and encouraging the subject to read a great deal of English lyric poetry. They feel eternal, yet vanish in a term or two, leaving only a faint sweet miasma of wistful embarrassment. If everyone concerned has been tactful, they can even mature into ordinary friendship.

Crushes are great. They fill the dull corners of daily life with a light that never was on sea or land. They are our clouds of glory, rags of our inward urge to seek the ultimate good, the entirely beautiful. Just because the ultimate good was represented, for a few months of the hockey season, by the sturdy form of Tabitha Ramsbottom of Lower VIB, and then mutated into Mr Gryff-Henderson in the chemistry department, and then Ron Boggs who

saved you from the bullies and later became an ordinary drinking-mate in your twenties – that does not degrade the currency. Adoration is an innocent and selfless thing, even when it is being squandered.

Or at least, it would be innocent if we could all keep our nerve. The problem is sex. I suppose the worship-instinct of small boys and nubile girls has always put them at risk; although I also suspect that the first frankly sexual pass usually kills adoration stone dead. It certainly did when Professor X put his hand up my miniskirt in 1968. You know who you are, professor, and your secret is safe with me. I accept that you just read me wrong: I wanted you to be the unattainable good, not the all-too-attainable Goat, see?

But the problem for modern crush victims is not in what happens (usually nothing) but in what the fretful world thinks.

The other week in *TES Primary* a newly- qualified teacher was worrying about a group of older pupils who leave admiring notes on her desk and cultishly follow her to the bus-stop to wave. The reply majored on the need to 'nip it in the bud' because the young 'may have no concept of the consequences or interpretations of what they are doing'. Oh sad, sad! Sensible, but sad! In the days when I had newly transferred my worship from the hearty heroism of Flora the

Goalie to the chiffon wistfulness of Mademoiselle French-Oral, nobody bothered with interpreting. I sighed, and carried her bags, and shot up my hand in the hope of being chosen to rub her dear participles off the blackboard with the cloth she had – gulp – touched.

Mam'zelle accepted, with equal grace, both the worship and the fact that it would be all over by Christmas. She didn't go writing off to the press for guidance. She could hack it: one fellow-sufferer actually cracked and spoke her love on a school trip; Mam'zelle serenely replied 'how kind!' and patted the supplicant's hand in a way which kept the poor sap going for the whole term.

Why was it so easy? Because of the safety of taboos. Because in those sweet, innocent days nobody had wrecked our bloody lives by telling us to get in touch with our sexuality. The moth yearned for the star, and the night for the morrow, and a kind word from the games captain could transport us far from the sphere of our sorrow.

Bring back repression, I say. It was much more fun.

SEPTEMBER 10 1999

A kick in the pants

'Hello girls! Today in the PSE careers module we are going to discuss a subject which may seem arrivial, but is important to the way society works and the signals we send one another. What's that, Kim? Look, I explained about 'sending signals' last term – remember? I know it sounds like semaphore, but it's a very important piece of jargon. Even the Home Secretary uses it. Stop arguing.

'Anyway, the subject is this: now that the great tides of history have brought equal opportunities and esteem to men and women in the workplace, how should a woman dress for work?

'Neatly? Of course. Carole, very good point. And practically? Well, yes, within the bounds of decorum. You don't wear a boiler-suit to go into a merchant bank even if there is a risk of spilling copier fluid. Comfortably? Well, of course – a worker has to be reasonably comfortable to function at her best.

What was that, Kim? You think women ought to be fashionable? Well, up to a point. It would look odd to wear something out of the remote past, like a poke bonnet or a bustle. But nobody is tied down to specific fashions these days. Just look at the skirt lengths down any street. And some high fashion isn't modest or comfortable, is it? Imagine if the inspector turned up in a PVC bondage outfit. Or even Lacroix.

'So we're all agreed: neatness, modesty, practicality, comfort. Now, let's move on – What was that, Kim? Do women wear trousers to work? Well, of course, plenty do. Not jeans as a rule, or skin-tight leggings – but trousers, yes. Women executives do it. Female bank managers and vicars do, MPs in the Chamber and Cherie Blair. And teachers, yes. Especially in winter! Look at mine!

'What was that again, Kim? WHAT? You have the nerve to ask why you aren't allowed to wear trousers into school? Great heavens, girl, wash your mouth out! What a disgraceful suggestion, it's perfectly clear that if schoolgirls wore trousers, civilization would come crashing down, bringing in its wake the destruction of all we hold most dear. Leave the room!'

I do not know, I really do not know, how certain schools can attempt to teach reasoning, tolerance, modernity and equality when they insist on hanging on to barmy and unkind rules. There has been widespread disapproval of the Equal Opportunities Commission's decision to back the Hale family in their forthcoming battle against 14-year-old Jo's school because it won't allow girls, even in mid-winter, to come to school in trousers – even the smartest kind and in the same colour as the school skirt. The general, and quite understandable, view in education circles seems to be that the law is the wrong instrument for such a matter, that the Secretary of State should also keep out of it because schools must be allowed to have their own ethos and not be pushed around; and that if parents don't like the way a particular school does things, they shouldn't have joined. There is a view that if heads don't even get their way over things like this they might as well pack up shop. And that what they say should go, when it comes to banning girls' trousers.

As a fan of local autonomy I am swayed by all that. But when the rule is harsh and stupid, when girls get cold chapped legs, can't run for a bus, get jeered at by boys for having thick calves, or just feel uncomfortable and bothered by the ghastliness of those ill-made, grey, shapeless A-line skirts which nobody in the land would ever voluntarily buy – then what?

Am I going to the barricades for the right of heads and governors to be sexist bullies, 1950s bigots, St Trinian's fetishists or just inconsiderate, petty-minded toads? Or am I going to raise a fist in salute to the Commission for taking them on?

The latter, on balance. But there are dark prognostications. 'If this case is won on sex discrimination grounds,' a male teacher told me, 'within a few weeks we'll have the first action brought by some Boy George or Marilyn type, demanding the right for boys to wear skirts in school.'

I can hardly wait. It will serve you right, you few jurassic heads, for not changing the rule years ago on grounds of plain common sense.

FEBRUARY 3 2006

Please sir, are you gay?

What on earth is A-level politics, let alone Year 8 citizenship, supposed to make of the great Lib-Dem sex uproar? On the principle of 'show, don't tell', the recent exposure of Mark Oaten and his liaisons with a male prostitute, followed sharply by the outing of Simon Hughes, seem unlikely to ease any juvenile confusion. They certainly won't help stem the tide of homophobic bullying or ease the miseries of gay teachers reported in last week's *TES*.

Layer upon layer of confusion mark our public reaction to such stories: it all reminds me of the week when Ron Davies was caught on Clapham Common and one reporter asked him four times running 'Minister, are you gay?' when the real question was, 'Minister were you cruising for casual sex?' Nothing wrong with being gay; lots of gay ministers do their governmental work no worse than anyone else. On the other hand, if you are in a responsible and confidential, position, there is plenty wrong with promiscuity, secret adultery and random risk-taking with strangers of any sex.

'All right then, we'll talk about it,' sighs Sir, or Miss, reluctantly. 'Class, I put it to you that Simon Hughes was perfectly within his rights not to tell the press whom he fancied. He'd always stood up for gay rights, OK? Er, yes, Jamie, except during the by-election when he beat Peter Tatchell. He did say sorry.'

Teacher sighs, crosses fingers, grimaces. 'But on the other hand, what about his apparent reason for not telling? His friends say he was sparing the feelings of his mother who is 'in her eighties and very religious'. Hands up who thinks that's a good reason? Are you being ageist? Why is a woman in her eighties deemed unable to take in new truths? He's not a murderer, is he? And why is a religious person regarded as too emotionally fragile to deploy forgiveness? Ask your RE teacher – isn't it supposed to be the other way round? Christians, they do this forgiving thing, right?

'And what about *l'affaire* Oaten: why are all the papers saying it's a tragedy for him? He had a free choice whether or not to do that thing with the rent boys – quiet, Kylie, yes, we all know what the websites say it was – no need for details. Yes, Duane, it's not wrong to be gay – we did that last week when we talked about Sir Iqbal Sacranie, but Mr Oaten is married after all . . . and there's the issue of paying the young men, all right, the sex-workers. No, Jolene, it does not mean that all gay men go in for the thing Kylie wrote on that bit of paper, yes, I saw, no, it's not normal gay stuff – what do you mean, how do I know? My private life is private, how dare you . . .?'

I do not envy anybody who has to try to lay out, for the new generation, exactly what it is that 21st-century British society thinks about homosexuality, and the acceptable norms of gay behaviour. The law is visible enough – no discrimination, no persecution, civil partnerships, and it seems that it isn't illegal to question the sexuality of a police horse. Far more difficult to be clear about more nebulous issues of approval, and about the freedom of religious groups to label thousands of inoffensive middle-aged civil partners as sinners and 'a danger to society'. Especially if in your own school community you have unmarried teachers being persecuted either slyly or openly, boys calling girls 'lezzers' when they won't sleep with them, and mockery and violence visited on any boy who doesn't snigger loudly enough through *Brokeback Mountain*.

Section 28 is dead and gone and there are policies against homophobia in schools, but anecdotally it is clear that many of these are pretty half-hearted. And why? Fear of parents. I'd guess. You try suggesting at your next governors' meeting that it would be a positively excellent thing to have settled gay partners on the staff, and invite relevant visiting lecturers to be casually open about their sexuality. Eeeek! Out come the concerned Muslims, the more devoutly obedient Catholics, and the sort of parents who are convinced that gayness can be caught like a cold. Better to jink around the issue and talk vaguely about respecting individuality and 'lifestyles'.

But then you run aground, sharply, when the news is full of stories about MPs, giving almost the same weight of shocked contumely to a troubled but fairly virtuous single gay man as it does to a husband and father who persistently frequents the seediest end of the sex industry as a predator. We have to decide what we think, be straight and uncompromising with parents, and stick to our line. And that means everybody in the staffroom. And that won't be easy.

Curriculum, curricula. . . .

My essay's in cyberspace, miss

'Pay attention, children. This is Mr Gates, who has come to talk to us about the future of education. Roy, stop flipping the cover of your calculator, you'll break it. Mr Gates says that all of you will soon have laptop computers instead of books.

'Mr Gates is going to tell us about the future of the laptop as a full-time learning tool backed by instant Internet capability – Leanne! I have told you about tilting your chair back, you'll topple into the radiator – soon you will all have these miraculous tools in front of you – George! There is a RULE about carving on the desks!'

Bill Gates is, of course, correct. The time will come when wired, confident boys and girls will be inseparable from their flat plastic friends, blithely getting online from the school bus.

It may seem wildly improbable in an age where the struggle is to equip even the teacher with a laptop, and anything under £1,000 gives you headaches; but even three years ago it would have been ludicrous to imagine teenagers with mobiles text-messaging each other across Pizza Hut.

Like every change since those early hornbooks for children it will come jerkily, driven by technology and pragmatism. Laptops will never, I think, entirely replace books but it is certainly on the cards that they will liberate schools from the tyranny of the stale photo-copied worksheet. Even diehards should be thrilled by the prospect of Internettable kids: if there is one thing you have to get right when you do Web searches it is spelling.

However, we old laptop hands have a few cautions. As a rural teleworker I am a veteran: my first one weighed as much as a Christmas turkey, had a flickering green screen and a one-hour battery which got hot enough to melt the casing. The one from which I now address you is a chic slender oyster, in turquoise and cream plastic, which delivers a picture better than a desktop machine for six untroubled hours. In between there were others, including a repulsive machine with a fold-out keyboard which proved allergic to its own programme and halved in value during the brief interval between my buying it and selling it back to the dealer.

The advances during those years have transformed laptops from a show-off toy or capricious business tool into something which makes you wonder why you bother with a big machine at all. Indeed, better-off students and sixth-formers don't even consider humping some great awkward monitor, keyboard and hard-drive unit around at the beginning and end of each term; they slip their A4 laptop into the rucksack and saunter off with a couple of leads and a miniprinter the size of a Swiss roll.

But the younger schoolkids? Like the technology, they are going to need a bit of modification. PSE will have to shove in a quick module on relating to your laptop, to bridge the gulf between advanced electronics and unregenerate children.

Meanwhile, the trade will have to make them much, much cheaper, without compromising the screen: even at £500 a time they would be too nickable to walk home from school with.

They also need to get more robust. So far, designers have only protected laptops against the kind of things which happen to business travellers – bumping into other executives in the queue for the Shuttle, the odd splash of cappuccino. Children have far more adventurous lives. If your day includes changing-rooms, conker battles, wheelies, duels with the dog, Dunkin Donuts and Big Macs then the laptop must be willing to share the experience. The Fantaproof keyboard has not, I can tell you, yet been developed.

Both junior school and secondary models will also have to be equipped with piercing, wailing alarms linked to a bracelet permanently fixed on their keeper; like those virtual babies which put children off pregnancy. There is only a very short gap between the end of childish inattention and the beginning of hormonal forgetfulness. The 21st-century version of leaving your books on the bus does not bear thinking of.

Actually, none of the excuses does. 'Miss, my cursor's frozen . . . Naomi put chewing-gum on my Trackball . . . I did all my project and it got wiped when my brother pushed the button . . . Sir, he corrupted my hard disk, s'not fair . . . Didn't you get the homework, Miss? I e-mailed it, honest, it must be your server, my Dad says Freeserve is pants, Miss . . .'

Hysteria and cakes

League-tables week always produces a pleasing flurry of hysteria. We connoisseurs of educational brouhaha particularly enjoyed this year's outbreak, heralded by the London *Evening Standard* headline: 'Cookery exams outrank physics'. The story was even more luscious than it looked, since the paper – followed by a posse of others, yelping in pursuit of the fox of dumbing-down – revealed that while physics GCSE at A grade gets 52 points for your school, a distinction in cake-decorating gets 55.

Fabulous. The harrumphing was deafening. Alan Smithers raised the spectre of students being 'nudged' on to vocational courses to raise a school's rating, opening up the delicious vision of a young Faraday or Newton weeping tears of frustration as a sinister director of studies locks away the gas chromatograph and sombrely hands him an icing-bag. The Department for Education and Skills waffled about 'old-fashioned educational snobbery' and said that 'the world has moved on', though it did not say whether it believes cake-decorating has moved it on faster than physics.

Perhaps there has been an outbreak of pacifism up there at the ministry, with some Old Labour CND firebrand leaping on the table and setting hearts aflame with a cry of: 'Look, if Einstein had only stuck to making delicate pink sugar roses, there would have been no bomb.'

Meanwhile, of course, nobody looked at the small print and pointed out that if the notional GCSE physicist gets an A* rather than an A, he or she acquires 58 points, a score not available to even the most inspired and distinguished creator of marzipan bridegrooms. So that's all right then. Maybe. Some of us might mutter that anything which undermines the credibility of league tables is good news anyway. Perhaps now we can go back to choosing schools by looking rather closer at them, and asking actual questions about subject success and teaching methods.

But my mind ran off at a tangent, reflecting on the whole business of school subjects and the esteem in which we hold them. A lot of it,

I fear, depends on the degree of dishonesty with which they are named. People seem woundingly ready to insult cookery and cake-decorating, for instance – fine and practical subjects with edible results – whereas only a few of us take the trouble to insult the vapidities and enslavement to the food industry of GCSE 'food tech'. Perhaps if they had called the cake-decorating qualification something like 'sucrose technology', it would have been less readily dissed by the papers.

But there have always been oddities, snobberies and illogicalities in our view of subjects. A medieval child of the aristocracy was expected to study astrolabe, rhetoric and Petrus of Spain's *summulae logicales*. Useful vocational subjects like archery rubbed along with fantastical balderdash, about how hyenas can change their sex at will, and how an elephant's only fear is of dragons.

In the era of *Tom Brown's Schooldays*, Dr Arnold's boys wasted hours every day on their 'construe', translating dim Latin texts (or more likely buying translations of them off older boys for crumpets and sexual favours).

The idea was that a 'grounding in the classics' would produce a gentlemanly boy, even if he knew nothing of the remotest usefulness.

Glance at education under various dictatorships and you find fantastical elements in the core curriculum, involving everything from 'gymnastic and military exercises' to Communist morality and Kim Il Sung studies. Nearer to home, it is not hard to find barking-mad approaches to subjects enduring right into the modern era. In my husband's 1960s grammar school it was ordained that German was a 'boy's language' and French was for girls. How they thought Marlene Dietrich and General de Gaulle got by is anyone's guess.

Meanwhile, just as Miss Prism instructed Gwendolen to omit the chapter on the fall of the rupee as too sensational, a girls' school of reasonable reputation, right up to the mid-1960s, used bowdlerized Shakespeare texts and would not allow the word 'womb' to be uttered in *Macbeth*. Macduff was, nonsensically, 'from his mother's arms untimely ripped'.

Future generations may look back and giggle at our curriculum contents. I revere physicists, and cake-decorators too. Let a thousand sugar flowers bloom.

OCTOBER 4 2002

Broad and unbalanced

Breadth. That's what it's all about. More breadth in the 16–19 school curriculum. That's why we've had the chaos of AS-levels, the scandar over A2, the Tomlinson inquiry row, hundreds of traumatised university freshmen sitting in undesired lecture halls wondering whether or not they were robbed, government witterings about now moving towards 'a sort of baccalaureate', and the concerted baying for Estelle Morris's head.

Breadth in the 16–19 curriculum! That was the golden egg, the Holy Grail, the McGuffin, the object of ravenous desire. Maybe there's another way. Maybe the big mistake was assuming that the only way to get breadth is to put in more exams.

Perhaps in real life, breadth is something you acquire differently. Perhaps it doesn't depend entirely on passing exams. Perhaps we could have approached the whole problem in a simpler way, leaving A-levels more or less intact.

Columnists exist in order to have scorn and contumely poured on them by those who know better. So here, as part of the ongoing national process of fretting ourselves into a stew over this matter, I offer a scheme. It involves no extra staffing, no new examinations, and only a modicum of extra time for pressured sixth-form students. It delivers breadth where it matters, which is between the ears of the pupil, and uses up very little stationery. It goes as follows.

Everyone chooses their A-levels, being as selective as they like between arts and sciences (I have to say this because my daughter fulminates in rage at the idea that people who are old enough to join the army or marry might not be allowed to give up maths).

Once they have chosen their three (oh all right, maybe four) subjects, they must pick one (or two) completely contrasting ones. In these, they take on the role of fellow-traveller. They have to attend as many classes as they can, watch what the real pupils learn, and make notes (however confused) for their own benefit.

Thus I would have sat, half-baffled but faintly interested, in the back row of physics classes – and botany nuts would observe

historians and musicians at work, and smile in recognition of occasional words on the French whiteboard which remind them of Latin plant names.

At the end of two years, just before their real A-levels, they would be required to write an essay – about 2,000 words, and as colloquial as they like – about what they think of this alien subject, what they most enjoyed learning about, what the real pupils seemed to get out of it, and what they found baffling or pointless. These essays would be marked – not very subtly, but on a pass/fail basis – by mainstream examiners who would find it strangely refreshing to have an intelligent, innocent outsider's view of geography, or psychology, or physics, or history, or whatever.

Essays might begin 'The only bit of the history classes I enjoyed was the bit about the Tudors. Those guys were mental . . .' or 'This molecule business is really odd . . .' or 'The amount of time people spend looking at just one short poem is incredible'.

All the examiners would be looking for is proof that the fellow-traveller has really tried to see the point of the alien subject, and made an imaginative leap into what it might be like to understand it and specialise in it. That, after all, is how most of us learn most of our breadth all through life. We listen to Melvyn Bragg talking to scientists, we read Sunday paper articles about a new Peter Ackroyd biography, we get into dinner-party discussions with people who understand quarks or cancer cells, we work down the corridor from an IT wizard from Cupertino.

We don't have to pass exams in these things, but if we have enquiring minds we make connections. Why ask any more of the sixth-former? He or she has specialist subjects, properly studied. But, working in a school environment full of other subjects, why not pick up breadth just where it lies?

There would be rules, obviously. Disrupting a class would be a sacking offence, and if you got a bad name for it then no other teacher would touch you, and you would be stuffed, since your real A-levels would be worthless to universities unless you had a pass in the 'breadth' certificate.

If you didn't understand at all, you would have to keep your questions till later and sidle up to the brightest geek in the group at break and ask for guidance on the baffling bits. This would be very nice for the geeks. It would all be very informal, very natural, driven by interest, and minimally – but seriously – evaluated in the reading of the final essay.

I'd have loved it. I'd have gone to zoology. I always wanted to see what really went on in that lab.

APRIL 29 2005

How not to go to university

I was hanging out at the City and Guilds the other day, chatting about the woeful fact that not enough people realise that it is good, not bad, when a kid decides to do a solid vocational training instead of racking up debt on a fifth-rate degree. And one observation from an old-stager pulled me up short. It is, he says, partly the fault of careers teachers. They don't know enough about vocational courses, and they don't push them enough.

But as he said it, an awful suspicion came over me, which maybe I should not have expressed. If it is true about careers teachers – and I have not studied the subject – there might be a hidden and disquieting reason. Let me throw it out to professionals for consideration. Could it be, could it possibly be, that some careers teachers with aspirational heads and pushy parents on their backs actually don't dare to promote the idea that it might be interesting to avoid university and learn a skill?

Maybe they see a danger in revealing to restive, pallid 16-year-olds that you can do a course in boatbuilding or photography, electrical engineering or embroidery, pottery or silversmithing or nightclub bouncing (yes indeedy, City and Guilds accredits a door supervisor course, do look it up. It's not as long and taxing as some, but it's there).

Perhaps the careers teacher shoves all these entrancing options to the bottom of the heap because he or she has an awful suspicion that if such delightful life-skills were openly on offer, they would not be taken up solely by the 'non-academic' cadre. There might be a lemming-like stampede of children marked down as potential academic high-flyers, thrilled at the idea of doing something that involves less writing and more handling of real-world stuff.

It could happen. I remember only too well how my own sixth-form friends used physically to drag me past the Army Careers Office, whimpering and pawing the air, simply because after an overdose of gerundives and the Thirty Years War I could imagine

nothing nicer than learning to grease a gun or put down smoke or march around in the lovely fresh air.

It wasn't patriotism, just the idea of a containable, masterable skill or two. Of course, being a girls' school they sometimes mentioned nursing to us, but no sooner had I become excited about learning bandage-rolling and plastering than someone would say: 'Of course, there's a lot of academic studying in modern nursing', and I would be turned off again.

At least my school taught compulsory needlework. Today things have gone further, and we ought to recognise that in the way education is now structured, there is a powerful risk of not only alienating the non-academic kids, but of wearing out the patience and the natural joyfulness of the academic ones.

Why else do they all take off on gap years, strapping rucksacks to their weedy, underexercised backs and leaving their books on the bedroom floor? Why do even the most apparently talented English A-level students stubbornly resist reading classic novels which are not 'set'? They are sickened, literally: they are in ketosis on an Atkins diet of the mind, overfed with rich cerebral protein, yearning for the fibre and honest bread of practicality. Even school technology gets less and less practical and more and more about folders; cookery has mutated into foodtech and woodwork into resistant materials. You don't even get to cut up pickled dogfish any more in biology. OK, it was disgusting, and the only thing I can remember 40 years on is the smell, but I do remember looking forward to it as a delightfully practical change from *Dictée* and the Diet of Worms.

Maybe the answer is that just as every schoolchild should do a sport, so each should do a practical skill. Tapestry, or bicycle maintenance, or bricklaying. That way, people like me would be reminded that they are in fact lousy at sewing and seriously bad with a screwdriver, and we would return with renewed vigour to shovelling words and ideas around because that is our only talent. Meanwhile, others would discover that they are gifted, and bombard the careers teacher with requests about how to take this talent further.

Whereupon the teacher could artfully point out that they might even run their own fashion house or garage, if they'd just settle down and learn to write a literate sentence and grasp the concept of percentages.

So academic basics would benefit, too. And you could cancel a few citizenship classes, because they'd all have learned the basic principle that everyone counts and everyone can contribute. Some would learn it by succeeding with the needle or the trowel, others by failing ignominiously (as I did) and learning a bit of respect for those who are handier. Result!

The bell won't ring on Friday

I love the idea of whole-day lessons pioneered by Leasowes school in the West Midlands, and endorsed by the chief inspector Mike Tomlinson at the Social Market Foundation. It is one of those blindingly obvious initiatives. Why should children always, relentlessly, all through the week, have to turn subjects on and off at 40-minute intervals?

Why should they be forever thundering along corridors to different classrooms, or in earlier years waiting for a series of teachers to thunder towards them, scattering folders, glasses, and cardigans?

Why encourage the idea that you can get clear of your most hated subject if you can only struggle through the next 33 minutes, with artful distraction of the teacher and guaranteed red-herring questions – 'Sir, is Beckham better than George Best was?'

Why let children grow up thinking that nothing need ever be concentrated on for longer than the span of dreaded Double Maths?

Why should your train of thought, the subtle progress of understanding of a new idea, be forever interrupted by the terrible clatter of desks, stuffing of bags and shoving in corridors, as the thumping feet of your less interested *confrères* dispel the idea which was just beginning to take beautiful new shape in the deep folds of your brain?

I know good teachers have as strong an instinct for the structure of a period and the passage of time as any broadcaster. I have watched them cleverly raising the intellectual temperature and then winding it down again to anticipate the bell.

But not all lessons can be so elegantly ordered. I can remember English periods where a poem was stopped in mid-reading by the shrilling of an electric bell and the banging of desks. And maths lessons when I had just begun to understand what the bloody bracket-things were for, when I had to stop and consider the Diet of Worms or demonstrate Osmosis Using Two Eggs.

There were religious education lessons when you were just getting to the nub of the matter of papal infallibility, with the teacher-nun defensively backed into a corner, and she was saved from defeat by yet another damned bell. Life doesn't break into equally-sized pieces. Why should school? The Leasowes experiment seems a modest advance. One day a week, Friday, is devoted to a five-hour block of teaching in which groups can be brought in and out at different levels, visiting artists or science demonstrators used most profitably, and large projects completed. Complicated Meccano can be set up to demonstrate maths principles, and not tidied away. Or the theme day can be used for an outside trip. But always the principle is there: on Fridays the bitty, stressful, scuttling pace of school life is altered. Not to something slower, but to something more coherently purposeful: a piece of real life.

Leasowes, according to *The TES* report, is communicating the idea and has got one other school going down the same road, and another likely to. But it is interesting that the headteacher, John Howells, says that even though he shows the ropes to many interested schools, few actually do it.

Of course it's an act of faith. All these learning-centred, innovative, blue-sky initiatives always are acts of faith. The interesting thing is to see how far a modern school, with all the grinding centralist pressures on its day, can be flexible enough to take these leaps, and think from the ground up. Presumably Leasowes must opt out of the new secondary literacy hour requirement for its Fridays. Clearly this is possible. But the more standardisation that is imposed, the harder it gets for heads to have ideas and, in the words of Greg Dyke, cut the crap and make it happen.

When I heard about the adventurous Meccano projects at Leasowes, I was, depressingly, reminded of a complaint from a four-year-old. His nursery school mentors were anxious to fulfil every corner of the 'pre-school curriculum'. Whenever he was just getting involved in a model of his own devising, he was made to put it away and join the prescribed Japanese-style session of chanting letters and numbers. 'Usually' said the child glumly, 'the model gets broken up when you put it on the shelf. I never finish my garage that I want to make, and I have to start again.'

So good on Leasowes. And thank God for a chief inspector who accepts ideas that look a bit different and weren't his. Let the green shoots flourish between the dead, heavy flagstones of the system.

Top marks for sale

How much does an A grade cost at A-level? Can I afford one? At last, thanks to the Centre for Policy Studies and the Education Research Trust, we have a ballpark figure. It costs £9,150 in a private school and £5,950 in the state sector.

In *Standards and Spending – Dispelling the Education Orthodoxy*, Dr John Marks explains that he got this figure by comparing the results of the top 100 independents with state sixth forms, crunching fees and funding, and spitting out the result in what the independent spokesmen huffily call 'a crudely mechanistic way'. It is part of Dr Marks's argument against the namby-pamby liberal line that spending more on education will improve it.

The story was flagged in one paper by the unsurprising headline 'State schools better value for money than private'. Well, we knew that. Quite apart from obvious economies of scale, it is axiomatic that if you put any mixed gang of top headteachers in a room together, sooner or later the private-school ones (shadowed by beady-eyed bursars) will sidle up to their state-school oppos and hiss: 'How the hell do you do it on the money?' The comparative meanness of spending-per-pupil in the state sector is legendary. Cash-strapped private schools gnash their teeth at the mystery of how well the good 'bog-standard' comprehensives manage. But really, it seems a cruel irony that the penny-pinching efficiency of state schools should be used against them in this way, to conclude that there is no point whatsoever in bringing them closer to a private-school spend.

The only attractive feature of the CPS report is the idea of introducing value-for-money in league tables. I back that simply because anything which makes the accursed things more obscure is to be welcomed. Then parents can go back to choosing schools on the basis of gut feeling, local reputation, and whether or not the head-teacher gives them the heebie-jeebies.

The trouble with the calculation over A-levels is twofold. First, you can't price an A grade because some of the pesky little varmints just won't get one, however much you spend. Pay £30,000 per subject and still some will be too idle, too slow, too bored, or spooked by Edexcel accidentally setting the question back-to-front.

The other problem is that the high spend of private schools does not all go on a kamikaze rush for high grades. Oh, they want them all right they lust for them, they coach and coax and police the course-work deadlines. But that isn't all they spend it on. There are other things which are unfairly lavished on private-school children while being denied to their state-funded counterparts. Things like music lessons, with plenty of instruments available, well-stocked libraries and laboratories, quiet chapels, playing fields, swimming pools, grass, fresh air, and pleasant classrooms in decent architecture with most of the paint still adhering to the walls. There are small classes led by teachers who stay a long time, are not driven demented by paper-work, and have a reasonable chance of knowing everybody's name. There are abundant school trips. There is individual help. There is also – in the less fiercely selective schools – often a better chance of chivvying the duller and more obstreperous pupils into some success.

Never mind the A grades, what about the triumphant and unexpected Cs? That's the real measure of a crack school. We all know privately-educated kids who, without huge amounts of expensive attention, would have quite understandably been despaired of or thrown out, but who are miraculously prodded through two A-levels.

Money is spent on all these things in private schools, because if it wasn't the parents would cut up rough. They're clients. In the state system we are also clients – all of us, with or without children – but it is harder to crack the economic whip.

The high pupil-spend of private schools might not, in the end, buy your darling a row of straight As, but it can help to provide other things: order, space, peace, personal attention, music, sport, variety.

Yes, it's unfair that some people can buy their children these things; but it's unfair that some people live in luxury and hire personal trainers, or have wider-screened TVs than the neighbours. And yes, there are lousy private schools (close them down) and yes, the best state schools also manage the peace, music, variety etc, often in catchment areas which make the achievement miraculous.

But there is something really creepy about suggesting that we should not bother to put better resources into looking after state pupils, just because it might not guarantee more A grades. Ugh.

Becky's ad break

This week's entry for my Education Hall of Fame is Becky Bates of Norwich, age 15. Step forward, young Becky, remove that chewing-gum, take a bow.

This is the girl who was told by her teachers that she was a border-line D or E candidate for her GCSEs next academic year having, by her own admission, 'messed about' during her school career so far.

She describes herself as 'not that academically great but very creative'. Admittedly one shudders on her poor teachers' behalf at the thought of all those years of creative messing-about in their classes.

But what is life about, if not the possibility of redemption and improvement? So read on. Becky, it seems, reflected on this dour prediction for a while and connected it with the grim fact that to be an air hostess, her life's ambition, you need good GCSEs. Having thought about it all for a while, she took firm and rather startling action. She advertised in the *Norwich Evening News*.

'Will someone take me on?' she inquired. 'Perhaps a patient retired teacher or someone bright who has a lot of patience? Can someone give me the time in return for me walking their dog or tidying their house? Or just take me on as a challenge?'

Even better, she added with Oliver-Twist hopefulness and a tenuous grasp of reality, they could 'pay for me to go to a boarding school where there is only 10 in a class and I won't be bullied'.

According to the rather startled newsdesk at the *Norwich Evening News*, Becky did not tell her mother she was making this plea, still less her school. It is in special measures, with a shirty sort of Ofsted report on its back and a long way to climb.

Naturally, on hearing of his non-star pupil's appeal, her head-teacher rather huffily said he was surprised, because the school has a Student Achievement Centre for people falling behind and 43 per cent of candidates got their five A–C grades at GCSE last year, so there. Again, sympathy veers towards the school. Life is not easy, not with so many Beckies wandering about.

The eventual outcome of the story is uncertain. The latest I heard

from the newspaper is that they have indeed had several offers of coaching, all sounding pretty genuine and teacherly, and are proceeding to arrange contacts with the family – albeit with all the caution appropriate in these suspicious days where sweet young 15-year-old girls are concerned. So it could be that Miss Bates will get her coaching, and her grades.

Cheeky little madam, or heroine of our times? I incline towards the latter view. Think how many lessons young Becky has taken in and acted upon, despite her history of messing about.

She has grasped what many do not – that you need exam grades to get ahead in life. She sees there is no future in turning into Vicky Pollard. She has understood the urgency of the situation, even though summer 2007 must seem aeons away. She has concluded that good teaching is the key and admits that it requires patience to deal with the likes of her. She sees that in a hard-pressed school in special measures, it is not that easy to provide the sort of personal concentration that she needs.

She has even, God bless her, grasped that teaching is a job with a value to it, and that her tutoring will have to be paid for with dog-walking or housework.

More importantly even than all that, the child has realised that glum predictions need not come true. I am well aware that prediction skills are now an unnervingly large part of teaching, what with value-added tables and universities doling out offers on the basis of nothing more than staffroom guesswork.

But I have never been comfortable with this form of soothsaying. One friend's son was told by staff at age 13 that he was a C/D candidate for GCSE at best. He subsequently changed schools and at 18 rattled off to a top medical school garlanded with As.

Most children, confronted with confident adult predictions, tend to go along with them as meekly as if they had the words 'not academic' tattooed between their shoulderblades. Becky Bates of Norwich, lairy though she may be, somehow maintained the ability to look into the future and resolve to shape it in her own way, by her own efforts, irrespective of the views of the adults.

Good on her, I say. She fulfils the magnificently stroppy county motto of her native Norfolk: 'Do different.'

Don't be a Jubilee sourpuss

Time to think about the Jubilee, I reckon. No, get out from under that desk, you can't put it off forever. I sense that there may be a touch of resistance to overcome here and there; something which I had not quite reckoned with until I had an incendiary conversation with a teacher last week. He is a department head, to my eye dedicated and clever, in a large comprehensive in outer London.

But he spurns the Jubilee. 'I'm having nothing to do with it,' he said crossly when the subject came up, apropos the excitements and free mugs of 1977. 'I don't believe in it. I never did. I'm a republican. Why should we celebrate the hereditary parasites? Come to that, why should they mess up the half-term dates?'

'But it'll be fun!' I bleated lamely.

'Yeah, right,' said the Robespierre of the staffroom. 'Fun for sad old codgers like you. Anyway, there's no time for schools to faff about with jubilees. Got a huge curriculum to deliver.'

He claimed to be backed by about a third of the staff at that school; I have no idea how widespread the phobia is in the teaching community at large, but a poll would be fascinating.

I think they are missing a trick. This is not because I nourish any burning devotion to the monarchy, nor even just because that Jubilo-phobes tend to be of the sourpuss persuasion. The real reason I was so startled is because the teacher concerned does history and English, and it seems inconceivable that in these damn dreary days any bright pedagogue would willingly pass up an opportunity to identify his or her subject with colour, gold robes, trumpets, horses, lions, unicorns, processions, pop concerts, and people with their faces painted to look like Union Jacks.

If you've got a monarchy with a fine tradition of dash, pomp, fanfares and general hoopla, you really might as well press it into service. Other do: my son gap-yeared as an apprentice deckhand aboard a Dutch square-rigger in the Pacific, and on the day of the Dutch royal wedding, a thousand miles off Honolulu with nobody else to see, the young crew decked the entire ship out in the national colour (orange) and declared a holiday and a round of deck games.

Quite apart from the mileage the history department can get out of crowns and monarchs, a jubilee is a fabulous teaching aid. Fifty years, after all, is a nice manageable span of time. It is 'when Mum was a baby' for the teenagers, and Granny's memory for the primary-schoolers. Every network will be stuffed with wonderful old black-and-white footage not only of the Royal family but of ordinary people leading monochrome lives in awful clothes; every town library will have the old postcards out on display, showing how different, yet recognisable, your home streets once were.

The PSE department can use it to consider changed social attitudes, dig out some hilarious cuttings from the 1950s, and help pupils debate the different values of a time of rationing, sexual hesitancy and prime ministers without saucy pictures on their shirt-cuffs. Media studies can interview the local over-60s about what a novelty television was at coronation time, and try to analyse the massive shifts of consciousness, knowledge, sophistication and attention-span between a generation without TV and a generation incapable of doing without it for one single day. Again, every Jubilee nostalgia programme will be a teaching aid as summer approaches.

Then there are the debates. No sixth form should be without its session of verbal fisticuffs on the motion 'This House hopes that the Queen is the last of her kind' or 'This house would rather be a citizen than a subject.' Meanwhile, the art department can set the juniors painting entries for the *Blue Peter* competition, and the seniors researching images of royalty in sculpture and painting, or constructing ironic homage from grubby Kleenex and plastic grapes.

And through it all, contemplating the steadfast dutifulness of the monarch, the vagaries of her family, the shocks and surprises and upheavals of the clan, and the general slow soap-operatic unfolding of their stories, marriages and family tree, children can learn the most difficult and useful lesson of all. They can observe that life is a very long and surprising business, requiring constant adaptation, and that the sooner you get used to the idea the better.

Oh go on – grit your teeth, do the Jubilee. It's a richer vein to mine than the boring old Millennium.

JANUARY 18 2002

Browned off

We all know about the classroom of the future. There will be electronic whiteboards fed by laptops, so that teacher can play Hogwarts, tapping with a wand to make diagrams rotate and videos flower. Children will go home with teeny pen-size downloads of homework, plug them into domestic machines, and return the following morning claiming that the dog ate the data module.

Great. The electronic whiteboard in particular seems to work, not least because of the sophisticated and responsive piece of apparatus which stands beside it and answers to the name of Teacher. It was always obvious that computer technology would only get really helpful when control of the machinery was prised from the hands of people with an unhealthy technical interest in it.

But it focuses the mind on other, older visual aids to making stuff sink into children's minds. Take the most basic technology of all, colouring in. I was well and truly told off by post the other day for including in a novel (*Passing Go*) a brief scene in which the 11-year-old son of the house is gloomily confronting his homework 'which was nearly all colouring in and copying and drawing. Kids' work. Resignedly pulling the folder towards him and starting to shade in a patch of steppe . . .' etc. My correspondent, an eminent geographer, said that geography is much more whizzily taught these days, and no longer imposes 'strategies of the kind you suggest'.

I wholly sympathise. It must be very annoying to modern teachers that novelists are adults, who therefore tend to portray homework as 10 to 50 years out of date. I take his point that geography has moved on since 1965. But that bit of homework was actually given to my own 11-year-old in the mid-90s and looked very tedious for a bright, but cack-handed, child well past primary school. The teacher at the time said that physical, copyist work was 'the only way' to get the general outlines of the world into children's minds. Similarly an RE teacher who kept sending the other one home with 'word squares', as featured in puzzle magazines, out of which the pupil was required to find such significant biblical words as 'Jacob' 'ladder' and 'angel'.

I have no real complaints, just a parental puzzlement which I find is quite widely shared by the naturally inartistic. Why are intellectual 16-year-olds still required to cut out pictures of roulades and tarts from magazines to illustrate their food-tech folder? Why do you lose marks in a cerebral subject like economics if your pie chart isn't perfectly circular and neatly coloured in? Why does a friend's fairly brilliant child, at a top-rated comprehensive, spend so much time tracing? In the age of the electronic singing whiteboard, will there still be such an emphasis on ruled straight lines in red and green Biro?

I am trying to think back, fairly, to my own education and how much all this visual drudgery helped. At primary school it definitely did: I can still see the shape of Italy because it was so damn tricky getting the heel of the boot right. Over 11, though, I am less sure. I remember that our RE teacher in the lower fifth was very keen indeed on making us do diagrams of spiritual matters – I can still draw a mean challice and a passable Holy Ghost – but beyond that, none of the things I remember have much to do with the things I drew, untidily and smudgily, in exercise books. Despite endless incompetent biology diagrams what I actually recall are things I was vividly told, or saw demonstrated on a defunct dogfish and a couple of hard-boiled eggs.

I never minded drawing experiments we had actually done, but maps of the human digestive system or circulation never stayed in my mind as biological facts, simply because the chief association is the sense of panic at having lost the red crayon and having to do the blood in orange.

I fear virtuality and the screen as much as any old codger: nobody thinks that prodding buttons on a computer and staring at pixels takes you to genuine understanding. And I have always had rather a yen for the style of maths teaching in which you all go outside and the teacher throws a ball at you and everyone shouts numbers. But of a the physical aids to secondary learning, the one I most mistrust is colouring-in. I wish someone would convince me that it works, because there's a lot of it about.

FEBRUARY 21 2003

A floating fantasy

A MAD old daydream sprang back to life the other day, spurred by a headline in *The Times*. I hadn't indulged this fantasy for years, and had a pleasant five minutes remembering all the details.

A gang of us used to elaborate them back in the 1980s, while we drank coffee out of paper cups at the leisure centre and watched our nine-year-olds' swimming lesson. (To tell the truth, we kept the poor sprats at it for years, doing swimming lessons they no longer really needed because we mothers so enjoyed our Friday teatime *conversazione.*)

The fantasy was this: when our children outgrew primary school, we would raise two fingers to both the troubled, overcrowded, league-tabled, government-bullied state system and the prissy, snobbish, tie-wearing local independents. We would start our own school.

The headline which brought this day-dream back said that 'businesses, charities and parents' groups' will be invited to run all new state secondary schools. Education Secretary Charles Clarke said that he wants 'the widest possible range' of school types, each with their own ethos. 'Let a thousand flowers bloom!', he seemed to be chirping, a bearded harbinger of spring. The effect was slightly spoiled a couple of days later by the news that parents would no longer even theoretically be able to flit, like choosy bees, to the flower they like best; but never mind. There is nothing quite like the fantasy of inventing a school.

It was going to be housed in an old but cunningly converted trawler, moored bang in the middle of the River Alde and Ore in Suffolk. The school roll might go as high as 50, and the uniform consist of blue jeans or canvas trousers, sweaters and oilskin jackets.

Every morning, pupils would be met on the jetty and taken upriver in a fast rigid inflatable, to clamber up the ladder on to the deck. This would give them some fresh air and excitement to start the day; each group would then hang up their lifejackets and scatter to their various tasks, which would include meteorological

observations and checking the dials on the ship's various systems –
refrigeration, heating, power, smoke alarms, etc.

When they had reported to the bo'sun (an employee somewhere
between caretaker and CDT teacher) and thus taken responsibility
for their own physical surroundings, they would be sufficiently calm
and focused for assembly. This would involve a lot of lusty singing,
possibly with an accordion.

We had worked out that among us all (a collection of freelances
and assorted homemakers with reasonable control of their own
time) we could supply a rota of non-teaching supervisors for free,
and also enough solid expertise to teach English to GCSE, cookery,
carpentry and (via navigation projects) the first couple of years of
geography. We had a cook, but each Friday one group of children
would be taken out of lessons to make lunch for all. Other teaching
expertise, we reckoned, could be bought in on a freelance basis.

Frankly, rural areas are full of career-break teachers with young
children, who could benefit from our mini-crèche up on the bridge;
and, more important, there is generally a good stock of burnt-out,
fed-up former teachers who are getting a bit bored with their early
retirement.

These, we reckoned, could be re-enthused by a smaller and more eccentric academy such as ours. We asked some of them, just for fun, what they'd charge, and when we added it up, it still came to a lot less than private schools.

After lunch, there would be one brief lesson – or performance, because we would be getting a lot of drama and music into the curriculum – and then games, which would involve up to two hours of heavily supervised and reasonably strenuous dinghy sailing, rowing, canoeing, summer swimming, mud-wrestling, and walking along the reedy bank. Children would then return aboard for an hour or so of prep round a roaring coal fire with cocoa and biscuits, thus saving parents the nightly hell of supervision. At six or seven they would be delivered back to the shore exhausted and glowing.

Our curriculum was a matter of debate, I favoured whole-morning, total-immersion projects rather than bite-size periods. We all agreed that a lot of education – from physics to poetry to natural history – would be assisted by using the ship, and the river, and perhaps (if we could afford an engine) the occasional trip along the coast. Discipline would not, we felt, be a problem given the number of adults around and the knockout effect of fresh air. What, in any case, could make a more suitable sin-bin than a steel fo'c'sle, or a more suitable detention than scraping rust or painting bulkheads?

Oh, all right. Mr Clarke would turn it down, and prodnose authorities would close us. But it was a nice dream. Almost the best bit of it was that when inspection time came round, we wouldn't necessarily bother to send the rubber launch to them from the jetty. If they weren't nice to us, they'd have to bloody swim.

In praise of clockwork

Grüss Gott! I address you from the top of an Alp, quite my favourite place at this time of year, though it rarely actually happens. I got imprinted with love of the Swiss during my teens when my Dad worked in Berne, and every few years the urge arises to grit the teeth and pay Swiss prices for the clockwork wonderfulness of a Swiss week. The trains work, the postbuses work, the snow-blowers work, the woodpiles are neat, the shopkeepers solicitous. And for those who observe the tangled world of education it is profoundly reassuring to watch the ski-schools. From my perch on the nursery slopes, I have been studying them as a seductive model of a particular kind of educational perfection.

For the Swiss believe, above all, in training. Everyone is trained for something. Plumbers, builders, electricians, decorators, carpenters and other craftsmen serve formal apprenticeships so rigorous that Swiss householders rarely attempt DIY because bodging is simply not done. Nobody makes even the most unpretentious hillside cheese without years of sitting at the feet of some tyrannical old mountain beardie who holds the timeless cheese wisdom in his gnarled fist. Bankers and checkout staff, hoteliers and maids, dressmakers and kindergarten teachers undergo so much training it would make your eyes water: the language skills alone required of schoolteachers are downright embarrassing to list.

So when it comes to enrolling in the Schweizer Ski und Snowboard Schüle, you can forget any namby-pamby rubbish about personal discovery or individual learning adventures and peer education. There is an instructor, and there is a row of learners, and the instructor's way is the way it will be done. Ordnung muss sein!

You watch this at work with the little children, three and four years old in the Pulvo Club pen. They surround their instructress, who rattles away in four languages with no apparent effort and demonstrates such basic skills as hopping from foot to foot, falling over on your back with your legs in the air, clutching the drag-lift rope and sliding downhill in your teeny boots and two-foot skis.

Voices are never raised, smiles never slip, but authority is absolute. No toddler defies Christiane or Liesl. Before long they are following her down the big hill, turning when she turns, going 'Whoo!' when she instructs them to go 'Whoo!', and lining up at the bottom again in the correct order, eyes front.

It reminded me of the period when, just before primary school, I craftily enrolled each child in turn in a dancing class of local renown. It seemed to me that after the freewheeling playgroup approach ('Do you want to come to the story corner? all right, dear, stay with the Playdough') it would be helpful to their reception teacher if they learned that orders is orders. For when Mrs Goddard said 'point your toes' you damn well pointed them, and they stayed pointed. There may well have been a touch of Swiss in Mrs G.

Anyhow, then you come to the adult classes, in which I nervously re-enrolled after a ski gap of 35 years. And it was just as I remembered from my teens: shorter skis but no variation in the teaching style. You watch the instructor, you do what he tells you. You do not try and do something more agreeable to your own instincts. If he says put your weight on the downhill ski, top ski forward, bend from the waist and keep your knees still, that is what you do. If you don't, even if you're still upright at the end of your turn, he slithers down the line accusingly and points a stick. 'You! Snowplough not wide enough. You! Weight more downhill!'

And if you think – as some impatient man in a woolly hat always does – that you would be OK in the higher class which goes right up the big lift, this theory will get you nowhere unless Hans or Werner agrees. The fact that you are paying cuts no ice. You can book a private lesson for three times the money if you like, but if Sir doesn't want to take you up the Grabben-Gruntcherberg lift, his word is law. You will remain on the bunny-run until he is totally satisfied with your traverse, turn, sideslip and stop.

And do you know, it is strangely restful? And at the end of it, you have internalised your instructor so much that an inner voice rebukes you sharply whenever ze knees slip out of line. Yes, yes, I know it would never do in the real, intellectual questing, child-centred world of caring education. I will be over it soon. But for one week, every few years, I get the heady sensation that I have seen the past – and it works . . .

JANUARY 19 2001

Don't be the best

'The trouble with ski instructors,' she said, limping into the hotel in her orthopaedic-style plastic boots, 'is that they're like PE teachers. They're never satisfied when you can just do it, they always want you to progress and go on to the next thing, and achieve (she spat the word out with hatred) *excellence*.'

Whereupon she fell over on the bed, and became a member of the international league of ski-school dropouts.

I had a certain amount of sympathy. Years ago, I got to the happy stage where I could almost do parallel turns but usually funked it on steep slopes, and could scare myself just enough on a moderate blue run to feel a sense of adventure.

But whenever I joined a ski class, the Lycra-clad Werner or Bernhard in charge would simply not be satisfied with leading us down a new and moderately interesting run, with views. Instead, he would head for some ice-face, confiscate our ski-sticks and devote two hours to getting us as bruised as possible. 'Vizzout pain is no gain,' he would say, with all the cheerfulness of the permanently upright.

You never quite dared to mention that you weren't that bothered about improving, actually, or at least not until you had spent three or four years getting over your cleverness at actually being able to turn corners without falling over. Eventually I learned to call this 'consolidation', and went off on my own to do it in decent privacy.

As the holiday progressed, we discussed this theory of PE teachers and their compulsion to press onwards and upwards.

'Take netball,' said one thinker. 'The warm-up, I find, is more than enough. It burns up calories, gets your blood racing and you feel nice and energised. But then they have to go and spoil it by making you play an actual game, with scores.'

'Swimming,' said another. 'Same thing. Now, I love swimming, do it every day on holiday. I can do a mile, easily. But PE teachers get worked up about stroke improvement and eradicating twists in your kick, and they're forever attaching bits of polystyrene to you and making you tow them around. Mystifying.'

A man in his forties raised athletics.

'I quite liked high-jumping,' he said. 'I could jump three foot three. But this Welsh gorilla who took PE was always at me to challenge my limits and do three foot six, so I caught my foot and hurt my arm. After that I used to forge sick-notes.'

'I liked hockey,' said a girl, 'when I played in the third team, which quite often lost something like 32-nil to the fourth team of the other school in town. We had a blast, and when we actually scored a goal it was like Christmas. But then this new games mistress came and decided to improve our wind by taking us for long runs and doing star-jumps in the mud. So two of the team went up to a better one, and the rest of us put our names down for library duty.'

You have to see the PE teachers' and ski instructors' point. In the world of sport, excellence and competitiveness are all. It must be agony to watch the rest of us lumbering around contentedly, uttering little cries of joyful surprise when we catch the ball. It would be as bad as being a geography teacher and having a pupil turn up term after term tremendously pleased with himself for still knowing the shapes of the continents. ('Wow! Africa! Can't fool me'.)

Or a maths teacher, whose pupils beam fatuously at him, saying: 'Guess what? I can still do seven-times-eight without thinking! Fifty-four, no, I tell a lie, 56. The teacher would sink into a slough of depression quite quickly.

But the PE teacher in a sedentary society has a double duty. Going for excellence and medals is not enough. The central point is to get the blood running round in a lively fashion, and bring a healthy glow to the skin. So the deplorable muppets are doing themselves just as much good as the finely-tuned athletes of whom the school is so proud. Probably more actually: good players use their muscles with efficient economy, so you get more exercise lunging hopelessly after the ball, or running the wrong way because your glasses fell off.

Good PE teachers, at all stages, know this. Ruefully, they accept that a lumbering team shrieking with enjoyment is probably a better tribute to their skill than a superbly-oiled winning machine. But it must be galling nonetheless. Salute them.

Release your hidden Miss Jones

Want a New Year's resolution? Easily realisable, perennially useful, utterly harmless, non-fattening, environmentally neutral and suitable for personal, school, or national educational use? I have just the thing for you. Learn to touch-type.

Or, if you already can, teach someone else. Or urge them to learn, courtesy of some friendly computer programme like Mavis Beacon.

None of you will ever regret it. One of the great blights of the new keyboard age is that because of ancient 1970s' snobbery about 'typists', not enough educated, professional people can type accurately and fast and without looking down. Educational apartheid meant that for decades, anyone considered bright enough to go to university was regarded as too grand to learn touch-typing. Hence generations of journalists, authors, executives, doctors and teachers were still pecking away with two fingers as the keyboard era dawned in a glory of email and word-processing.

And instead of using their heads and saying 'Right – this is the moment to unlearn the old inefficient habit and use all eight fingers', they bury their head in the sand and carry on pecking. Meanwhile, Mavis Jones from the Secondary Mod, who trained on old Remington manual uprights in 1962, can sit down at the lovely new keyboards and rattle off emails and best-selling novels while the intelligentsia fiddle around giving themselves RSI and ignoring the ergonomic marvel which is the standard QUERTY keyboard.

Millions of hours are wasted by this nonsense. And, shockingly, very few schools think it worth their while to encourage children to touch-type. The national curriculum prefers getting them to design disgusting pineapple pizzas in Food-Tech, or acquire waffly 'key skills' without ever remembering to include the keyboard one.

I was lucky. In an otherwise appalling year at a bigoted, violent convent school in the old South Africa, I found that girls were expected automatically to learn to type: not because anybody foresaw the computer age, but because in that culture being a 'sekketery' before marriage was the natural destiny of anything with a womb. Moreover, as a foreigner I was allowed to skip Afrikaans lessons, so I got extra time in the Typing Room. The machines were upright, ornate as old sewing-machines, with a heavy touch which required you to bring down your whole hand with a crash, fingers poised. You put a check duster over your hands, positioned your little fingers on the a and the colon, and consulted a diagram above your head while struggling through 'The quick brown fox jumped over the lazy dog' – initially taking 10 minutes then, as the brain became programmed to associate letters with movements, advancing joyfully towards a fluency as beautiful as any Chopin prelude.

It even improved my spelling. Every new word or name, to this day, causes my fingers to drum out the spelling on any handy surface, imprinting it on the mind by physical movement. Coming home from Johannesburg after a year, I was given my father's old portable typewriter. Five years later it came to university with me, and wrote all my essays, poems and Union speeches. It doesn't make you think any quicker, but to be able to type out quotations or second drafts without looking away from the source saved endless time. Later – thanks to articles written on the faithful old portable, and spells spent as a temp audio-typist – I could afford an electric typewriter. And, eventually, the computer.

I have not looked down while writing this: I have thrown my head back, looked at the birds outside the window, and abolished any grammatical infelicities spotted on the screen, without having to peer down. My hands are not tired, nor my shoulders tense. It is a most basic, useful, life-enhancing skill. Moreover, for us duffers at other physical skills like cooking, DIY and playing the violin, it provides self-esteem.

The only time the old reflexes let me down badly was during a gap-year spell knocking out letters in a German bank. The Germans – because they use zum and zu and are not fond of the letter 'y' – transpose Y and Z on their Querty keyboards, so all my letters ended with a broad Somerset accent, Zours Faithfully. But I daresay the bank's customers got used to it.

So go for it. At first it will slow you down and make you cross. Persevere, and it will change your life.

Urge it on your gap-year children. Start a prize award in your school. Come back, Miss Jones. You're beautiful!

APRIL 15 2005

Essays-r-us

I am not often shocked, but the *Times Higher Education Supplement* and the *Daily Telegraph* managed it the other day. It was the report from Loughborough university on plagiarised internet essays; the hair rose on my scalp like quills upon the fretful porpentine.

The gist of the story was that cheating isn't worth the money: Charles Oppenheim, a professor of information management, ordered up some essays from companies with names like Essays-r-us and Papers4You and found that they were lousy. One barely got a pass, one scraped a 2:2. The companies responded huffily that marking is a subjective business, and that: 'We are sometimes asked to write at an overseas student level and the mistakes are done on purpose. We have thousands of essays at different levels . . . the client gets what he/she wants.'

Gawd. I am not shocked that the essays are bad, just that nobody seems embarrassed about their existence. I have no law degree (though a few quid in the right direction could presumably get me one) but I would have thought that you could cobble up a charge of inciting and abetting a fraud on the public purse. These students are having most of their tuition fees paid, after all, by local education authorities. The least you would expect would be that they would be forced to repay every penny the LEA spent on their idle and fraudulent studenthood.

You would also expect, as a legally innocent Martian observer, that the companies would be brought to book, rather than allowed to make indignant self-justifying remarks about how flexible they are. Yes, yes, they will piously claim that these are only 'model' essays, never intended to be handed in as your own work, O perish the thought: but in that case why on earth would they offer to 'write at an overseas student level', or to put in deliberate mistakes, eh?

Because it has to be done, this essay-writing business. Some cheeky geek from EssayWorld or Insta-Desmond or whatever had the nerve to tell the reporters that it is actually the universities' fault for not teaching students to write essays. There may be a slight point there, but sixth forms should have broken the back of this particular task long before, and A-levels should have tested it, properly and without multiple-choice get-outs or downloadable coursework.

We all know that writing essays is hell – especially the first 10 lines. For some of us the misery doesn't end with finals: writing columns is just as bad, what with blank-page fever and scratching out and rephrasing and worrying about structure and whether it makes sense and whether it's boring (this last being something students don't have to think about too much). Writing company reports and management analyses is presumably pretty awful too, which explains why they are so dull. As for press releases, about half of them are so incompetent you could weep.

Political speeches are a bit better, having larger teams working on them, but even then the basic laws of rhetoric are shakily understood. Only the press carries the torch: journalists may be smug slimeballs, but they get their essays in on time, and they are readable.

What is to be done about the decline of the essay? If the quality is low even from shysters who sell them to lazy, frightened students for 300 quid a pop, we really are in trouble. Perhaps training should just start a lot sooner. Small children at primary school write cracking essays, full of vim and originality. Obviously, something happens to them at puberty to inhibit the natural flow, much in the same way as their drawing suddenly deteriorates.

All parents have trunkfuls of fabulous blue elephants and green sunsets and wild ships and surreal fish in swirling water, yet most 13-year-olds draw badly, hesitantly and without élan. All babies sing to themselves rather tunefully, but few teenagers. Infants are poets as soon as they can speak, but decline into grunting.

Maybe it is the same with essays. It may seem a long way from 'What I did in the holidays' to 'Consider the impact of Italian Unification on the development of European identity', but it ought to be a smoother curve than it is. Unless, of course, you believe that everything is going to the dogs. In which case there will soon be a website where seven-year-olds can download model essays on 'My favourite pet', or feed in six facts on what they did in the holidays and get it back in convincing roundhand. It could happen. Anything can happen. Eeeek!

Old enough to know better

Is it 11, or is it 13? When is the caterpillar truly ready to be a butterfly? Where should we put the fold in the map of youth – when should Big School start? Does a six-year-old have more in common with a 12-year-old than one aged 11 with one aged 17?

If such a thing be possible in the snarling jungle of British educational theory, we have the makings of an interesting debate here.

George Marsh, head of Dulwich College prep, told his members at the Incorporated Association of Preparatory Schools that 'tweenagers' up to 13 should be educated with 'a space of their own and a staff of their own'. They need 'protection' from older children and from pressure to grow up too soon. 'They deserve a childhood. They above all need a prep school or junior school environment away from 14 and 15-year-olds'.

His listeners must have clapped loudly, because there is a gentlemanly arm-wrestling match going on in the independent sector about this. Most independent preps take children up to 13 and get furious when they transfer to senior schools that start at 11.

But it is not just a matter of bums on paid-for seats: Mr Marsh has experience in state middle schools, and champions those too. His remarks coincide with a battle in Oxford over the ending of their middle-school system, and unease in the few remaining pockets of middledom elsewhere. The alarming thing in both contexts is the number of pro-middle speakers who talk as if the problem with transfer at 11 lies not so much with educational matters as with the need to 'protect' the tender young plants from the older pupils.

'It is simply not appropriate,' said someone 'to have such young children in the same institution as 18-year-olds.' The tone suggested that you might easily replace the words '18-year-olds' with 'Siberian man-eating tigers'. Mr Marsh himself said that 'above all' these children should be away from 14 and 15-year-olds.

I defer to experience, of course; but is there not something vaguely creepy about this argument?

I can remember well my own qualms when our children went to

big schools at 11 (Great louts! Big busty sluts! What have they to do with my little precious angels?). But for heaven's sake, what is a family, a neighbourhood, a community, a civilization if it is not a forum where diverse ages learn to rub along together?

And if a school can't guarantee decent respect between children without putting up institutional firewalls every four years, what sort of admission of defeat is that? If the 14 and 15-year-olds are over-sexed, predatory, bullying little swine, then that surely needs sorting out directly, rather than merely by removing anything that looks vulnerable to a fortress several miles away? And what good is served by creating – as a middle-school system does – a number of secondary schools with small sixth-forms or none at all, where 1,000 13 to 16-year-olds are mewed up together with their hormones, bereft of the civilising influence of sixth-formers and of responsibility for younger ones? A good school works differently.

You go in at 11, terrified, and find you have mentors and protectors within your house, or whatever vertical division is made.

You look at distant heroes and heroines, and observe how authority and responsibility overtake others, and will come in turn to you. There may be formal mentoring schemes, or paired reading, or games under sixth-form supervision; you see that not only is the adult world there to protect you from feral tendencies in the dreaded 14 and 15-year-olds, but that 17 and 18-year-olds are on the side of civilisation, too.

Then you grow up yourself, and learn to laugh at the endearing follies of the smallest boys and girls. The whole thing becomes a kind of family: a model for the future. That is how it works in a good, happy school. They exist in both sectors.

Obviously, in a bullying, badly-supervised, institution there are dreadful pressures put on the little kids by the big, loutish ones, and such schools also exist in both sectors. But, if the relationship between age-groups is the litmus test of good school morale, I would have thought that the last thing to do was to throw up your hands and expect the worst.

Mens sana in corpore sano

Much virtue in a jumper

Out of the mouths of babes and Year 5s there often comes a great
and embarrassing truth. The embarrassment is usually rooted in the
sudden adult realisation that we have been getting something completely wrong about their feelings, wishes, needs and attitudes. We
have been underestimating, overestimating, or (most often) pointlessly hiding something from them which they have known about
for months. If we have any grace, we blush. If not, we bluster. But
sometimes the only graceful response is an embarrassed gulp and a
throwing of the hands into the air in surrender.

Nine-year-old truthteller of the month is an anonymous boy in a
survey by the magazine *Zero2Nineteen* about students' views on
school councils. A report published last week suggests that children
don't think much of the consultation process, especially where
expenditure is concerned. This child says, in tones any parent can
easily recognise as authentic: 'They've bought us proper football posts and nets. They cost loads. We used to use our jumpers as
goals and we were quite happy with it.'

Alas, I do not know what he would have preferred the money to
be spent on. Gym-balls or fantastic theatre trips, or a climbing
frame, or something so inventively childlike no adult would ever
guess it.

But the boy was right. They should have asked the consumers, the
children, and they didn't. They probably thought that 'proper'
goals would look professional and make parents think that the
school had wonderful facilities.

There is often a spendthrift sterility about the way adults make
provision for children, and we should bow our heads and acknowledge that we are bossy and do not always know best. It begins when
we spend 20 quid on a specially designed 'baby gym', and then go to
visit some experienced bohemian multigravida and find our baby far
more entranced with a soft plastic bottle filled with glitter and a few
dried peas to rattle.

Babies need a fast-changing variety of interesting objects, not one or two overpriced designer rattles. Yet we surround them with things that look good to us, and we are ashamed to see them play with grubby old rag-dolls. I used to buy beautiful soft toys, witty toucans marketed by wildlife charities. They were eclipsed for years by Mister Blue Lion, a hideous baby-blue dog won at a fair.

On it goes. We look at nurseries and primary schools, and once beyond the basic checks on cleanliness and safety we focus stupidly on the kit – its glossy varnish and tasteful colours and the elegant Corbusier-style portholes of the Wendy house. We find it harder to look dispassionately for evidence that children use this stuff. We are upset by school buildings that look like bits fallen off 1960s air terminals, and impressed by pretty Victorian schoolhouses or dove-grey cloisters. We see a playing-field with 'real' goalposts and nets, and think, 'Aha! Excellent facilities', whereas the real sign of excellence is children charging around in a friendly fashion, even if they are kicking goals between jumpers (jumpers are good because you can adjust the size of the goal to your own nine-year-old, concept of the game). Of course, we should spend money on children's environments – but the obvious, impressive things are not always what they need or want.

I went to a lovely primary school playground in Southampton recently. It was beautifully divided into quiet areas, rowdy areas and a walled ball-kicking area in a way which reflected not a desire to show off to parents, but a real understanding of the variety of children's tastes. I'll bet they were consulted at some stage.

Of course, we should not skimp on things which really make exercise and teamwork possible – but in their terms, not ours. How many times has a local authority combined economy with an obsession about 'facilities' and sold its school playing-fields to builders who promise to provide a leisure centre? But ask the children, and as often as not they will mourn their lost den-building and ball-kicking ground. And, anyway, they can't afford many visits to the leisure centre to play sanitised games of squash or badminton.

And when they trail indoors to the school library, perhaps some are sorry that a whole bookcase full of shabby blood-and-thunder stories which they used to take home has been chucked out to make room for a bank of computers that keep breaking down. Someone should have asked them. And listened to the answer.

Locker-room scandal

Sometimes it takes a national back pain association to alert you to a philosophical difficulty in education. The other week such a group, Back-Care, brought out a report on the loads children carry. Whereas Italian children – the other pack-horses of Europe – carry between nine and 20kg around with them, British children come near the top of the league with up to 25kg in their schoolbags. One in 10 regularly carry 13 per cent of their bodyweight around in books, files, PE-kit, sandwiches and the rest; and some tote more than a quarter of their weight, like Marines.

The organisation pointed out that adult workers are not allowed to shift such loads without frequent rests and special training in grips, knee-bending, hugging to the chest and all the rest of it. The Post Office restricts 16-year-old employees to weights of up to 9kg. Adult workers confronted with the lifting and carrying inherent in the average secondary school day, would go straight to their union, and thence to the courts.

Yet still a lot of schools do not think it necessary to provide lockers for all, nor safe supervised areas to store bags during the day. Many do not even provide lockers for PE kit. Rarely indeed do the wizards of timetabling feed into their baroque calculations such questions as 'Is it better for 40 11-year-olds to cover 100 metres, twice, carrying a quarter of their bodyweight each, or for one 40-year-old to cover it once, carrying only 40 marked essays, a confiscated packet of Silk Cut and a copy of *Silas Marner*?'

Even if they are driven to school (and vilified by transport gurus) tens of thousands of schoolchildren have to carry great lumpen bags around with them up stairs and down, along corridors and across courtyards, with all the material for every lesson. And since the younger children have more different lessons, they carry bigger loads than the sixth-formers. It is giving them bad backs.

It is good to have these things pointed out to us sometimes. Parents touring secondary schools are often quite surprised by the way that things are organised: teachers lurking in dedicated areas waiting in state for the next gang to arrive, and classes having no secure base to leave their possessions at the start of a day.

The best schools have lockers, at least, in a central position, and a foolproof system of codes or keys; but in those that do not – often very well-regarded schools – the parent realises with a small shock that little Jemima or Jake will have to trudge around all day with the schoolbag whose hard, cornery weight gave them such a shock when they lifted it off the kitchen floor that morning. The parent, however, is told that this is the way things are done at Hubris High, and meekly nods acquiescence.

It was the industrial comparison that was most interesting. For in a school, who is the workforce? The teachers, obviously; but are the children not a workforce too? They have to turn up, fulfil jobs, meet targets; just because they are not paid, that is no reason to deny them the dignities of the worker.

You could argue that because of the philosophical notion of staff being *in loco parentis*, the children are actually better loved and protected than if they were regarded as on a level with employees. They are clients, which is better than being on the staff. But in fact it would be closer to the truth to say that the children are regarded as a product: a raw material to be processed into credit-points for the organisation; on which funding may depend.

If this is indeed the unspoken philosophical underpinning of the school, then it follows that bad backs in future life are of no particular concern to the management because in future the child is not going to be either a credit or a debit to the organisation. Whereas the comfort of teachers is reasonably important, because teachers are the machine-tools which are needed to carve and mould the children into acceptable product. You maintain your machine tools in case they break down; but the pile of raw material will keep on coming, so you can afford to be a bit more cavalier with it.

All of which, of course, is a disgraceful caricature of the most demoralised tranche of schools. But it gives the restless parent a new question to ask of a prospective head: who's the workforce? Who's the customer? And where, exactly, are the lockers?

We are the losers

It's the Boat Race this weekend. The 150th, and the last ever one on the BBC. Well, you probably knew that: either because you are looking forward to it and plan to watch it while wearing a straw boater and striped blazer and clutching an old college oar, or else because you think it is a disgracefully élitist anachronism, and you wouldn't dream of sullying your mind by caring.

This could either be because you are a rowing purist, and feel that Oxford and Cambridge aren't even the best rowing eights in the UK, let alone universities, though they get all the glory; or it could be because even without the taint of 'Oxbridge' you don't intend to waste your life watching overbred giants with geography degrees sweating their way along a muddy river while braying geeks exclaim pointlessly into lip-mikes.

Either way, you can't escape it. What with vintage boat races and the celebrity reconstruction and the ITV takeover, it's the Boat Race's big year. Might as well sit back and enjoy it, as generations have. My husband, reared in a working-class family in Sheffield in the 1950s, remembers that everybody always knew whether they were 'for' Oxford or Cambridge, even if they had left school at 14 for the steelworks. It is one of those national sporting events that by tradition is permitted to grip the unsporting – like the FA Cup Final or the Grand National.

I have to admit that I am a closet fan, an old fascination having been lately revived by becoming the mother of an oarsman, albeit a lightweight one and not one of the huge Pinsentosaurus Rex creatures in the big race. When you have rowing in the family you learn a bit about the extraordinary focus, the subtleties of tide and pace, the extraordinarily effortful training, the inter-relationship of eight men who cannot even see one another's faces, and the heartbreak of failure. You learn respect.

You watch *True Blue* on the video. You groan and cheer. And, when it comes to the race itself, you feel every twinge of agony in your own bones.

Last year, with the neck-and-neck struggle and the final victory of Oxford by one stroke, I fell off the sofa with emotion, alternately shrieking 'Oxford! You can do it! Go!' from the macho half of my brain and from the maternal side, racked by the pain on the close-up cameras 'Careful boys! You'll have a heart attack! It's not worth it!'

And then there is the moment, pure and intense, when joy floods through the half-dead winners, and bitter, unassuageable sorrow comes over the losers. For here there is no second place, no *proxime-accessit*, no silver medal, barely any congratulations for a near miss. You win, and are blessed, or you lose and look back in sorrow at the waste of all those 5.30am starts, all those hours in the gym, that grim winter training on the icy waters, the drinks and rich dinners rejected.

I suppose this, too, is education. We ought to be opening doors on to parallel universes, older worlds, Spartan moments lost to soft modern society. We at the liberal, soft-hearted end of things have built a world for plucky losers, personal bests, relative successes and value-added improvers. We have forgotten – except in the narrow world of sport – the hard old values of winner-takes-all, and the ancient bitterness of the loser who slinks into the dark.

Children know it instinctively; the early disappointments of not winning a race draw the corners of their little mouths down in pure antique Spartan sorrow. We rush to reassure them, to commend their failed effort, to belittle the winning and laud the taking part. We are right to do it, we are civilised, we are kind, we know we must help them pave the way for the next effort and never let the word 'waste' cross their minds.

But they know really. They know that a loser of a close, hard-fought competition undergoes a stab of misery. They know how much it costs losers in self-control to do that smiling Tim Henman handshake or take that long walk to the pavilion without flouncing. They know how fabulous it is to win, to hold that cup aloft. It is hard-wired into all of us, it is primitive, it is necessary.

And the Boat Race – most black-and-white and edgy and unpredictable of sporting events – speaks to that deep knowledge. We need those cameras tracking on sweaty masks of tragedy and joy, to remind us what it is to be alive and striving.

Why winners need the rest of us

He leapt up and down by the rope, yelling encouragement. 'Go, go go!' We all joined in, howling the niece's name. She is, after all, the standard-bearer for our extended family, none of whom in recorded history have previously done well enough in heats to feature in the athletics events of a conventional school sports day.

Well, I tell a lie. My daughter did throw the discus once, but it shot off in the wrong direction once too often and she was binned. Otherwise, we belong to the proud yet obscure tribe who, by losing in the preliminary heats, enable the athletes to feel good about themselves. Without us game losers, there would be no victories, would there?

Anyway, the fleet-footed niece, being the smallest and youngest in her event, arrived at the tape second last. Her leaping father was not depressed by this. 'Wa-hay! Fantastic! *You didn't come last*! You beat that other one!'

'Dad,' said the runner, patiently, trotting over towards a hurdle appointment, 'she did her hamstring in yesterday. That's why I beat her.' They have a sternly realistic approach to life, do children. It's the parents who are so deluded. We all went back to our picnic, knowing that the proper way to enjoy a sports day is not to give a damn about trophies, but to keep the strawberries and sneaky cans of readymix Pimms coming, meet your children's friends, gossip with other parents, and enjoy an occasional shriek of pretend excitement when someone you know streaks past with a reasonable number of others behind him.

I see that the *Daily Mail* has been having a go at Tessa Jowell launching Sport England's latest wheeze of a 'toolkit' for 'inclusive' sports days in which there are fewer winners and more people get exercise.

'Egg and spoon are axed as schools bring in soft-boiled sports!' shouts the headline, although the toolkit is a voluntary exercise. The paper's political correspondent (note, not the education cor-respondent) announces the 'death knell' for traditional races, as

Sport England suggests problem-solving exercises and all-ability team events instead of the usual system where, as a spokesman put it: 'a small proportion of children take part in activities while the majority sit around and spectate'.

Oh, it's a hot one, this: the Campaign for Real Education is frothing at the mouth, and the Tory MP Andrew Rosindell says, 'competition is a vital element of everyday life', although the suggested games actually seem to be quite competitive. I would have thought that being in a stroppy team forced to complete damn silly assignments is just as much like life as wobbling along with an egg on a spoon.

It's a hot issue for two reasons. First, because we suffer a massive collective guilt at the sheer lack of exercise inflicted on modern battery children. Driven or bussed to school, banned from running and biking on the streets from fear of traffic and paedophiles, deprived of playing fields as government after government cavalierly sells them off, short of public adventure playgrounds which even when they exist are becoming dumbed down for fear of lawsuits, they then have their school PE squeezed to almost nothing. Next to this epidemic of under-exertion, it is ludicrous to worry about whether or not sport is competitive enough. Get the little beggars jumping, running, rolling and stretching, and that'd be a good enough start.

The second reason is more complicated, all tied up with class and ethos and the legacy of empire. To some honest, well-meaning educationists the very idea of winners and losers is still anathema. A generation that was bellowed at in draughty shorts does not forget lightly, not when the memory is all jumbled up with adolescent discoveries about revolution and utopias and the superiority of intellect over brute muscle as exemplified by PE teachers.

There is still a generation – quite a lot of them headteachers by now – who turn purple and throb with indignation and shame if you creep up behind them and hiss provocative words like 'Victor Ludorum'. They are not, as a rule, personally responsible for the utter decline in school sport – shortsighted greed by local authorities and government stupidities have more to answer for there – but this generation did, at the very least, fail to fight for games because to them – OK, to me – games were pretty ghastly unless you were a star.

Now we fight back up the slippery slope, with difficulty. That reluctance needs overcoming. Probably the younger teachers and heads and parents don't have it at all, because theirs is the leisure centre generation for whom sport and games hardly happened at school, but are fun things you do at weekends. But the winning is still a problem to many.

Sports days in the future will probably be more fun, and use up more children. But until we all accept with a cheery shrug that there have to be losers in order to have winners, we shall have more of the present outbreaks of loopy overreaction to simple, helpful ideas. We have to grow up.

SEPTEMBER 20 2002

Teenage inscrutability

Some Cambridge academics at the Autism Research Centre have brought out a DVD of actors doing distinctive facial expressions, to teach autistic children to read other people's emotions.

I applaud anything which eases the barrier of incomprehension which autistic children live behind. I hope it helps. Being able to hear the intonation of the actors' voices probably makes it clearer.

However, I have to admit that looking at the stills reproduced in *The Times*, I got five out of six wrong. The right answers were 'insouciant, hysterical, terrified, concealing, luring, brazen'. What I wrote down was 'smug, delighted, terrified, maternal, smart-alec, drunk'. It is easy to see how you could mix up drunk and brazen, but a bit worrying that the face which was supposed to mean 'concealing' looked to me like a mother gazing adoringly down at a baby, and that the 'hysterical' face just looked like one of those pictures (so beloved by editors in late August) of pretty girls opening their A-level results and screaming for joy.

My failure reminded me, though, of one of the reasons I am not a teacher. Whenever I go to a school to do a group session – about radio, or journalism, or whatever – I find one of the hardest things is knowing what on earth they are thinking, and whether I am getting through at all.

Young children, of primary-school age, are easy: they have the beautiful transparency of babies, so I can quickly tell the difference between giggly, inattentive, frightened, worried, inspired, and bored, and adjust my routine accordingly. My own children, obviously, I knew well enough to read their mood all the way through their teens. Sixth-formers are nearly adult enough for me to make an educated guess at whether they are enjoying the session or not.

But with unknown children, between the ages of about 12 and 16, my experience is that unless you actually question them one by one, it is unbelievably hard to work out anything at all.

You look and look, and cannot know whether they are listening,

whether they care, whether they understand, whether they are storing up mannerisms to take the mickey out of you later, or whether they absolutely hate you. The girls put on impassive, Siamese-kitten masks with big staring eyes and unreadable mouths. The boys all look sullen. Only if they actually jeered, stared out of the window all the time, or wrote text messages with little bleepy noises, would the situation be clear.

Since I generally only go and see nice groups of nice children, nicely filtered by canny headteachers, they don't do those things.

But until they can be coaxed to speak, I still have no idea what's in their heads. Perhaps it is a specialised form of autism: the inability to read teenagers' faces. Anyway, it would clearly never do for a teacher. You are experts, you have to know what's going on behind those masks, you have to spot incomprehension and unhappiness alike and decide who to focus on with a question and who to have a quiet word with after class. I asked some real teachers about this. One looked puzzled and said: 'Oh, it's just practice, like with your own kids.' Another said: 'Well, I can do it better with pupils I really know, but I admit they do get a bit opaque in Year 9 and 10.' A third, I regret to say, said: 'Frankly, I don't care as long as they keep quiet.'

Turning the situation round, and with the mellow hindsight which attaches to the first term since 1986 when I haven't had to buy anybody new rulers and pack them off to school, I realise that perhaps in the past I have been a bit unfair to some staff. It is natural for a mother to feel censorious about teachers who appear insensitive to the moods of her children. 'Mr X is putting him/her under such stress . . . surely ought to see how counter-productive all this anxiety is . . . these remarks in class may be jokes at the time but they're really upsetting the kid . . . when I bring it up at parents' evening he doesn't seem to have the slightest idea.' 'Insensitive pig' we chunter.

But perhaps this teen-related autism is widespread, and poor Mr X was genuinely unable to read the signs. He just saw the usual row of sullen, unreadable, unchanging masks. He meant no harm. He was doing his best. Perhaps a DVD should be produced for teachers showing a range of teenage emotions: insouciant, bored, hysterical, brazen, attentive, stressed, asleep, or doped up to the eyeballs. Student teachers could do a touch-screen recognition test, like the driving theory one. I'd fail. Real teachers would pass.

Fat is fine

It's enough to make you burst out of your lederhosen in indignation. The state of Bavaria, home of the killer sausage and the foaming stein, has barred the employment of teachers with a body mass index of over 30: that is stout ones. Teaching is civil service employment, and claiming to be fearful of the high costs of illness and early retirement, Bavaria has put its foot down.

Lard and learning, says the state authority, do not go together. They can't do much about those already holding civil service status, but trainees and short-contract staff aspiring for permanence must get the weight off. The individual cited in *The TES* report, Gisela Neubauer, is annoyed. At under 14 stone with an index of 33, she is being told to lose one-and-a-half stone, although she does a sport three times a week and feels fine.

I don't know enough Bavarian teachers to pass a judgment (though it has to be said that the further south you go in Germany the less space is left on your train seat) but this seems to be going either much too far, or not far enough. To be logical, you've either got to police everything or nothing. Heaviness and unfitness are very subtly related: some fat people are scant of breath, puffing and perspiring from the mere effort of getting up on the stage for assembly, others are bouncy and flexible and walk with a spring. Think of the Roly Polys tap-dancing. Some thinner people are indeed fit and toned and set to live forever, others are weedy chainsmokers, or following high-protein diets so mad that their breath would knock a horse over and their livers will pack up any day now.

If Bavaria is only weighing its pedagogues, in this carefree hit-and-miss way, it is missing a lot of tantalising health-screening opportunities. Granted, the very stout have disadvantages as teachers, particularly when they obscure the whole whiteboard or crash through the podium and have to be freed by the Year 8 PSE group. But there are plenty of other, less strictly visible human problems that should be worrying an enlightened state just as much.

What about the smokers, coughing their way through maths

exams and putting the children off their stroke? What about the sex addicts, with their chain of debilitating infections and their tendency to yawn uncontrollably through the morning? Or the spookily flexible yoga-bunnies who feel a need to wrap a leg round the back of their neck in sixth-form seminars, thus causing intense distraction from the topic in hand and possibly costing their pupils several A-level points?

Why not screen out the dangerous sports enthusiasts who limp in from piste or rally-track on Monday morning with so much adrenalin ripping round their bodies that they can hardly string a sentence?

And then there are the incurable romantics, who sigh and dream and look out of the window and get platonically distracted by the timeless beauty of Mavis McGorgeous' long blonde hair. Screen them out, before they start setting far too many sonnets for homework and messing up French *dictée* by choking tearfully at the sad bits. And what about the careful hypochondriacs whose bodies are temples, and who are thrown right off their stroke if the staffroom has run out of herbal teabags? And how about the fitness freaks whose ability to teach economic geography with conviction is seriously compromised by their secret indulgence in Pilates abdo-crunches and pelvic-floor contortions behind the desk? And what about the young parents, eh? Covertly phoning the crèche every 10 minutes from the stationery cupboard, and trying to transmit the culture of centuries on an hour's sleep a night and a diet of leftover pureed parsnip?

No, give me a cheerful fatty any day, full of sausage and sauerkraut and self-confidence. This screening philosophy just won't work. Teachers are human beings, and share the vast, fascinating, struggling diversity that goes with the terrain. A good teacher is a good teacher, however many legs, arms, chins, spare tyres, quirks and private neuroses come in the package. A good teacher is far too precious to waste, and shouldn't be quibbled over.

The Bavarians, frankly, are lucky to have enough choice to be so damn fussy. Over here, from recent news of the supply agency world it would appear that heads are supposed to be grateful for anybody who knows the subject, turns up in the morning, and more or less keeps her hands off the tequila slammers and the Year 10 boys.

Motivation and the mottled thigh

Never mind the International Baccalaureate; let us talk about schoolgirls' legs. They seem to cause just as much upheaval. If they're not placing career-wrecking temptations in the way of ambitious male staff, the said legs are causing outrage in the *Daily Mail*, with several full pages and many pictures devoted to the great debate about whether hideous grey school skirts should be worn one, four, or 18 inches above the knee.

Schoolgirl legs hold a perennial fascination, all the way from the spidery black stockings of St Trinian's cartoons to the cards in King's Cross phone boxes. Perhaps it is because girls grow so fast, causing the legs to elongate and shoot disturbingly out from under last year's school skirt just when you least expect them. Even a stern moralist like myself cannot blame the chaps for their confusion: one minute you have a little romping moppet, and the next you are humming 'Zank 'eavens for leetle girls' and turning into one of those bluff old chaps who used to give us crypto-fatherly pats on the shoulder (the front bit of the shoulder) while quoting: 'Standing with reluctant feet/Where the brook and river meet'.

Some men get quite annoyed when their daughters' generation blooms. An upper-crust friend exploded: 'One minute I was organising party games for her little friends, then the next holidays she brings home all these unrecognisable *busty sluts*!' Plagued by legs, what can a chap do but hide in his study until it's all over?

However, it has taken the Professor of Youth Sport at Loughborough University to point out the real problem with schoolgirls' legs. They are not moving around enough. A study linked to the Girls in Sport initiative revealed the long-ignored fact that puberty makes girls resent PE.

God bless Loughborough, I say. It was time someone listened to the radiator-huggers in the girls' changing rooms; certainly nobody did in my day. Goaded by cries of 'Get your skates on!' from Miss McNally, we huddled on muddy pitches with bent sticks, or were penned in netball courts to hop drearily up and down .

Moreover the school – normally dedicated to pleated skirts that touched the ground 'all round when kneeling' – insisted that even for cross-country runs in full public view we wore large brown bloomers and tiny divided skirts showing great tracts of purple-and-white mottled thigh. They also had this ridiculous idea that we were out to assist the school in its futile mission to be better at throwing balls around than anyone else in Kent.

I thought things had changed, and have a daughter whose track-suited mates seem happy doing aerobics and the vigorous but ratty team games in which merry insults are hurled and anyone who lets through fewer than 47 goals is derided as a control freak.

But from the complaints made to Loughborough researchers by 11 to 14-year-old girls, it seems she is lucky. It appears that most are still being systematically alienated from exercise by daft clothes, barking teachers, public showers and a competitive ethos in which people get cross if you're hopeless.

'Girls,' says Professor David Kirk of Loughborough, 'are much more likely to be motivated by fun.' Knight this man at once.

It even appears that he, and the Youth Sport Trust, have grasped that growing girls have a code of modesty. However tartily they may dress when posing at bus stops, they feel that the budding female body jigging around doing exercise is best kept shrouded in the decent mystery of tracksuits and floppy T-shirts. Certainly not revealed in a straining aertex blouse and repulsively flirty little games skirt. Look round any gym; the females in Lycra thongs and high-cut lime leotards are all well over 25. The teenagers are in floppy grey T-shirts, which they keep on even when swimming.

It is vital to find girls forms of exercise which they won't skive out of. Using your body properly, whether in kick-boxing, dance or hockey, wards off eating disorders, depression, stress, low self-esteem, and the tendency to believe boys when they say you are a dog, or frigid.

Hell, some of those effects might even combine to reduce teenage pregnancies: now if we could persuade the Government of that, the girls-in-sport pilot scheme would go nationwide before you could say: 'Get your skates on!'

Media messages

TV in translation

Over the years, being a media type, I have had five different schools ask me whether they should agree to let a television company make a documentary about them. Teachers are natural performers, and touchingly proud of their pupils, so it is tempting. So is the idea of free publicity, to dazzle your LEA (or pull in more paying customers, depending which sector you are in). Therefore the letter on the headed notepaper is a tremendous lure. Memories are short, and the odds are that the tempted head, hesitating amid dreams of fame and glory for the school, has genuinely forgotten the last time a perfectly decent educational institution got shafted by the cruel skill of the TV editor.

My reply, therefore, generally includes the word 'bargepole'. But just in case anybody is currently considering such an approach, I thought I should provide a little glossary of what the film-makers really mean.

'**Explore issues in education today**' – ferret out the embarrassing bits, and convey a strong impression that the teachers are at breaking point and the children learning nothing whatsoever.

'**Lively portrayal of the daily life of a school**' – film as many rows, assaults and tantrums as possible, and intercut them satirically with highflown speech by head at assembly.

'**Give a voice to the children**' – encourage the little sods to show off by slandering the staff and whining on and on about some injustice wrought on them six months ago by an exhausted chemistry teacher.

'**Explore the challenges of education in our times**' – we will film a PSE class and focus on a very pretty underage girl struggling to put a condom on a banana.

'**We use lightweight, unobtrusive handheld digital cameras for minimum disruption**' – we use rather small spy cameras that run silently, so nobody will notice they are on until it's too late.

'**Our production team have won/been nominated for many prestigious awards including BAFTA and Prix Italia**' – Look, we are cleverer than you are. We will run rings round any conditions you try to set, and end up with a very, very funny and unfair film which will upset you dreadfully, but all the reviewers will love and write about at great length, especially if you are an independent school with high fees and therefore a haven for posh bastards of the type that everybody loves to hate.

'**We hope to empower the children by providing a number of them with equipment to make their own 'video diaries'** – We will be able to identify the awkward squad with unerring accuracy, since our own producer got expelled from Holland Park some years ago for arson. We will give these little swine easy cameras, flatter them copiously under the guise of training, tell them that spying on their friends is called 'cinema verité' and will launch glamorous careers, and suggest they get a group of friends together to discuss sexual attitudes among teenagers. We will also slip them the price of a few beers to lubricate the result.

'**We will reflect the pressures on the modern teaching profession**' – as above, giving cameras to the three most discontented members of the staffroom.

'**. . . and of course on headteachers**' – we will make you look like a pompous arse, never doubt it.

'**In conclusion, we hope you will join us in this exciting opportunity of conveying to a wider public a deeper understanding of schools today**' – We hated our own schooldays because we were stroppy little cleverdicks even then. Now we are making our way in television, we are glad of the opportunity to take revenge. Particularly since there is nothing more alluring to the torpid Middle England viewership than lots of fresh-faced young people showing a lot of leg and reinforcing their prejudices about the new generation. We can't lose on this one. And it'll be wonderfully cheap. Oh go on, you know you want to . . . and who cares if nobody respects you in the morning? Certainly not us. We'll be in Aviemore by the time it goes out, making a low-budget programme about the sex lives of ski instructresses.

The UNI image

I spent an enjoyable half-hour this week with the new educational Lad-Magazine FULL ON, part-funded by assorted London borough councils in an attempt to persuade disaffected boys that education equals power, cool, respeck!, etc. It's rather good. In between the Garage reviews and pictures of girl skateboarders with pink hair, my eye fell on a lurid page headed WHY UNI?

I read on, gallantly suppressing my middle-aged snobbish hated of the expression 'Uni' (if you can't be bothered to finish one word, what hope for your degree, eh? Harrumph!). The students talk – in snappy little broken-up wordbites on violent coloured blobs – about doing 'a subject you really enjoy' and scatter the words 'cool', 'gig', and 'club' (though mercifully not 'wasted' 'fit birds' and 'doss'). One boy rather worryingly claims that the work is 'much easier than I thought it would be'. But actually, the page makes a reasonable case in few words, which also include 'career you're passionate about' 'qualification' and 'power and choice'.

It set me thinking, though, about what image of university usually gets conveyed to both boys and girls of all types and tastes by the most popular media. A quick tabloid scan of newspapers revealed that the most common aspects of student life reported are drunkenness, drugs, debt and debauchery. If the poor student concerned has met with tragedy or been arrested for rape, this is leavened with references to shining promise and dedicated hard work. Otherwise students surface intermittently in the local papers having rag weeks, taking part in bizarre experiments dreamed up by academics desperate for a headline, or getting crippled by debt.

The 'trouble' is that in most entertainmant media, university is the end of the drama: the sad goodbye to the boyfriend, the moment when the empty-nest mother starts a scorching affair. Studying – being woefully static – is done offscreen. Lectures would involve a lot of expensive extras with nothing to do but scribble on a pad on the arm of their chair. The most prominent student in a soap at present is Toyah in Coronation Street, who occasionally mentions 'uni' while apparently spending all her time sorting out her mother's doomed love-life, serving in the café or picking up Croatian asylum seekers in Blackpool. What she is studying remains mysterious.

So we are left with the cinema, which offers an unsettling montage of university life. There is IRIS, in which academic activity is confined to beautifully lit lectures on Platonism by Judi Dench, and the fabled inability of dons to get round Tesco without embarking on explorations of the meaning of 'whole' in 'wholegrain mustard'. Apart from that, you throw yourself into the river in the nude, dance like a Bacchante, smoke in a significant manner and are allowed to keep a very untidy house.

Fair enough. But then you go to the next screen and see A BEAUTIFUL MIND, which makes it clear that the point of Higher Education is to scribble obscure equations on venerable leaded windows, cut lectures to study the territorial behaviour of pigeons, and hallucinate about being followed by CIA spooks in big black hats. If you stay on and get really eminent in your field, you go through strange ceremonies with fountain-pens and nobody minds about you walking backwards ranting at imaginary flatmates.

Otherwise – unless you go back a long way to BRIDESHEAD REVISITED – university dons are boffins, who get visited by the action hero in search of some lethal secret. They are rarely seen lecturing, let alone conducting seminars. They never do it in ordinary modern buildings, or even redbrick. To function correctly, Professors in the movies need either futuristic labs or sandstone turrets and cloisters.

Oddly enough, the only current youth-friendly film I can think of which offers university realism is LEGALLY BLONDE. You get an admissions procedure, grungey students competing about who did the most right-on gap year, and a couple of terrifying seminars complete with put-downs, raised eyebrows, and assignments you were meant to have done but never knew about. You get hard slog in weary late-night bedrooms, anxious jockeying for summer placements, growing passion for the subject and ultimate reward.

Hearteningly accurate, really. Which is curious, considering that it is about a lovestruck airhead Barbie-doll in fluffy mules, who follows her man to Harvard Law School and wins her spurs in court by knowing more about Prada and perms than the prosecution.

DECEMBER 13 2002

The monster spoke

I have been thinking a lot lately about radio history: both in the broad sense, and in a reminiscent way. It is because of a book, and the need to answer questions about it around publication time; but the result has been some extraordinarily vivid dreams.

Many of them involve Music and Movement. I searched vainly on the BBC website for any evidence that Music and Movement still bends and stretches and skips its way through modern childhoods, but the nearest I can get is Dance Workshop and something called Hop Skip and Jump. Since these go out on Radio 3 in the wee small hours, along with Mr Grumpy's Motor Car, Mental Maths 3, Scottish Resources and stories from Guru Nanak, I don't tend to hear them. In the old days, schools programmes went out in the afternoon on a Radio 4 wavelength, enabling nostalgic adults to sit in their cars shouting out the answers to Mental Maths and singing along to 'Three little speckled frogs'. Now, like so much in education, they are hidden from curious onlookers.

But the role of Schools Radio in bygone education was huge: possibly more significant even than video and film are today. I can still remember verbatim long passages from the schools broadcasts of my childhood, but none from film or TV. I can remember a song called 'Farewell Manchester' which was made much of in the music programme Rhythm and Melody, and if I know all the words to 'D'ye ken John Peel' this has nothing to do with any hunting background and everything to do with BBC Schools. And as for Music and Movement, to this day if that commanding lady's voice were to say, 'Now find a space – and sit in it!' or 'Make yourself into a long shape!', I would immediately do so, casting dignity to the winds and ignoring all middle-aged twinges. The programme stopped in the Eighties, after 30 years, but I bet that if you were to pipe it into any pinstriped office today at moments of stress you would get countless greying, red-faced men bending their pinstriped shapes into Giant Steps, obediently bunny-hopping, or curling up very, very small. It had authority. I have long suspected that this is how Lady Thatcher acquired such mastery over her Cabinet.

The thing about Schools Radio, as against schools TV, digital CBeebies, Online Curricula and all the rest of the modern razzmatazz, is that it demanded absolute silence and concentration. The big radio – at my first village school it was a walnut-cased monster with red valves glowing in its innards – focused attention. Whether it was a drama about Vikings, a poetry reading or a singalong, it was something too precious and fleeting to be wasted by Alfie Knights making rude noises or Keith blowing his nose incessantly. Round that radio, we all behaved.

And we concentrated. The ability to listen, without visual excitements, is something extraordinarily valuable, and in a noisy world it is the radio (and its sidekicks, story-tapes) which give children the best chance of learning that skill. Sometimes, it was the worst kids who listened most reliably to Schools Radio in the classroom, because it was different from a teacher just droning on. The teacher was a foe, an authority-figure, to be baited. The radio voice wouldn't know or care if you didn't listen. So you probably did.

When I was a young studio manager in training, I used to love working on Schools. The dramas were brief and comprehensible; the imagination of the producers considerable. One of my favourite moments was when the senior operator present couldn't think of a way to convey the look of the Albert Bridge at night with occasional bulbs out: we needed to play music with sudden, popping drop-outs to give the feeling of interrupted light-strings. Fresh from my training course, I invented a way, by clicking a tape destination switch in and out. It sounded like the bridge looked: perfect synaesthesia. I am proud to think that somewhere out there are adults who remember the Albert Bridge Song, and others who were stirred to the idea of a trotting horse by my adroit manipulation of coconut-shells, or who shivered in sympathetic cold when I turned the handle of the wind-effects machine in the programme about Scott of the Antarctic.

Radio is a psychological miracle. It conveys wonders, yet the real wonder of it is inside yourself, aged seven or so: the ability to be still, listen and imagine and dwell in a parallel world, free of your wriggling body for once. Magic.

APRIL 27 2001

The humiliation game

Oh, how I detest *The Weakest Link!* It baffles me why the education world does not rise in protest against the licensed, poisonous culture of contempt, the demeaning of knowledge, the parody of school-marm disapproval!

Well, actually, it doesn't baffle me at all. The education world, quite understandably, is afraid of being cast as humourless, pompous and devoid of smart post-modern irony. The few voices which bleated about the quiz encouraging playground bullying were silenced with just this sort of response. *You don't see the humour? Poor you!* No, on the whole it is not safe for professors or headteachers to point at a phenomenon of popular culture and go 'Yuk!' More trouble than it's worth.

I, on the other hand, am just a simple hack and can say what I want. Even more so because it should be clear that there is no resentment of the ginger dominatrix involved. Personally, in an age when media fortunes come chiefly to the very young, I heartily applaud any trend which enables women journalists of a certain age to become rich by reading off cue cards while looking deeply unattractive. I would not wish to cut off a lifeline that I might need myself when university fees go up.

But I have watched about four, gamely trying to get the point, and hated it. The heart of the problem lies in the trivial dumbness, the cultural nullity, of stupid questions randomly mixed in with real ones. This has bothered me for years in various quizzes, but comes to a head now because of the staged sneery response to contestants who get them wrong. If you couldn't tell Chris Tarrant 'Which singer's albums include Listen without Prejudice', he would just giggle. 'Ah well, good try, it's all a game.' But if you fail in front of Anne Robinson, you're told you have no brain, are the weakest link, and must take the 'walk of shame'.

But what the hell is so shameful or brainless about not knowing who is the lead singer of the Smiths, or the rules of snooker? Where is the intellectual deficit in not knowing who married the Bee Gee

Maurice Gibb, or plays lead guitar in E Street? Like most quizzes now, TWL is rife with questions about the stars of *On the Buses*, which Lethal Weapon film is which, the identity of the red Teletubby, Claudia Schiffer's hometown and the identity of Michael Jackson's child's godparent (Macaulay Culkin, by the way. I wouldn't like *TES* readers to go round all day worrying).

If it were all trivia, this would be fine. There is a certain buzz in being the only person in the room to remember who was the final member of Dave Dee Dozy Beaky Mick and Tich, or which musical 'Good Morning Starshine' comes from. At a pub quiz night you can all have a good roar of ironic despair when your team fails to give Giggsy's correct boot size. The problem begins when such questions are randomly mixed up with the kind of real general knowledge that an educated adult ought to have like whether a tench is a fish or a frog, where the San Andreas fault runs, what metal is in a thermometer, or highlights of the canon of great literature and music. And it gets worse when – as in TWL – ignorance of either kind of knowledge is equally lambasted as brainless ignorance.

Last year's football star and the greatest Verdi opera, physics and the cast list of *Hi-de-Hi* are all jumbled up higgledy piggledy, in the modern quiz world. Then, to compound the crime, they are all labelled 'trivia' together, and you are considered a spoilsport if you point out that while some of them are indeed trivia which will be clean forgotten in a few years, others given equal weight are deeply serious matters about the life of Nelson Mandela or the conquering of disease or cruxes of art and history which changed the world. Pointing this out is bad form: a keen reading of *Hello* and hours spent dribbling popcorn in a multiplex are put on a par with the kind of educational effort which enables the respondent to know whether Horace was Greek or Roman, what glass is made of, or where in the Mediterranean you might find Nicosia.

This irritating, value-free dumbing down has crept everywhere; even into school general knowledge quizzes. But even that crassness didn't matter too much until we got Anne Robinson and a flock of imitators, pouring contempt equally on those who don't know celebrity godparents and those who can't work out the square root of 49. *'Oh, wake up! . . . Not very bright, are you? Oh, you got one right – was that a mistake? Threw you out of Mensa, did they . . .? Pity you worked on your body not your brains . . .'* Dumb, nasty, degrading of the concept of knowledge, not even particularly funny. Yeuch. Oh, how glad I am that I am not a headteacher saying this. I would be mocked to the rafters.

Something in the disinfectant

Forgive the straws in the hair; I am enmeshed in a fictional playground. The latter stages of a novel, the bit where it starts to fly, always produce a surreal frame of mind. The plot swerves around, the characters wrench the wheel from the trembling authorial hand and every device must be employed to keep control. So when in doubt, I always tend cut the scene to whatever imaginary school my imaginary family favours.

Frankly, quick scenes in school are invaluable to any plot, and I am amazed that more contemporary fiction writers do not do it all the time. Once I set an entire novel in a school, where the fiendish head of English, Molly Miles, plots against the idealistic maverick hero with a dark secret. I wrote various bitchy and tense staffroom scenes, enjoying myself hugely but ashamed of actually knowing little about the milieu from experience, and assumed I was getting it all wrong.

But then, a teacher accosted me at a literary dinner and said: 'Have you been hiding in our stationery cupboard? How did you know how bloody irritating science teachers are behind closed doors?'

Since then I have felt free to toss in school scenes whenever it suits. And if you are writing about the dynamics of a family, school is an excellent chorus and commentary. *Meanwhile at Nobb Street High, a pulse of rain swept over the bleak tarmac. Year 7 scattered for shelter. 'Gracious,' said Miss Fazackerly, looking out of the staffroom window and sucking at her coffee, 'Do you think there's something wrong with young Damien McTavish? He's standing all by himself near the dustbins . . .'*

Well, one polishes it up a bit, you understand. At the moment I am amusing myself by echoing a crisis of gender politics among the adults by having a pestiferous little girl called Joanne harass a group of boys who absolutely do not want a Violet Elizabeth Bott clone hanging around while they discuss dead pythons at break. I like to feel it adds a pleasing touch of chaotic realism.

What set me brooding on this was the final episode of Lucy

Gannon's *Hope and Glory*. A couple of years ago I waxed eloquent about the opening episode in which a failing headteacher goes ape and shrieks abuse at assembly, whereupon wise, kind Lenny Henry takes over and resolves to get the school off special measures. It was magnificent melodrama, but in subsequent weeks tailed off a bit into an everyday story of only mildly psychotic teacherfolk. For its finale, however, the author pulled out all the stops.

Science teacher gets disillusioned, fails to do his paperwork, tanks himself up from a smuggled hipflask, barricades the classroom door and begins berating his class in a manner which my husband considered utterly normal, until I explained to him that you aren't even allowed to grip them by the shoulder these days, let alone chuck them around.

Eventually Mr Barmy threatens to throw himself off the roof in the middle of sports day, so heroic Lenny Henry rushes onto the roof to talk him down but himself collapses dead of a much-signalled dicky heart. Splendid stuff.

Schools are the cauldron of social problems. Dramatic and sometimes terrible things happen there, as so do immensely funny things. They have limitless possibilities as a chorus on how the main action seems when retold in a corridor smelling faintly of disinfectant.

Yet they don't figure nearly enough, except in American high-school movies which portray a world unrecognisable to the British. We set scenes in pubs, nightclubs, offices, TV studios, everywhere but schools. Why?

'Because they're not sexy,' says my publisher friend. 'The moment you think about teachers you picture corduroy jackets with leather patches, and scrubbed women with good manners and tidy writing cleaning recorders with Dettox.'

Not enough minxes and Madonnas in the staffroom, see; not enough rangy studs greeting the new PSE teacher with a twirl of their moustache and a drawled 'Well, hello!'

So I was pleased to hear that *The TES* staff are currently fighting over a proof copy of a forthcoming novel which includes raunchy scenes between an OFSTED inspector and a lissom superhead, including an intimate scene involving a 12-inch ruler engraved with the Kings and Queens of England.

I just hope they clean it with Dettox afterwards, that's all.

Dumbing up

Long ago, before the Flood, there used to be a thing called the *Children's Newspaper*, which middle-class parents gave their disgruntled children instead of *The Beano*. I have yet to meet anyone who will admit to having enjoyed the thing. No Bash St Kids, no Mekon, what's the point?

Yet its restless legacy remains to haunt the earnest adult mind with a fitful, irritable conviction that it would be a 'good thing' if the kids read newspapers instead of getting all their information from Bitesize TV. Nothing pleases a pedagogical parent more than the sight of a child engrossed in a broadsheet. I felt a bitter pang of envy the other day, escorting young teens to a Meat Loaf concert, when one of the boys wanted to stop and buy the new *Economist*. I have not been so choked with intellectual envy since we went to *Phantom of the Opera* and the two most musical eight-year-old girls in the party rushed to the shop at the interval to buy not T-shirts or CDs, but copies of the score.

But why this sense that reading newspapers is education? I had a running argument with one primary head who kept sending home little notes about how even the youngest children must 'keep up' with current affairs. I used to barrack the poor man, on the grounds that at the time the headlines were about Tory in-fighting, sleaze, interest rates, and Chancellor Nigel Lawson.

'Why should the poor little toads bother with this stuff?' I would cry. 'Look, they don't even have a vote for 10 years, by which time Thatcher and Lawson will be dead old meat. Why depress them now? They have thousands of years of stuff to learn about first! Teach them about Marathon and Waterloo, about Wilberforce and Nelson and Charlotte Corday. Teach permanent things, like photosynthesis and the circulation of the blood. To hell with newspapers! Why measure out their lives in coffee-spoons before the clouds of glory have even faded?'

He thought I was mad. I thought he was. Amiably, we left it there. Gradually, though, my own children got older and I began to observe that they looked at newspapers sometimes, if only to check what time *The Simpsons* was on. Older still and they start reading odd bits in order to work out what the jokes in *The Simpsons* mean. At this point I persuaded Puffin to let me write a little book explaining the news media to the seven to 11 group.

It is my proud boast that this was possibly the first work ever to explain to such innocents the concepts of the photo-opportunity, the press release, and publicity stunt. It had nifty little exercises like subbing out waffle from an agency report, and reading headlines like 'Scouts to cross channel on giant rubber duck for charity' and working out who gave the story to the paper and why.

When I ran through some of the exercises with real children, I found out two things. One was their scornful conviction that newspapers lie. They were amazed to hear about the existence of sub-editorial checks, the law of libel, and the Press Complaints Commission.

The other thing was how serious-minded they were. A gang of six to 10-year-olds in a bookshop were set one of my exercises, which was to look at three headlines and decide in a news conference which one to put on the front page. The first was 'Cure found for cancer', another 'War declared in Afghanistan' and the third 'Queen chased up tree by gorilla'. With a magnificent disregard for circulation figures, the children unanimously put the cancer cure on the front page, and wouldn't run the stranded Queen as top story even when I told them a) that we had pictures and b) that she had been up there all night. A cancer cure, they said repressively, was Much More Important.

Well, it never caught on and the poor book was pulped. Serve me right. But today – with real and ghastly war news rolling and crashing around their heads – I slightly wish it had. What is a child to think, with so many different voices expressing everything from gung-ho patriotic militarism to accusations of murderous ineptitude in our leaders? At what age do teachers and parents encourage newspaper reading, and which newspaper, and how much of a context do you provide?

And if they bought the *Children's Newspaper* back now, might it not turn out to be too sober for most of the adult readers in the market?

Let Bridget be a lesson to you

If you can't beat them, join them. If your Year 7–10 girls are struggling to look 15, and the female end of the staff room is covertly on the phone booking cinema tickets, best to make the most of it. The new Bridget Jones film is rolling over us like a tidal wave of syrup and whipped cream: now is the moment to build a PSHE/careers lesson deconstructing the education of the fictional Ms Jones.

I know her well; have followed her through the newspaper columns, two books and both films. She is a fine comic creation, but it was a shock when single women started wailing 'She's just like me!' and declaring her a role model. It is as if men started going around saying 'Hey, I *am* Adrian Mole' or 'I dream of being Mr Pooter in *Diary of a Nobody.*'

The cleverness of Helen Fielding is that Bridget – while good-hearted and capable of occasional sharp observations – is revealed at every turn as a prawn, a klutz, a dumbo, a creature who is so self-obsessed and needy, infantile in her dependence on silly friends and silly books, that it is no wonder men run a mile. That's the joke. Or so I thought. She's not an ideal – she's an awful warning.

Scattered through the canon are plenty of clues to how her education made her. She was at school somewhere in the Home Counties, where she had just enough ambition to avoid 'marrying Abnor Rimmington off the Northampton bus'.

Her A-levels were a disappointment: she missed her place at Bristol and read English at Bangor. We are not told whether she did much work, but she never refers to any classic work of English literature (apart from the TV version of *Pride and Prejudice*) and never compares her own situation to that of a fictional heroine (most English graduates do, compulsively). She never goes to the theatre and mainly reads *Vogue*, celebrity magazines and vapid dating manuals. Nor does the outer world interest her much, unless it comes in boyfriend form: she is famously unable to point to Germany on a map, and only reads newspapers when forced to.

When Mark Darcy takes her to the Law Society dinner in 1997,

Bridget understands not a word of serious conversation, but announces that everyone normal votes Labour because it stands for 'kindness, gays, single mothers and Nelson Mandela'. Mark Darcy bleats that her views on his cases are 'refreshing', but only because the poor sap is sexually infatuated, and insecure enough to like his women dumb.

She has managed somehow to land a job working for a publisher, but only ever refers to one author's book (*Kafka's Motorbike*) and spends the day sending flirty emails. She does write press releases, which take her an inordinate amount of time, and has no discipline whatsoever working from home, spending the short morning changing into different bras and falling asleep all afternoon.

When she gets a chance to do a star interview with Colin Firth, she gets tipsy, fails to pick up any of his cultural references ('What is neacher?') or to read the book of the film he is making. When she comes to write it up, she spends the day on the phone to her friends and finally has to hand in the tape, having written nothing.

When her mother swings her a job as a daytime TV researcher she is equally feckless, gets sent off to a court case having read nothing about it, and is out buying a Twix when the verdict comes through. Darcy rescues her, whereon she is convinced that she is a star. In the newspaper column, she finally gave up TV to do aid work in Africa (as her creator did in real life). But in book and film she merely falls into Mark Darcy's arms and Holland Park mansion, to be a dilettante dependant. In real life the marriage would probably not last long, leaving her a discontented, drunken, desperately dating divorcee.

This woman has less general knowledge, wisdom and ability to organise herself than the average bright sixth-former. If you strip away the warm, fuzzy Zellweger charm, Bridget is frankly hopeless. School and university have left her with little in her head, and she has seen no need to put anything else there in the intervening decade. She does not learn, barely reads, has no skills or solid ambitions, and it is a toss-up whether she will be able to set aside her self-obsessed cravings for long enough to raise a child. She is prey to every crystal-waving self-help charlatan in town. A happy ending is, alas, unlikely.

Go on, live dangerously. Zap them with that little lot.

1950 was hell – official

For a grumpy hater of 'reality TV', I have been strangely hooked on *That'll Teach 'Em!*. The parody of a 1950s school was set up to embarrass modern curriculum planners by proving that even the smartest modern 16-year-old could not do O-level, and to cheer up grumpy parents by showing hip modern kids being put through the pointless discipline we all remember with loathing.

It fulfilled its first brief, although I had reservations about the French. While it is perfectly true that O-level French pupils in the 50s could say 'J'ai, tu as, il a', accomplish a *dictée* with fewer than 30 mistakes and identify a past-pluperfect at 50 yards, what was not stressed was that owners of a French O-level were famously useless at actually speaking it. Whereas the modern GCSE kid, ignorant about pluperfects, can order a beer in Calais with insouciant confidence. In English language and maths, however, embarrassing deficiencies were laid bare, to general fogey rejoicing.

But the really interesting bit was the discipline: the hysterically absolutist banning of contraband biscuits, the glum silent mealtimes, the chalk-and-talk teaching, the pompous assemblies and the embarrassing interviews in the headteacher's study. The reason it was interesting was not the kids – they adapt to anything, and besides, they knew that nobody would dare to hit them. This invalidated any claim to 'reality', and enabled the boys, in particular, to send the whole thing up in an admirable manner, especially where the contraband biscuit tin was concerned.

The really fascinating thing was watching the teachers. For they, of course, were not in a 'reality' show, not being tested or experimented on. They were acting. To be precise, they were hamming it up. And did they ham! The head-teacher was plainly under the influence of the some very, very old films and a sketchy remembered reading of Stalky & Co, while the others had modelled themselves firmly on Teecher in *The Beano*. The only ones with any vestige of normality were the beautiful and dignified English teacher, who accordingly was seen less and less as the series went on, and the manic ginger-haired French teacher, who was in fact the inimitable Mr W from my own children's school. He specialises in showy ranting, but is invariably forgiven and prized for his vigorous impressions of glamrock stars. All he had to do for this programme was to turn the ranting up a notch, and refrain from laughing.

Watching the other teachers was the truly hilarious bit. Relish those dire assemblies; that pompous reiteration of the high standards of the school: it is every rebel's dream to have a head so humourless to kick against. The persistent verbal abuse in class was vintage, too – 'I am horrified . . . I repudiate you . . . you are a disgrace . . .'. Some of them tried sarcasm, but it failed to work on the bewildered modern kids, who merely bowed their tidy heads and glanced sideways with a sort of awed pity, towards the gloating camera. Many of the tellings-off reminded one inevitably of the joke about the inflatable schoolboy who went to see his inflatable head in the inflatable school, and was told: 'Boy, you've let yourself down, you've let me down, you've let the school down.'

As for the appointment of the head boy and girl, and the dormitory searches for contraband, these were carried out in a spirit of parody worthy of the most advanced Sixties experimental theatre group; booking Lord Tebbitt for speech day was nothing short of genius.

Look, it was tough at times back in the 1950s, and you did have to do grammar. But it wasn't all that bad. Some teachers actually laughed. Many were inspiring. Breaking rules in a boarding school did lead to a certain amount of tedious hectoring, and the constant claim of heads to be 'disappointed' is perennial (as my daughter once said, why do these people think we *care* about their disappointments?) It was just life, bits of it better than now, bits of it worse.

What we need now is another series, in which adults who were at school in the 1950s are put into a simulacrum of a modern comprehensive, and have to cope with new maths, modern tech, oral French, investigative history, political correctness, school-gate drug gangs, deprivation of games and fresh air, endless government tests, and the dispiriting discovery that your school is bottom of the local league table and the *Daily Mail* says your exam results are worth nothing.

See how they cope!

APRIL 23 2004

Child labour no fairytale

I am not in the business of recommending teachers' resources – God knows, the national curriculum would be in ruins if you paid any attention to most of my enthusiasms, what with Meat Loaf and drag chanteuses and square-rigged ships and rightly-forgotten melo-dramatic novellas.

But a Radio 4 programme last week struck me with such force that I want every child over the age of nine to listen and discuss it, and every humanities teacher to use it as a springboard for, well, everything really. Literature, art, history, drama, morality, psych-ology, the nature of childhood, the illusions of adults, the nature of social campaigning. It was barely 28 minutes long, but I cannot urge the profession too strongly to hit the Radio 4 internet site, push the listen-again button, or failing that harass the network into putting it out as a CD. It was a documentary with dramatised inserts, entitled *Footlight Fairies*, and like all the best radio programmes it came with few pretensions.

Susannah Clapp, the critic, merely presented the story of Millicent Garrett Fawcett's reforming campaign against the exploitation of child actors and dancers in the Victorian theatre. In 1889 she won: to this day, a network of chaperonage and education and limited hours protects children in the theatre. Stagestruck moppets with their eye on the next Annie will already be aware of this; but the tale of the fight is one of those typically doughty 19th-century battles which in itself warms the heart.

What was particularly riveting, though, was that the programme did not dodge the fact that this army of stage children – some only aged five – were sometimes thorough professionals, who liked doing it. Ellen Terry looked back fondly at her days playing Prince John and Mamillius, and spoke approvingly in later life of a particularly good director who would wallop her to make her cry convincingly. 'Master Betty' was such a star that the army was called out to control the crowds on his opening nights.

Nine-year-old Rose, one of Fawcett's interviewees, spoke of her terror of 'mashers' trying to pick her up at the stage door late at night in the West End, as she shivered in her scanty costume, and of the long lonely journey back to the suburbs; yet she indignantly opposed the idea of restricting her hours. Evening, she said, was 'the time when the public expect their diversions, Mum. Our manager says we must always please the public, it's our duty.'

Meanwhile, the utter fascination of Victorian theatregoers with child fairies, monkeys, mini-demons and ghosts, and the regular presentation of all-child versions of Gilbert & Sullivan and Shakespeare offer in themselves material for a whole term's psychology if you're in the sixth form, and a lot of concerned discussion if you're 12 and starting to realise that you are no longer automatically 'sweet'.

The pleasures children and audiences got from this craze are bravely acknowledged; but then we hear of a 14-year-old 'gaiety actress' who attempted suicide, jumping into the Thames; of parents who gave up working in favour of drink because they had three small daughters bringing in 35 shillings a week in the ballet, and only ever came to fetch them from the theatre on Friday nights because that was pay night. We heard MPs (and *The Times*, alas) resisting change and harrumphing that 'if these children are not in the theatres they are in the gutter . . . some of the girls go to the bad, I admit it . . . but there must be small fairies!' It was riveting.

Clapp's conclusion takes it wider: 'creatures onstage are shadows, and who legislates for shadows?' You could play this programme, with children's voices and issues firmly at its centre, to a citizenship class. Then you could discuss drama, parenthood, children's rights, stage illusion, employers' liability, exploitation, opportunity, how campaigners can change the law, and whether there are modern parallels to be found in the pushing of child models or underage pop stars. Then you could put it all down as a module of Victorian social history. Magic.

OCTOBER 18 2002

Word on The Street

I know you are proper grown-ups out there, far too busy to watch TV soaps. You rely on me to keep you up to date on the image of serious education as viewed through the multicoloured prism of *Coronation Street*. It is, after all, a popular prism.

I have grumbled before that the only university student in the series never does any studying or talks about it, and clearly the grumble has been heard. Not only has Toyah the lone student actually done an art project but – with its gnarled northern finger firmly on the pulse of current controversy – the Street last week barged into the great university entrance inclusivity debate. Signs are promising for a continuing strand of plot, provided they don't lose their nerve, or grow bored and turn the focus back on the story of the serial-murdering financial adviser.

What happened is this. Todd is the younger and less dashing son of Big Rough Eileen, the taxi-dispatcher with a heart of gold and a tongue of sandpaper. Todd has been lovesick for 15-year-old single mother Sarah Louise (stepdaughter of the serial killer, pay attention there at the back!).

She has spurned him, preferring to snog with a creature in an eyebrow ring who hot-wires cars. Todd's lovesickness, though, has just been alleviated by his form teacher dropping a bombshell: he has been told he is 'Oxbridge material'. Eileen is so excited she is doing extra shifts to help him pay the expected vast costs of a 'uni' away from home. Most Weatherfield kids go local or not at all. And Todd, as she says, is not only the first in the family to consider university but 'the first who could do joined-up writing'.

Now, there are a lot of interesting places the scriptwriters can go from here. At worst it could just fizzle out, treated as yet another story of broken dreams, in which the Street specialises. It could be a brief ploy, caused by the young actor demanding to be written out so he can become a pop singer.

But it could – cross fingers – go the whole way. Now that, I would love. And so would Oxford and Cambridge university authorities, and those of every other élite university in the land.

We could see Todd frowning over his UCAS form, and borrowing Sarah-Lou's chatroom computer to surf for courses, identifying the whereabouts of dons who specialise in his area. We could follow him off to interview, where to his happy amazement he would find other kids not unlike himself, as well as the inevitable chorus of posh Henries and Henriettas. We could see him questioned, tested, left to stew in the JCR for hours then interviewed again, by a selection of terrifying dons (possibly including one who says 'Coronation Street? By 'eck, lad, I grew up round corner in Bessie Street.' We could see him come back home, to battle against the general view in the Rovers Return that Oxbridge is for 'snobs'.

If he's lucky, their attention will be diverted then to a couple of fresh adulteries and the unmasking of the murderous financial adviser. Then, in the Christmas Special, Todd could get his conditional offer (my, how the colleges will be fighting for that honour! Having a *Coronation Street* character is better for your credibility these days than having Prince William or Euan Blair).

He could work all year, earnestly, even refusing the blandishments of Sarah-Lou to put more hours into his personal study. Then there could be a dramatic regrading showdown with the OCR exam board over whatever weird and unwholesome procedure they go in for next year, and at last, next autumn, we could have the scene where Eileen commandeers one of the company minicabs to deliver Todd to the old stone cloisters and pointy spires of his new home – where he will discover to his amazement that several of the Hooray Henries didn't get in, whereas he did.

Vice-chancellors would ply Granada scriptwriters with the very best college port in return for a plot-line like that.

Then we could just have occasional snapshots and visits from Todd, growing ever more confident and baffling the minicab office with light references to tutors, mods, collections and subfusc.

Perhaps he could bring home a girlfriend from Roedean. Perhaps he will get a first and come back north to do postgraduate studies at UMIST.

Perhaps higher education will at last gain Street credibility . . .

(LATE PS: Of course, it didn't. Todd decided to be gay instead.)

Sassy Fanny

The other night, slack-jawed with horror and amazement, struggling with hilarity, I watched the new film of Jane Austen's *Mansfield Park*.

I have always been strangely fond of this book; strangely, because my 1970's school and college contemporaries regularly flew into a passion of irritation when they read or studied it. In the age of Germaine Greer and Reclaim the Night marches, women bristled at Fanny Price. She was, they averred, a drip, a prig, and a weakling.

They wanted their Austen heroines to be Austen herself, with the cheek of Elizabeth Bennett or the bounce of Emma Woodhouse. Reading *Mansfield Park* they were infuriated by the way Fanny sat still and suffered snubs, and by her timid aversion to the coarse sexual energies of the Crawfords. Her adherence to prissy moral principles over amateur dramatics annoyed them even more, and they were not moved even when she steadily rejected Henry Crawford in the face of Sir Thomas Bertram's wrath.

I rather relished all that, in much the same way that I relished Griselda, in the *Clerkes Tale*, exhibiting the patience of Job in the face of a tormenting husband who wrecks her life and deprives her of her child to test her loyalty. My tutorial partner at the time, now a leading feminist writer, used to go ape over that one too, and shriek at me for saying that it was only a story, that it was a sort of Christian allegory about Man and God and vows, that there was enough irony there if you looked for it, and that, anyway, this was the 14th century so it was unreasonable to expect Griselda to carry on as if she were being advised by Anna Raeburn on a radio agony slot ('Leave the bastard. Leave him, now!').

I argued that it is actually very interesting, historically and psychologically, to read works of bygone fiction which betray strange, dated attitudes. I thought we should try and understand why Fanny was so horrified by 'lovers' vows', just as we should struggle to understand courtly love, or virgin martyrs, or the Private of the Buffs, rather than dismiss them as imbeciles.

In the same way, even though I had lived miserably in South Africa and was passionately, furiously anti-racist and pacifist, I relished *Prester John* and *King Solomon's Mines*. Although half our family friends were Jewish, I learned to take perverse pleasure in the hearty John Buchan heroes who murmured that at the heart of every international conspiracy lay 'a white-faced little Jew in a wheelchair with an eye like a rattlesnake'. I thought – I still think – that it is educative to observe the prejudices of another age, even when you emphatically do not share them. Still my feminist friends would start throwing chairs at the very mention of Fanny Price.

Well, I thought in the cinema, they've got what they wanted now. The film not only makes explicit the nature of Sir Thomas Bertram's slaving business in Antigua (not a bad idea, actually) but bestows on us a modern, 'feisty' Fanny, speaking the waspish lines of Jane Austen herself and flashing her eyes at all and sundry. This Fanny has not a timid bone in her body, gallops her horse (legs astride!) through the dusk when thwarted, French-kisses Henry Crawford on the Portsmouth seafront, agrees to marry him then changes her mind overnight, catches him bonking Maria and – no, I can't go on.

In an age when teenagers think GCSE English revision can be accomplished by lying supine on a sofa with a video of Colin Firth in a wet shirt, what on earth is going to happen once *Mansfield Park* comes round as a set-book again, and harassed parents pick up the video in the corner shop? Will examiners have to put up with analyses of the moment where Mary Crawford says to the assembled Bertrams: 'Huh, this is 1806, after all!'?

On my way home from this weird ordeal-by-anachronism I switched on the radio to hear Peter Bazalgette of Bazal productions, which makes *Changing Rooms* and *Ground Force*. He was in a ferment of indignation because an Australian cable channel was doing a gardening programme suspiciously similar to his weekly masterpieces of grinning Titchmarshes and saucily swinging Dimmocks. It was, he said, important that TV formats should be safeguarded because they were 'intellectual property' every bit as much as novels and deserved the same respect.

I laughed so much that I had to pull the car over to the verge.

Ministerial madnesses

All going on a summer holiday

Ooh, they set your teeth on edge! There is much to like about the Government's commitment to schooling, but there are moments when its righteous, prissy, bossy instincts drive you insane. They make you want to grow hair to your waist, drape yourself in cheese-cloth and rechristen the kids Moonbeam and Earthchild before taking them off in a psychedelic van for lessons in the woods.

Take the latest threat: fixed penalty fines for taking the kids on holiday in termtime. Using the language of industry, the DfES claimed that '4 million school days are lost every year' by parents removing their children for family trips. A spokesman insisted that 'Any unauthorised absence is truancy, whether it is taking a child Christmas shopping, a Mediterranean holiday in school term or just letting a child roam around the local housing estate'. It would be double standards, he said piously, to distinguish between 'disadvan-taged' feckless parents who let their children roam the streets alone, and those who take them on foreign trips. Another spokesman claimed 'the law says children must be in school'.

No, it doesn't. Section 7 of the Education Act 1996 makes par-ents or guardians ensure that a child receives an efficient full-time education, suitable to age, ability and aptitude, 'either by regular attendance at school or otherwise'. Home educators are constantly fighting their corner against LEAs who cannot grasp this. But it's the law – they're our children, we bring them up, and as long as we educate them to a minimum standard (which can't be high, since nobody prosecutes duff primary schools for turning out 11-year-old illiterates) we can do what we like. We can send them to nuns or monks or yogic flyers or Summerhill. Nobody can even force us to teach the national curriculum.

Against this background, threats are not impressive. Don't get me wrong: I like schools. They're a good way of educating and socialising children, and passing on culture, knowledge and skill. At their best, they are inspiring communities. Even at their worst, they are usually better than watching MTV. It is clearly best if term-time removals are sparingly used, by agreement. But school is not all a child needs, nor does it offer a complete education.

There are moments when reasonable parents reasonably decide that it is better for a child to rejoin the tribe, even in term time, for a family celebration or journey. Heads may not like it but they must lump it. And to equate measured, deliberate family decisions with parents who condone unattended shopping-mall truancy is insulting, and probably not legal. I await the first case in which a parent argues that the family project was educationally superior to just another school day.

Of course, not all the absconders are off to the Louvre. Of course, there are inexcusable serial holidaymakers who are a pain in the neck. But even so, there are questions to be asked. Such as, why are state school terms so much longer than independents'? How much actually gets learned in the last fortnight of summer term? And does the spirit flower more readily while doing boring national tests to help school reach its 'targets', or by seeing Greece? And what matters most, the child or the school?

The other interesting question is why, in a society where children rule the roost, do these alleged victims play along? Primary school children may not have much say in whether they are taken out in term time, but secondary pupils have powerful views: I once struggled to persuade one of mine to come out three measly days before halfterm. If thousands of parents meet no resistance when removing teenagers in their exam years from weeks of education, one must ask oneself the same question as we do about real truants: what is wrong with their school life, that it seems so dull and irrelevant?

Learning is individual and elastic, not wholly programmable. Children catch up after illness, after moving house, after family crises. They are expected to survive the disruption of missing the start of school years because the LEA hasn't found them a place, or of having classrooms closed by leaking roofs and periods cancelled for lack of teachers. It would obviously be nice if parents did not add to the general confusion by taking them to Spain; but if they choose to do so, then there is neither morality nor sense in fines.

Persuade, identify, nag if you will; prosecute the truly negligent. But leave families some dignity. Either Government wants us to take responsibility for our own children, or it doesn't.

Hogwarts' horrors

I see no reason to wait until the midsummer solstice before knowing the plot of the new Harry Potter book. There are clues, because JK Rowling's publishers are so plainly anxious to make sure we all get hooked again that they have released some information about the next 255,000-word epic.

We know that the book begins on the hottest day of the summer, in Privet Drive, with 'a teenage boy lying flat on his back in a flower-bed'. What he is doing flat on his back we do not know, but anyone with a rudimentary knowledge of teenage boys can guess that he is either thinking about teenage girls, wondering where to get hold of some money, digesting a family-size Swiss Roll, or else he has just fallen off the roof.

Which is not much help. On the other hand, someone auctioned a postcard on which Rowling summarised the book in 93 words including, we are coyly told, 'Ron, broom, sacked, house-elf, new, teacher, dies, sorry'. Still only a faint clue. It would be nice, though, to think that the house-elf (the one who looks like Vladimir Putin) will get a job as a fast-track food tech teacher.

The really telling fragment is a scene between Harry and the all-wise headmaster. 'Dumbledore lowered his hands and surveyed Harry through his half-moon glasses' it begins, raising the tantalis-ing question – lowers his hands from what? Tearing his hair? Trying to disentangle a phoenix from his hat? Or is Dumbles on a fitness kick, doing chin-ups on the ancient carven beams?

The fragment continues by hinting that there is something the headmaster has been keeping from Harry, and concludes 'Please sit down. I am going to tell you everything'. Aha! It is obvious that something had to change at Hogwarts, and now we have evi-dence. If I close my eyes, I can hear the sonorous voice of Professor Dumbledore revealing that at long last, the modern age has caught up with Hogwarts school.

'Harry, you have devoted much of your time here to fighting Lord Voldemort and all he stands for. It is not that we are ungrateful, but you must understand that as we enter the 21st century it is no longer possible for certain old-fashioned, élitist values to govern what we do here. Frankly, the Weasley family have been a less than suitable influence. Their values are very Old Labour. I suppose it is because Mr Weasley used to work for the Ministry before the recent outsourcing of his duties to Grabita PLC, a subdivision of Death Eaters International. Mrs Weasley has steadily resisted all efforts to return her to the workplace, and benefits for their large family have been a drain on common resources.

'Between you and me, the Treasury Goblins are devising a welfare-to-work programme which will have Mrs W scrubbing industrial cauldrons on the minimum wage before the year's out.

'The important thing I have to tell you, Harry, is that your vendetta against Lord Voldemort must cease. After very fruitful negotiations, I am happy to tell you that Death Eaters International, and its online curriculum subsidiary Darkarts.com, have signed a very advantageous agreement with Hogwarts. This imaginative public-private partnership will bring the dynamic business values of modern Voldemortism right into the classroom, creating useful links with the Death Eating community and providing an ongoing recruitment base. Mr Lucius Malfoy takes over as chair of governors, and Professor Snape has already redrawn the 14–18 curriculum in line with the forward-looking philosophy of our new partners. We are abandoning the Ordinary Wizarding Level exams at 16 in favour of the Vol-Bacc, a more relevant curriculum in modular form, with the incentive that those who pass each module are permitted to continue, while others undergo Transformation into a Vocational, or House-Elf stream and transfer to the kitchens.

'Defence Against the Dark Arts will be replaced by modules in Sorcery Studies and Understanding Satanism. I do regret the departure of such staff as Professor McGonagall, who felt unable to take on the new challenges and, following discussions with Lord Voldemort, is embarking on a new career as a yellow spotted frog. But our staff numbers will be kept up by employing a number of ghouls as classroom assistants. You may have heard the screaming.

'In short, Harry, Hogwarts school is moving forward confidently into a new era.'

Tories on the turn

Trendspotters will have noticed the latest buzz in educational matters. Hard on the heels of 'wraparound educare' from Charles Clarke comes a Tory promise of 'turnaround schools'.

This mania for portmanteau words with a vaguely cuddly suffix can only grow: though it could go quickly downhill with the possibility of bossaround schools for training tough heads, sleeparound schools for the liberated, and muckaround schools for the hardline AS Neillites.

I have been brooding, though, about the Conservatives' new big idea, schools for the excluded. What would life be like at St Turnaround's? A blazer badge showing the marks left by a skidding U-turn, the gilt motto 'Never Too Late', the school song 'Jolly Asboating Weather' and a uniform incorporating tasteful electronic ankle-tag in house colours?

Might it work, and if so what would be the chief engine of change? Should it, perhaps, be wraparound as well as turnaround, since we now know that boarding schools can work astonishingly well for children of chaotic families? Should there be a nightly tuckaround from a cosy Matron?

On principle, I have to admit that I prefer the idea of well-resourced withdrawal units attached to real schools, if only because it is easier to feed reformed offenders back into the system if they are on the same site. But laying that aside, what most assists the turning-round of the troublesome? Asking around, I collected a few pearls of advice. Few of them, alas, come cheap or without grief.

The first, according to prison educators and ex-prisoners, is that people are like those flip-over toy cars: nothing makes them change direction quicker than banging into a wall. The moment you hit the concrete is when you finally go 'Wooah! Something must change!'. Ask any recovering addict. Chaps start learning to read in prison who-never cared about learning anything outside. Drug-dependent women separated from their children feel as if cold water has been dashed in their faces, and may abruptly wake up. However, a

criminal record and a prison sentence have too many disadvantages to be actually recommended.

It is clear, though, that a sudden dramatic change can have a remarkable effect on the speed of learning. Every year we read stories of asylum-seeking kids who get here with barely a word of English, and two or three years later brandish a hatful of A* GCSEs or a place at Cambridge.

Obviously, they're clever; but further down the line you get equally striking examples of uprooted children hurling themselves into rapid learning. As a travelling diplo-brat I arrived at my French school at nine, not speaking a word beyond the 'Madame Souris' book, and two years later came top in French dictée and composition. It's something to do with newness, and concentration, and having something to prove, and being thrown in at the deep end rather than bored witless by slow, slow years of routine classes.

So a bit of despair and a complete change . . . what else? We speak keenly of mentoring; but thinking over the rogues, scallies, misfits, louts, rebels and stroppy little madams I have known, the interesting thing is that the mentors who change their academic and behavioural record for the better are often the ones who have nothing official to do with either. They are football coaches, swimming teachers, expedition leaders, tall-ship bo'suns, choirmasters; adults who give your horrid-looking rock group somewhere to practice; scruffy old guys down the road who give you a beat-up guitar or show you how to dismantle a motorbike; employers who give you a paper round or Saturday job and expect you to toe the line, but don't make any wider, pompous psychobabble-y judgement about you.

Or sometimes it's the great outdoors and animals which do the trick: it is sad that the prison service is short-sightedly giving up its Suffolk Punch stud, which has a record of calming, cheering and empowering difficult young offenders at Hollesley Bay Colony.

High art helps, too, and higher than you'd think. Ask the London Shakespeare Workout, fabulous actors who go into prisons and entangle the inmates in 17th-century language and imagery until quite unexpectedly some silent glowering figure bursts out in unwontedly verbal self-expression and writes riffs and codas around Macbeth, relieved to find rhythms which say the unsayable. Or ask anyone who has watched terrifying-looking kids getting excited about a ballet or opera project, hurling themselves into it head-on because they know so little that they don't yet know it's posh.

So there's your turnaround school. It's got music and sport and adventure trips and opera and theatre and valued work and minimal psychobabble and clear good-humoured boundaries and lots of staff and rolling broad acres and the odd animal.

Oh, blast! I have accidentally invented a rather expensive private school circa 1965. Probably not quite what Mr Howard was thinking of.

APRIL 4 2003

An ideal infant

At budget time – well, nearly all the time – the jargon has it that schools must operate like businesses. Business buzzwords fly around: line management, value-added, target-setting, efficiency gains, cashflow enhancement, performance-related pay. The idea is always seductive: the values of trade are brisk, profitable and predictable. Bums on seats and full order books mean dividends. New ideas can be tried. Failures can be written off to experience. When it comes to raw materials, unreliable or sub-standard suppliers can be berated, nagged, hammered with penalty clauses and blacklisted.

Schools, however, meet a few snags not experienced by businesses. One year's botch-ups cannot be cancelled out by next year's successes: they live on to rebuke you, and their failure resonates down future decades in human failure and unhappiness.

Quality control and estimates of performance are wildly difficult, because every product is an individual. The benchmarks of success – as provided by exam boards – are themselves suspect, and are crude tools at the best of times. Much success is hidden, not to surface until years after the product has left the production line, and emerges triumphant in some distant field of endeavour, saying in interviews: 'It was Mr Thrumbleton, who first got me going.' But above all, unless you're a selective independent school of the most hawkish variety, you simply don't have any proper control over suppliers of your raw material: children.

Instead of a stream of reliable goods, you have a crazily diverse rag-bag of families. They randomly send you these untested children, none of them properly standardised or quality-controlled, many of them with bits missing or dangerous sharp corners. You have to keep adjusting your assembly line to accommodate whatever turns up. It must be maddening. It is enough to make anybody give up trying to operate like a business and go back to the fusty, old-fashioned idea that a school is a community and children are individuals. Which would never do, would it?

Still, it set me thinking about what sort of ideal raw product a primary school would specify if it had the chance. We are bombarded with surveys about the effect of the first four or five years in a child's life – nurseries good, nurseries bad, the importance of stories, of fathers, and so on. But what, I wonder, truly gladdens a reception teacher's heart when it rolls off the family production line and is left in the loading-bay of St Crumb's county primary? You will undoubtedly tell me, but here are some guesses.

The obvious baseline is the traditional advice to parents: make sure the little bleeder knows how to get its shoes on and off, manage knickers in the lavatory and blow its nose. The failure of suppliers to attend to these details wastes hours of worker time at the chalkface. But beyond those basics, it is tricky.

Nursery schools pride themselves on delivering to primary school a steady supply of children pre-loaded with a comprehensive ability to recognise letters and numbers and paste wonky shapes on to paper plates. But hang on: suppose they are too good at it? My own daughter pitched up at Year 1 with a stern and unforgiving outlook: asked to do cutting and sticking, she said beadily: 'I've done that, I'm bored with it.' Heaven knows what mayhem she would have caused if she was also tired of the first six books of Roger Red-Hat. There are limits to a reception class's ability to absorb boffins.

Emotional security is definitely a plus point, so perhaps the tot need not have been in nursery at all, but might have hung out with a keen parent and a lot of storybooks. Remote hill-farm children, I am told, are a joy to teach, as well as having an encyclopaedic knowledge of lambing.

The other thing to consider when ordering your supply of perfect children is the sort of parent they drag behind them. The theory is that middle-class parents are 'good' for a school, and they are damn useful when it comes to fundraising and hauling in favours. But how good are they for teachers? Is a bright, focused, pre-educated five-year-old worth the hassle of an overbright, overfocused, educationally hawkish mummy who will be outside the school gate every day with a desktop-published list of complaints?

I dunno. You tell me. What's the best favour a parent can do for a future reception teacher?

I'm a celebrity, get me a child

Let's leave immediate politics out of this: you do not want me frothing at the mouth all over the tranquil back page. But did you see those television pictures of the Prime Minister in Iraq? He was at a primary school or nursery, and picked up a sweet little boy – aaah! – who can't have been much more than five years old. The child, oblivious to the unanswered questions that keep the rest of us awake, joined in the televised excitement of the moment by planting a kiss on Mr Blair's cheek. Then he did it again, with even more emphasis. Well, even I almost melted. Tony Blair, daddy to the world!

But then it set me thinking about the whole business of celebrity visits to schools. Kids do furnish a room, we know that, and are a peerless backdrop for those who wish to seem nice; but what is the etiquette on visits, what are the rules, are they laid down anywhere? Do you do modules about it at teacher training college? Do parents have to give written permission, for example, before their children are used as decorative backgrounds in political photo-opportunities (remember the PM, again, in front of a stained-glass window and an angel choir at St Saviour and St Olave's). And just how disreputable does a celebrity need to become before a cash-strapped, back-to-the-wall city comprehensive will turn down an opportunity to have the said celeb launch a new book or record with an artful photo-op with Year 7, or a well-publicised chat in the sixth-form centre?

And indeed, when it comes to sixth-form debates and talks, do you lay down any rules of engagement to the stroppier, more politically or socially aware pupils? If Lord Falconer is turning up to drone on about careers in the law or whatever, how do you make sure – or should you? – that someone isn't going to start asking lots and lots of pointed questions about how much money the Dome lost?

If your local Lord Lieutenant or some passing minor royal graciously agrees to present the prizes, are you going to censor your Republican tendency on pain of detention, or do you honour the ideals of the teaching profession and welcome the free exchange of ideas and beliefs at all times, even if it causes the Lord Lieutenant to turn bright purple and choke on his cucumber sandwiches?

We poor parents at home know little of all this. The younger child comes home saying vaguely, 'We had a visitor today. About Parliament. Whass for tea?' And only then do you realise that your hated (or, indeed, revered) local MP has been out winning hearts and minds for the next election but two. The older one may be even vaguer. 'There was this cool drug guy', which could mean either a pop star in rehab or a particularly fashionably dressed police sergeant with some anti-cannabis leaflets. Royal visits, I suppose, are better signalled, and I also suppose that most teachers, not wishing to have an apoplectic chairman of governors come down on them like a thunderbolt, will instruct pupils to be very, very respectful and speak when spoken to. But suppose mummy and daddy are in the GM food industry, or cutting-edge architects who disapprove violently of fox hunting?

What is to prevent a bright child responding to a hearty 'What a nice drawing!' from the Prince of Wales with a pointed diatribe on where he is going wrong? We do, after all, encourage debate, here at St Swine's . . .

Oh well, very good, headmaster. Very fortunately the sixth-form Republican society and the Leon Trotsky group have a large overlap in their membership with the film club, so we have organised a special trip for them to see *Belle de Jour* on Wednesday afternoon during the Duke of Edinburgh's walkabout.

All right, it doesn't usually happen. Children are strangely susceptible to the idea of 'Very Important People' coming to visit them: by and large they sit up straight and mind their manners.

Years ago travelling under escort with a producer in China I was taken aback to be met by a class of 50 chorusing 'Welcome, foreign uncles and aunties!' and breaking into a song entitled 'I grow up in a socialist garden'. It made a change, you could tell, from the everyday routine. But at least they didn't kiss us.

I feel that somewhere in Iraq there is a primary head who is even now wondering how he or she can tactfully phrase a warning to the class that if President Bush drops by, smiles are perfectly in order but it might be a good idea not to kiss him. At least, not until they find the weapons of mass destruction.

DECEMBER 16 2005

Creative about crime

I grow ever more fascinated by Judge Cicconetti, of Painesville, Ohio. He is the judge who – under some American permission irreproducible in our fretful land – amuses himself by devising interesting punishments for everyday crimes. A woman who abandoned 35 kittens in a wood was made to spend several hours out there herself, in the same freezing temperatures, to see what it felt like. A man who called a police officer a pig was made to stand for two hours in a pen in the town centre alongside a hog, holding a placard with an arrow pointing at it saying 'THIS IS NOT A POLICE OFFICER'. A man found with an illegal gun was made to go and look at dead bodies in a mortuary. Teenagers who defaced a nativity scene paraded through town with a donkey wearing a sign saying 'SORRY FOR THE JACKASS OFFENCE'. Noisy neighbours got sentenced to a day of total silence in the woods. General pests are robustly sent to shovel snow.

Reports suggest that the community is not displeased by this, that former offenders write grateful notes, and the judge's wacky sense of humour has been met by approval, unopposed local re-election and the presidency of the American Judges Association.

It takes you back to the days when schoolteachers and other mentors of youth had just this sort of gonzo, freewheeling freedom to suit the punishment to the crime. Mouths were washed out with carbolic soap to teach you not to swear, uneaten rice pudding was served up meal after meal with no thought for bacterial advance, and Dickensian moppets stood in shame with placards round their necks saying 'THIEF' or 'LIAR'. Not, on the whole, days one would wish to hurry back to: though I do know a family of lads whose mother – of my generation – washed their mouths out with soap for telling an elderly babysitter to 'Fuck off'. They were six and eight when it happened and while it would probably count as child abuse now, it must be said that they never did such a thing again. Say what you like, it was quicker and more effective than the 'withdrawal of approval' and sanctimonious nagging prescribed for parents today.

I can also remember the times when school prefects had the power to invent interesting punishments – not all of them sadistic. We are not talking Flashman here, just debonair and witty management of middle-sized misdemeanours. I once spent a whole Saturday afternoon at boarding school down in the basement washing out the vast collection of smelly silver milk-bottle tops the school was saving for guide dogs. It was, I recall, a punishment for brewing alcohol – a misguided attempt at 'bluebell wine' in a plastic shampoo bottle which exploded all over the bedroom wall. I think the idea was to help me understand the less attractive side of fermentation. Running round the playing field was another common punishment, with the additional merit of getting you fitter, so that next time you could run faster when you saw the prefect.

At another school, thinking that old-fashioned lines were boring and pointless, prefects used to set essays of 500 words on topics of their own invention: 'Describe the inside of a ping-pong ball' or 'Write a poem in praise of nothing'. These were outlawed as 'unusual and humiliating punishments', which seems a shame, since such exercises are surely the ideal warming-up routine for facing those famous Oxford and Cambridge interview questions such as 'Tell me about a banana' and 'Is this a question?'

Children like novelty. They appreciate creativity. They understand also that a great many crimes and misdemeanours are not a sign of evil but of being a wally: merely antisocial and annoying, cause as much for mockery as for po-faced head-shaking. It seems from Judge Cicconetti's experience that adults feel that way, too.

Schools, of course, are woven into a national net of po-faced headshaking and restraints on retaliation, so your hands are tied. But hang on – there could be a let-out clause. The Ohio deal is that once convicted the offenders are given a choice: conventional jail or a 'creative sentence'. They mostly choose the latter. So perhaps schools could offer the same. 'OK, Samantha. You know the punishment: a week's exclusion and a negative entry in your school record. But if you'd rather I got creative, just say so . . .'

On which politically incorrect note, I flee the scene with a faint cry of 'Merry Christmas!' Might give you teachers something to fantasise about over the holidays, though.

Inspiration

A Schools' best friend

The TES revelations about the usefulness of dogs in the class-room have met with great media interest, which can only grow once the Department for Education and Skills grasps their true import.

My own first reaction was 'Schools, have I got the dog for you!' as Treacle, panting lightly, lay across my feet in her usual attitude of generalised pleading. I tell you, this lurcher is just what any school needs. Her psychologically-soothing qualities were recognised some time ago when she was headhunted and auditioned for a role as cottage hospital visitor dog to cheer up the old and poorly. She failed only because she has a very long tail, and her wagging behaviour was thought to be a threat to drip-stands. But schools are more robust: and I tell you, anywhere from key stage 1 to A-level this dog could put in a highly productive working day.

She would begin during assembly (unless she was needed for singing) by carrying out a thorough anti-obesity programme, nosing through all the packed lunches in the cloakroom and carefully removing anything containing sugar and fat. She dislikes cottage cheese and has never been known to steal a rice cake, and fruit means nothing to her, so her lunchbox censorship would be broadly in line with government guidance.

Once in the classroom, she would happily agree to lie across the doorway to prevent pupils leaving. In geography fieldwork she would accompany students and dig invaluable holes, and provide cash-strapped biology departments with a good supply of free rabbits already partly dissected for ease of study. As for motivating pupils, she can muster an unusually moving look of doleful sadness to fill young people with remorse at not having done their homework. Conversely, she enjoys nothing more than delivering notes in her mouth, growling cheerfully as she does so: so she could be put in charge of commendations and certificates of merit. Children would be far more impressed by getting a distinction if it was brought to them by a beaming, wagging golden-haired dog than just by some knackered-looking teacher. Since she likes everybody, and is quite

dim, it would be perfectly possible to manipulate her favours and convince the children that she really likes the sensible ones best. On the other hand, the pain of failure in exams or national tests is never more effectively alleviated than by the unquestioning admiration of a dog. Underachievers and struggling non-academic pupils could be put right back on to the rails by half-an-hour's adoring gaze, accompanied by a sympathetic paw on the knee.

But we must be forward-thinking: this educational revolution could go further than even Treacle can manage. Dogs have shown far more subtle skills than hers down the centuries, from guiding the blind to organising sheep or digging up casualties. I advise the Kennel Club to start immediately on a programme of selectively breeding the perfect school dog. All the above qualities are obvious winners, but you could add a few. For instance, a seriously plumy retriever tail could, if accompanied by a handy ramp, remove the need for anybody ever again to bother with a blackboard rubber. The art of sniffing out explosives and drugs is clearly useful in the modern inner-city school, and the detective duties of the dog could be extended to the examination room if it was trained to respond to the high inaudible sounds produced by illegal calculators and furtive texting. And never underestimate the help that a properly bred and trained eduhound could provide to the staff. Quite apart from dissuading pupils from nipping out at lunchtime, it should be easy work to train an intelligent rottweiler to shadow Office for Standards in Education inspectors from room to room, uttering occasional low, discreet but unmistakeable growls and sniffing at their clothing in a way that indicates that they know where the inspector lives. At parent-teacher evenings the dog could double the roles of bouncer and arbitrator. As for meetings with the local authority or the more tedious sessions with the governors, a labrador has limitless patience and readily agrees with everybody, and could therefore stand in for the head at many routine meetings. If tricky matters came up, it could be trained to pad out from time to time with a set of minutes in its jaws and return with the real head's comments. The trend can only grow. Eventually schools will have one dog per year group, and in the more trying areas a trained pack of bloodhounds to round up truants. And calm your fears: not one of them will ever eat anybody's homework. That would be too far-fetched for words.

The barmy babes

When we moved to this house 10 years ago, the children were aged seven and five. Now we are moving out, and a whole crowded history must be sorted and sifted. In the attic is a box of papers bringing the temptation to prolonged, brooding educational meditation. Even 10 years on, even in a mood of unsentimental packing panic, the stuff they brought home from primary school has the power to jump up and stun you senseless.

Some things are familiar: they have never been out of daily sight since first brought home. I cannot easily imagine a kitchen without the multicoloured paper bird whose name was Checkamore. But most of them have not been looked at since; and now that the clouds of glory have faded and the wild weird children are frowning over A-level courses, I am dazzled.

They are from another world. Primitive as they are, they have more vision than the Turner prize and more prose vigour than the Booker. Half an hour with them makes you understand the normally mystifying question of why primary school teachers stick it out so long, what with the pay and the constant badgering by government. They are plainly permanently dazed groupies, slip-streaming in the creative flow of the glittering minds around them.

I doubt that my children were exceptional: certainly neither has turned out to be an artist or a precocious teenage novelist. So you have to conclude that every parent has a similar boxful. Their teachers were particularly punctilious about binding and presenting each child's best story in the form of a card-covered book, protected with good old sticky-back plastic; these have stood the test of time, and provide an important lesson in how to give children pride, and make parents see that the solid point of education is not only the learning you pour in but the ideas you draw out.

The pictures, too, are decently mounted on poster-paper, with some care taken to match the background paper to the prevailing tones of the painting. I am particularly taken by a vivid depiction of the dog-headed god Anubis, carrying a ladder for no clear reason, standing out with terrifying vividness against black.

The stories are short, vivid and allowed to shock ('The snake was in the living room. Eating my Dad.'). As the years move on, arresting use is made of presentation: a 10-year-old's space epic is contained in a capsule made from a silver-painted toilet-roll middle.

From even earlier, we found their logbooks of our sailing trip round Britain, full of telling Polaroids and brief oracular statements (dictated by them, and the letters traced after being pricked out in dots by us for the four-year-old): STRONG WIND IS NASTY. MUMMY WAS ANNOYING.

One of the pictures I particularly remember shows a wall in Brighton designed to disperse the force of waves. At the time, I queried the odd shape of the blocks: a bit Salvador Dali. The artist led me round the corner and pointed, and sure enough they were accurate. My eye had not seen how odd they were: expecting ordinary rocks, I saw them. None of this is remarkable. What is remarkable is the way that adults forget all about it – unless, presumably, they are primary school teachers, kept permanently awed.

All the recent government discourse about education in the early years seems to work on the principle that young children are uniform, stackable empty vessels into which certain key-stage skills must be 'delivered' by a quality-controlled system of approved valves and tubing. Certainly, the writing of barmy stories needs literacy, and painting needs the switching off of the video. But do we properly venerate the extraordinary, explosive phase of creativity that precedes the most formal learning?

The only place that we find it described is in fiction, or particularly intense early-life autobiography, usually accompanied by the memory of a snub (best recent example from pop musician Joe Jackson, who remembers being told not to be stupid when he inventing a space hero based on Dan Dare called Xavier Megan).

The trouble is, if someone does start valuing this phase we shall get a new set of key targets for imagination. 'At seven years old a child must: a) have invented at least one spooky imaginary friend; b) have written a story so weird that the teacher starts giving the parents funny looks at home time; and c) show an ability to make confident use of inappropriate colour, eg, red grass, green sky; and when asked about this, laugh satanically and run away . . .'

St. Crookbacks

I commend to all weary trudgers in the educational byways the tape of the first *People Like Us* series on BBC Radio 4, written by John Morton.

The first programme, featuring Chris Langham as the hapless reporter Roy Mallard, is 'The Headmaster': a straight-faced mock-documentary in which our hero spends a day in a comprehensive school, following the dim head Mr Peacock and his disaffected and mildly hysterical staff. I am particularly fond of the conference with the parents of one 15-year-old delinquent whose 'challenging behaviours' include assault, trouserless arson, drug-dealing in maths class and supergluing the music master to the harp.

'In the end' reports the breathless Mallard, 'it was decided to tackle the problem in stages. First the boy would be supervised at break times and lunch. Then he would see an educational psychologist. Then he would be expelled.' If you haven't heard this cruel, tone-perfect take on schoolspeak, get hold of a copy.

But as I was driving home the other day with that tape playing, something new occurred to me. The first subtle joke in the programme is the name of the school: the Richard III school.

But actually, come to think of it, why aren't there more schools honouring the late Richard Plantagenet? I could find only one: an infant school in Leicester, more honour to it. Otherwise, every kind of Edward, George and Elizabeth seems to be commemorated, but not poor old Crookback.

Perhaps school authorities are afraid parents would associate the offer of a place at Richard III High with a willingness to shut awkward children in towers and suffocate them with pillows (a strategy which, as far as I know, has not featured even in the briskest of Ms Kelly's mini-manifestos).

Yet why not? Richard III's reputation has been washed clean for decades. Shakespeare, following the lead of Henry VII's Tudor spin doctors and their willing dupes such as Thomas More and Polydore Vergil, immortalised the myth of the hunchbacked monster king.

Although the recent revisionists – notably Josephine Tey in *The Daughter of Time* – may have painted the last Plantagenet as improbably saintly, it is well established that he was, if anything, unusually humane for his times and gentle on his enemies. He was loyal to his brother Edward and had a reputation for fair dealing when he represented him in the North.

His claim to the throne was legal under *Titulus Regius*, though Henry then destroyed that document; the campaign against Richard's reputation in subsequent years was all about legitimising the seizing of his followers' wealth and bolstering the Tudors. It is a perfect example of the old saw that history is written by the winners.

What more educational, what more inspiring name and theme for a secondary school? Imagine the first assembly, the first PHSE class, the induction ceremony for newcomers. Teachers, warriors for truth and upholders of Fact, would thrillingly and gorily tell the story of a man born in a difficult time, who did his best amid familial upheaval and base treachery close to home.

They would invite the children to consider a man whose reputation was assassinated, who was accused of murdering children no older than they and became a byword for brutality. Then they would tell the story of the scholars – from 1646 onwards – who began to question the reputation; they would praise the painstaking uncovering of what was fact and what was fiction, and record how by Bishop Morton's influence the great and sainted Thomas More was taken in and became a low spin doctor with the rest.

They would be invited to consider how the rest of his reputation helped to make More the accepted source, even though he was a small child when the alleged crimes happened and heard only the gossip and the politically expedient lies.

Finally, as the bloodstained old tale fired up the children's innate sense of justice and reputation, the teachers would hammer home the importance of checking dates and timelines and questioning facts, and the dangers of regarding all old history – the way children often do – as having happened at vaguely the same time.

You could have Richard's life acted out for the newcomers by a group of seniors, raised on the tale of their school's patron; then finally, as the lights dim over Bosworth field and a thrilling blast of trumpets echoes round the assembly hall over a recording of Sir Ian McKellen reading something resonant, you could give them all a school goblet of Ribena representing malmsey, and invite them to drink a toast to research, truth and justice and the exhilarating qualities of education.

It would, at least, give them something to tell their parents when they ask: 'What did you do on your first day at school?'

The Pedants' Revolt

There was a great Frenchman on the *Today* radio programme last week, hailing the delivery of a 20,000 signature political petition, unimaginable in Britain. It was signed by assorted scientists, writers, lawyers, actors, poets and professors, unanimously protesting against the 'anti-intellectualism' of the French government, notably the Premier Ministre, Jean-Pierre Raffarin. 'He is always speaking,' said the Frenchman witheringly, 'of "*La France d'en bas*". He wants to oppose the people to the intellectuals.'

There is, the petitioners complain, a government policy against the arts, scientific research, creation and true education, and in favour of 'the military and rich people'. The intellectuals are fighting back, with an unselfconscious rage so magnificently alien to Anglo-Saxon behaviour that one can only gasp in admiration.

For, in Britain, to call someone an intellectual is an insult. It implies effeteness, ineffectual vapouring, pretentiousness and a lack of human sympathy. There are, of course, covens of samizdat intellectuals who admit their true nature to one another in dusty corners of university common-rooms or Hampstead, but the outer world is unforgivingly cold to intellectuals, to a degree the French protesters could only conceive of in nightmares. 'Oh, it's very clever,' we sneer. In Britain you can just get away with being a leading scientist if you admit either to being too daffy to do up your own buttons in the morning, or else being fond of football or some other populist pastime.

You can be a playwright or novelist provided you remember to keep saying that you are first and foremost an entertainer. The most serious classical actor must learn to shrug embarrassedly and pretend to be a simple-hearted wandering player, interested more in emotion than ideas. When a character with some sort of intellectual curiosity and inner life appears on *Coronation Street* (in the shape of the marvellous Roy Cropper) he is universally regarded as a comic weirdo.

Tom Stoppard has somehow got away with intellectualism for years by being funny and using deep camouflage. When he wanted to do a play about philosophers (*Jumpers*) he wisely dressed them up in gymnastic Lycra and had them leapfrogging, stepping on tortoises and sleeping with one another's wives. David Hare disguises himself as a political firebrand, expressing emotion loudly in case anyone should suspect that what he is really doing is thinking.

Moreover, unlike the French intellectuals who seem to be able to sink their differences and unite in gangs of 20,000, ours are weakened by mutual suspicion, with right-wing philosophical wonks hating left-wing ones, and scientists and artists pretending to be of different species.

Politicians in Britain have been playing the equivalent of Raffarin's '*La France d'en bas*' card for years. What else is the current insistence on 'the people'? Diana was 'the people's princess' not only because she was kind to the unfortunate, but because of her steady insistence that she was 'thick as a plank' and her pleasingly lousy academic record. 'Be good, sweet maid, and let who will be clever' is not often said these days, but it is certainly thought.

The Millennium Dome, which Ted Hughes wanted to be made into a representation of the human brain and its marvels, and Stephen Bayley planned to fill with art, had its contents dumbed down by pressure to be 'accessible' to any idle fool, and by the ridiculous Peter Mandelson announcements 'surfball' as the game for a new century, even though nobody had actually invented any such game. That is not, one feels, how chess was born.

But Conservative governments hated intellectuals, too. They preferred business, moneymaking, and the encouragement of consumption. Ministers like Keith Joseph, who thought too hard and had mad hair, were supplanted by self-confident thugs and simplistic disciplinarians. Education, under the control of anti-intellectuals, became reduced to tick-boxes, lists and tests which almost exclude the possibility of independent thought. As for universities, God save us: whenever some Oxford or Cambridge admissions tutor invents an interesting question to test a candidate for signs of independent intellectual life, there is a howl that such questions encourage 'élitism'. We are all the poorer for it, because a cerebral awkward-squad is necessary to any nation.

Time for a revolution. Time for a petition. Perhaps it should start in the schools and colleges, with a strike by staff and students refusing to co-operate with any government directive which is insultingly simplistic, illogical, ungrammatically phrased or populist. Let there be bonfires of stupid pamphlets and ruthless insistence on precision of language. Step forward for the Pedants' Revolt!

Down on the farm

At this time of year I remember the thing which I miss most about having a farm: the school visits. In our 10 years of running a small, organic, horse-operated farm we did, if I may say so, a damn good school trip. We liked doing it. We said 'Yes!' to every request. It reminded us of why we bothered with all these recalcitrant animals and wonky crops in the first place. And we very much liked the poems the children sent us afterwards, and have kept the one beginning:

'It was good to see
close to me
a big suffolk punch
which had just had his lunch.'

My husband, Paul, had a particular routine of harnessing up the working horses. He would get the smallest child to step inside the horse collar, to prove how huge it was. Then the two strongest were invited to try and lift it up, which dented any machismo they might have been suffering from. Having established that the horse was enormous and strong he led the creature out, to general ooohs and aaahs, and finished the harnessing. All the kit, old and polished with decades of use, was handled by the children. The solid, leather and brass reality of it entranced them.

The lambs were good value, too, since lambs behave in a way thoroughly approved of by schoolchildren: leaping up on hay bales, running around in circles, butting their mothers and staring fixedly at strangers. Cows are less popular, because the closer you get the more worryingly angular they are.

Calves are better. But the star turn was the piglets. Ours were shiny, black and wriggly, and swarmed over the comatose sow like storm-troopers until she lost her temper, lumbered to her feet and swatted them away with her long nose until they went flying through the air, squeaking. We would point out that pigs have a national curriculum, and that the sow would supervise them in rooting-lessons, swatting any idle piglet which was failing to turn over its quota of earth with its little snout. We took a piglet into the village school once, probably in defiance of health and safety regulations, and let it career around in a pen made of desks laid on their sides, while Years 1 to 3 wrote odes to it.

Once, we had a camp. A school ran a thing called 'field week' every summer term, when pupils and parents could choose between several sets of activities at different prices and degrees of adventurousness. Some went boating, some to adventure camps, the more nervous ones did day trips and the bravest embarked on crazy foreign exchanges (at least, it later turned out they were exchanges: in return for having one little eight-year-old girl kept up in restaurants till midnight by an extrovert Florentine family we found ourselves a year later housing two enormous 17-year-old rugby players called Diego and Valerio, who wouldn't get up in the morning).

Anyway, one of these field weeks was a cycle camp, which we installed on our top meadow under the harassed supervision of two teachers. Every morning a posse of a dozen assorted children vanished over the hill in a whirr of pedals, and every evening they returned, exhausted, to lean on the horses, pat the sheep, collapse surreptitiously in the hay-barn and make a gigantic campfire. You could hear the singing three fields away. On the last day the teacher-in-charge carried down two large Porta Pottis, and emptied them with ceremony into our septic tank (ah, what it is to be a versatile professional!). The whole thing was splendid, and for years afterwards that field was known as Ballentyne's Meadow, after the leader.

The other good thing was the year we got a tank-type swimming pool, and offered it as a stopover on a primary school cycle run. More puffing figures, more whirring pedals, and at lunchtime – with eight or nine miles under their belts – a cloud of children and teachers in Lycra shorts filled the lawn, unpacked picnics and hurled one another into the icy water for half an hour before picking up their litter and whizzing off again.

It was wonderful. I suppose it was a bit like grandparenthood: all the fun of young life without the unfading responsibility I just thought you teachers might like to know that out here, in the sultry summer days, there are some hosts who probably look forward to school visits rather more than you do.

Groundhog days

We treasure fresh thinking, right? Even if it is potentially slightly mad? If we want to clear the way for blue-sky reforms we surely have to allow a bit of battiness? So I felt a bit sorry for poor old Martin Stephen, of St Paul's, calling down odium on his head with the suggestion that academically brilliant teachers should be given special contracts, with their work focused entirely on top-set groups, and that the poor dears should be 'reassured that they will not be asked to teach groups for whom they have no understanding'.

Mr Stephen clearly comes from the sort of lonely, adventurous minority who get their kicks bungee-jumping over alligator pits. One can see why the education world got so cross: after all, every day of the school year certain gallant teachers stagger out and stand in front of groups of children for whom even a mother would be hard put to it to have any understanding. Given that these heroic teachers often succeed in enthusing the most unlikely pupils, there was something monstrously, almost endearingly, preposterous about the idea that sensitive and highly-paid superteachers who really, really love maths (or whatever) should be shielded from idlers and dimwits. Why should anything calling itself a schoolteacher be released from the central teacherly task of drawing out talent from stroppy hormonal blobs?

Unfortunately, though, Dr Stephen's Geek-Power idea rather overshadowed another suggestion he made, which ought to be given a bit more thought. He wants more grammar schools, but without selection. Anyone could go. The only caveat would be that every child would have to satisfy academic criteria in order to advance to the next class; if they didn't, they wouldn't be thrown out, but simply made to repeat the year. For as long as it took.

Now, I grew up partly in France, where such arrangements at the time were common. And I saw how my peers felt about it, so I know exactly why British schools have been reluctant to go in for repeat years. Quite apart from the incongruity and potential disruption of having a hulking creature glowering in the back row, the children themselves absolutely dread it. Being 'kept back' is seriously embarrassing. Your mates move on without you, your circle of friends is compromised, and the nearby desks fill up with a lot of little pipsqueaks to whom you thought yourself superior simply because you were born sooner than they were. You re-open the dreary old textbook your mates have abandoned, still with your old doodles in the margin; you look up glumly at the familiar teacher you tormented all last year. You endure a whole year of groundhog days.

But things you hate can have a useful side to them. The fear of being kept back is a tremendous incentive to pass your end-of-year exams, and therefore you are more likely to listen to the teacher, despite his or her irritating preoccupation with fractions or Shakespeare or diagrams of dogfish. You realise that there is no longer any chance that you can just drift on vaguely up the school until you and your mates are 16, whether or not you learn anything.

Children are pragmatists: if they realise they are trapped in a quagmire, they will try to get out of it. If the only way is learning something, that is what they will do. That ticket to the higher class – ah, how I remember this from France! – is a cherished passport. When my good friend Veronique, wickedest girl in the Quatrième Classe, was told that she would after all be able to join us in Cinquième, we all rejoiced together. We had before us the awful spectre of Chantal, who now trailed miserably astern of us, still wearing the shaming pink pinny of the Troisièmes.

I am not sure whether holding-back would ever work here, among our cadre of pupils and teachers and human rights lawyers. But I can tell you one thing: it delivers a clear message. It lets you know that school is not just a chronological process which will release you according to age whether or not it has left any mark on you. School is a workplace, a career, a ladder. You won't get on, get up, and get out until you have let it have its pedagogic way.

Children understand that sort of thing. No computer game, after all, would ever sell if you were guaranteed to rescue Princess Bustina from the Dragon's Lair after half an hour's playing, whether you deserved to or not. You have to go through the levels, keep your eye on the screen and your finger on the button, and earn every inch of advancement. Think about it.

Ars Longa

Last week I spent two days in Windsor Great Park, hot-housing and think-tanking in a formiable thicket of arts professionals, social philosophers, critics, educators and deep thinkers (no, I am none of these. I was the hack chairperson). From lofty BBC gods to the magnificently quarrelsome arts editor of *The Scotsman*, they were attempting to define and discuss the role of the arts in society. What's it all for, then? Music, theatre, fine art, literature, film, television, Internet, everything? Why do we bother?

A lot came out of it (some of it in raised voices). There were genuinely moving statements of faith in transcendence, and genuinely aggrieved snarls about subsidy. But among the mêlée of messages was one message which – if you have the nerve to dwell on it – turns the concept of educational need upside down forever.

In every area there was a sense of clamour, of clutter, of arts and forms of communication which can no longer be tidily contained in categories and curricula and schools-of and -isms. The notion of a canon of acknowledged masterpieces, always a slightly wobbly concept, was being disowned even by apparently conventional and traditionalist thinkers. Nobody wants to ditch Beethoven or Shakespeare, but everyone has to acknowledge that with time rolling on and arts production at a frenzied level, it is already impossible to think in terms of the old idea of a 'thorough grounding' or a convenient overview of the arts. Never again will there be a Kenneth Clark to tell us exactly what matters and how much. Today we have a free-for-all: one speaker used the image of the old centre cracking and new art 'breaking from below'.

So the question came up: how do you teach the new generation, the Web generation, how to search? Not research, *search*. Research is relatively simple to teach, because a researcher, whether six-years-old or 60, knows roughly what he or she is looking for. But someone groping for the consolation and inspiration of the arts – when the arts are so various, the new books such an avalanche, the digital channels so infinite, and the stretches of CDs fade into the farthest horizon – can quite well blunder around for years without finding anything they like.

There was a time, I suppose, when art was scarcer and beauty more consensual, when the sad or puzzled heart could wander into a church, gallery, library, or a concert hall and – even if they didn't like it instantly – get comprehensibly plugged in to a national, or European, cultural canon which would lead on to the next thing.

When the clerk Leonard Bast in Forster's *Howards End* went to Beethoven's Fifth he had a clearish idea of the 'high' or 'good' inspiration he was trying to get a grip on. Today his choice would be far, far wider and his income and education might be better; but if he took his cosmic puzzlement and thirst for beauty into the Tate and fell over Tracey Emin's bed, or to a modern experimental opera which sounded like cats scrapping in the IKEA saucepan department, he might decide to head back to the pub.

For, as arts proliferate and common standards of taste erode, it is inevitable that an ever larger proportion of artworks will seem, to an ever larger proportion of their public, distasteful, disgusting or boring. It is a tribute to our diversity, but also a hurdle for the earnest seeker; the seeker who is not instantly satisfied by what is served on familar TV channels, by three or four familiar authors and the local poster shop. You need grids of reference; you need to be taught to search, both physically and in cyberspace.

I idly speculated on what would happen if you got on the Net and typed into your search engine the words 'Comfort my sad heart', 'Is this all there is?', or 'Is beauty real?' When I got home, I tried it and got a list of side-effects of Prozac, an advertisement for a Phi Kappa ski trip, and a US drag queen contest.

But, because I already know about Shelley and TS Eliot and Philip Larkin and Mahler and Alan Bennett and Verdi and King Lear and Henry Moore, my comforts are secure. I can start from there and grope outwards for new stuff. But if the idea of 'the canon' and the 'acknowledged masterpiece' is crumbling – and it is, it is – how do you make sure that a new generation knows enough about searching to find their way to whichever of the above, or of 10 million other offerings, rings their personal bell?

NOVEMBER 14 2003

Engage brain and gossip

Yawning dumbly over breakfast after a bewildering week, I spent some time on a report from University College London about which activities preserve mental agility in a person's middle years. It did a study of 10,308 civil servants, over a period of 17 years, which should interest anybody who, like me, has started putting the cheese away in the washing machine and holding the dog's rubber bone to one ear when the phone rings.

I always assumed that education is the best way to keep your brain turning over into old age. This is based largely on the ancient, wrinkled sharpness of university academics in my youth. I was taught Anglo-Saxon by the late Professor CL Wrenn, who died in his nineties but who the week before his death, half-blind and barely mobile, was terrifying me and my tutorial partner with his pouncingly critical mind. When we heard the news, the unworthy thought flashed past that now we wouldn't have to finish his unspeakably difficult translation; I am happy to say that we both did it after all, out of a mixture of respect and fear that he might haunt us.

But education isn't everything. The UCL bar charts prove that. Some results are not too amazing – DIY and gardening do not seem to do much for the short-term memory and verbal and number skills they tested, which is no surprise to anybody who lives with a spouse wandering around holding a trug or screwdriver and muttering 'Now, where did I leave the thingummy for those whatsits?'. Cards, scrabble, etc, score high, as do reading and music. Which is a comfort to anybody inclined to stay indoors, ignoring the compost-heap and loose guttering in favour of a good book and some Bach. 'Sorry dear', you can say, yawning comfortably, 'I'm working on my mental agility'.

The results are split by gender, and while women get less mentally agile while using a home computer, men get more so (we shall come to that in a moment). Moreover, when women go out to pubs and clubs, it markedly improves our brainpower (presumably because we gossip), whereas men undergo an equally marked decline (presumably because they drink and grunt about football). So far, so predictable.

But the shock comes with 'educational activities'. Men who do courses shoot ahead in the mental agility stakes – it is better for them than computers, and nearly as good as reading and music. But women register less than a fifth of the benefit. It comes below going to church, and streets behind 'visiting friends and relatives' (which, interestingly, doesn't improve men's minds one bit).

What's going on here? How can it be that men flex their middle-aged minds in adult education five times more than women? Sitting side by side in classical civilisation or astro-navigation at the local FE college, can it be true that Mr Jones is making fabulous new neural connections and re-plasticising his brain cells, while Mrs Jones is getting less cerebral benefit than she would if she popped round to her sister-in-law's?

Well, it could be. Refer back to the weird finding that when men use a home computer it gees their brains up, whereas with women it has the opposite effect. I fear that the answer may lie in something only too familiar to schoolteachers: male challenge.

Perhaps all these men in the educational courses are arguing a lot. They are challenging the teacher, asking 'Why?' and 'How do you know?' and generally being macho and combative. In the same way, my husband spends hours updating his computer software and exploring the technical possibilities of his machine, while I just use mine as a typewriter and Google-powered encyclopaedia, and howl pathetically for help when the screen goes blank.

It is possible that females get less benefit out of adult educational courses because we don't argue with the lecturer enough. We are good girls, we take notes, tick boxes, finish the coursework, accept that teacher knows best. Whereas, of course – glancing up the bar chart again – when 'visiting friends and relatives' we argue incessantly over the way that our acquaintances should lead their lives, raise their children and colour their hair.

How very worrying. Of course I may get a flurry of letters from adult education lecturers saying 'Wrong, sexist, rubbish Libby, the men are docile and the women drive you nuts with their smartass questions'. Oh, I hope so.

Strut and fret . . . . theatrical triumphs

Clothes remaketh man

At last, a blow has been struck for the underage transvestite! Raise a cheer for the Centre for Language in Primary Education and the courageous English adviser, Sue Pidgeon, who has had the sheer bottle to inform a cringing national newspaper that little boys who dress up as girls are 'learning a different viewpoint', and congratulations also to the institute's director, who told the journalist (who was following up a story in *The TES* on May 7) that cross-dressing could have a beneficial effect on boys' willingness to read.

Go, CLPE, go! One of the great oppressions of our neo-Victorian world is that in a lot of families and not a few schools, boys are forced to be boys, all the time. What hell for them! A small girl can dress up as a knight or a pirate or Superman and nobody turns a hair. I refused to wear a dress for years, until forced into pleated skirts by pitiless nuns, and clearly remember how this alleviated the injustice of only being allowed one gender.

My butch phase was tolerated without any trouble, as any girl's normally is. But let that girl's brother spend more than a few larky minutes in a skirt and wig, and the surrounding world – depending on its class – either starts dialling psychiatrists, or else just shouts 'Poof!' until the poor brat gets back into combat trousers. If his sister hasn't pinched them. The only outlet for liberating fantasy is the school play (I remember my 10-year-old brother in silk breeches, courting his friend Sean in a full crinoline). But co-education has spoiled even that. I shall know I have found a truly free-spirited school when I go to its production of *Oklahoma* and find that Miz Laurey is Kevin from Year 5 and Jud the hired man is a strapping lass in chest-flatteners and a stick-on moustache.

Oh all right, it might go too far. But it seems to me that in our cheerless Gradgrind educational world we seriously underestimate the intellectual liberation of the dressing-up box. Like all ignorant adults who have forgotten real childhood, I used to think, idly, that it was mainly a girly thing. Over five, I reckoned, boys became soldiers and Ninja Turtles and quite rapidly lost the bits of the costume in the garden, while girls did the Princess thing.

All this changed on one fateful autumn evening when we had a joint birthday party, a mass sleep-over of six 10-year-old boys and six eight-year-old girls. We all went swimming to wear them out; then all ate pizza in an equally vain attempt to weigh them down a bit, then played games to fill the gap till bedtime. At this point the boys started idly fighting and the girls pursed their lips and turned aside from the main action to play chess in a marked manner, or toot recorders. Butter wouldn't melt.

So I unleashed the final weapon. We have a big dressing up hamper, plentifully supplied with drapes and wigs and bits of old fancy-dress costumes, topped up by my 1970s wardrobe of droopy Afghan things, bright yellow flares and Indian subcontinental tat. As anarchy levels began to rise, I shouted:

'Right! On the landing is a hamperful of clothes. I am giving a prize for the silliest costume!'

I had expected the eight-year-old girls to go for it and the street-wise older boys to snigger and hold aloof. Wrong. The boys stampeded, threw themselves into the hamper and began digging like dogs, ripping wigs in half in their urgency to cast off their male images. Ten minutes later, my restorative drink was interrupted by an ingress of astonishing figures. The girls looked fine – princesses or pirates or fashionplates, according to taste, but nothing unexpected. The boys, on the other hand, were sublime.

Beaming thuggish little faces peered through harem veils, bare navels wiggled above oversize Arab trousers, Pocahontas hair cascaded over Chinese robes. One had put on a drop-waisted sequinned dress with a furry bear mask and silver bra worn outside. The notoriously butch son of a professional footballer had done himself up like his own great-aunt, and one boy had even fastened an orange sponge and a yellow cloth from the bathroom as an ornament on his crown. They were creatures of fantasy, gender-bent glories from a parallel universe, briefly free of the tedious bonds of masculinity.

But when I showed the Polaroids to other parents, more than half of them looked very boot-faced. At least today I could have told them it was an advanced reading-recovery scheme.

Still crazy for plays

My personal theme of the past week has been rushing home to see end-of-term plays at schools that my children no longer attend. How sad can you get? Should a parent really be taking up space in the primary school assembly hall when her youngest is 18? And even for a school governor, is it not a bit over the top to attend both the technical rehearsal and the closing night of *West Side Story* without so much as a niece in the chorus? No, I stand unrepentant. Both were fabulous and set all sorts of educational hares running through my head: within seven days I saw both ends of the school performance spectrum. It went all the way from four-year-olds just about remembering to mime sturdy digging motions while singing a song about buried treasure, to 18-year-olds doing *Officer Krupke* with full-on athletic choreography and appropriate dramatic sneering.

It was education in action, a living exemplar of what drama can do and why you should never, under any circumstances, enrol your child in a school which says it 'doesn't do plays' because they are a distraction from the curriculum.

The other satisfying thing is that even though these were amateurs and children – who by all received wisdom, are only appreciated in performance by their parents – both shows genuinely achieved the haunting quality which stays with you afterwards. The leads in *West Side Story* had a particularly memorable sweetness – well, they are the right age to convey dangerous, headlong passion, and at that school they sing like angels – but some of the 116 children in the Coldfair Green first school play had the same quality.

And, even without input from Bernstein and Sondheim, so did the songs. The theme was Suffolk treasures, Roman and Anglo-Saxon: we have Mildenhall, Hoxne and Sutton Hoo. And a playlet at the end about Seaxmund of Saxmundham celebrated 'one of our greatest legacies these ancient peoples left us, the names of our villages and towns'.

Tags still haunt me: the tiny boy playing Gordon Butcher, a ploughman who found 34 pieces of Roman silver plate in 1942 and had it confiscated – and not reported to the authorities – by his farmer boss. They did it in a 'this is the house that Jack built' style, all the way through to the judge in the court case and the public visiting it now in Bury Museum. Every time it got to his part in the finding, the child elbowed forward and yelled 'which GORDON found!', reducing the audience to fond hysterics. You could see it dawning on the boy that the joke was better than he had realised, and he milked it more each time.

Another played Eric Lawes, who was out with a metal detector in 1992 looking for a lost hammer at Hoxne and found 14,000 coins, gold pepperpots and bangles (played by dancing Year 2s) 'but I never did find that hammer'. Class 3 did Sutton Hoo, with all the melancholy, foggy funereal majesty of that site; and the top class, aged nine, portrayed evil King Niohad, Weland the Smith and assorted Ethelwulfs, Swineherds and warriors.

Ever since my own eldest began there in 1987 I have noted how this school's plays (which, on principle, give a part to every child in the school) always hold behind the songs and glitter an understated moral structure: care for each other and for the earth, respect the past, be brave, hold fast and be faithful even through trouble.

Parents with small children who don't yet know the hardness of the world are very vulnerable to simple sentiments, and I cannot remember any play at that school which didn't at some point bring me to tears. Even now, the archaeology song that linked all these playlets brought an old, familiar pricking behind the eyes, celebrating not only the showier treasures but the shards and fragments: 'Pots and pans and plates and knives, Proof of other people's lives!'

And if I snivelled, that's the magic. These are small children, unconsidered except by their parents and close relatives. Yet together, and individually with the punch-lines, they command a hall full of strangers. They hear the laughs, and sense the emotion pricked into being by the simple words and songs. The teachers stand back, working the lights: the children dominate.

At any age, but especially for the smallest, the result can only be empowering. You prepare, you practise for weeks. Then you tell your story, and in the sound of the applause you have proof that the world has a place for you and can be made to hear your voice. It is theatre magic. It is education, education, education.

Right on, Cinders

In Hampshire, primary children are studying *Cinderella* in the context of the United Nations Convention on the Rights of the Child, 1989. A reporter listening in heard bright little mites saying 'They kept her in a cellar and made her work like a slave, which infringed Article 19' and 'Her stepmother denied her right to be protected from abuse' and opining that she should have gone to the ball under Article 31 'because children have a right to play'.

Apparently the children love it and Hampshire, which imported the idea from Canada, says it will transform their behaviour. In one exercise, children are encouraged to write a letter to the police complaining about the way in which Cinderella is being neglected. What will happen when they over-enthusiastically post the letter to the Southampton police station I dread to think.

Several thoughts spring unbidden from this fertile soil, the first being that it seems a bit sad if modern children can't see the evils of cruelty without banging a clause number on to it. In our day, wicked stepmothers were just wicked, and no one sent us to look up the precise clause under which they were infringing an international treaty. But let that pass. The second thought is what a brilliant wheeze it is to teach children their 42 basic rights, not least because they might notice that these rights do not include a constant supply of high-fashion trainers, TV in the bedroom, photophones, personal DVD players or £50 tickets to upmarket moppet discos.

But the third thought is simply what swampy ground they are on with *Cinderella*. This is dynamite. I can't believe they have reached the end of the story yet, or there would be howls of confusion from Hampshire night and day.

Consider. The first bit is straightforward enough: Cinders suffers discrimination (Article 2) and it is unlikely that sleeping in the grate and eating crusts conforms with the safety and nutritional standards established by the competent authorities in Articles 3 and 24. Her right to evolve her capacities (Article 5) and to express herself in art or print (Article 13) is clearly infringed. If you can count a palace ball as 'peaceful assembly' then the sisters have got a problem with denying it to her in Article 15.

But then she gets taken off to the ball by the fairy godmother (and I am not at all happy about the safety of any coach drawn by mice – I used to keep mice, those little bleeders have a will of their own). She is also dressed up in a ballgown not of her own choosing, which you could interpret as 'sexual exploitation' under Article 34; and once she gets to the ball, things grow murkier still.

Discrimination is outlawed under the UN convention, whether on grounds of race, colour, sex, language, religion, politics, ethnic origin, property, disability, birth or any other status. Yet Cinderella is chosen by the prince on the hatefully discriminatory grounds that she is golden-haired and more beautiful than the day. He whirls her round in his arms all evening. The rights of pig-ugly girls who might rightfully have hoped for a dance with HRH are trampled under her delicate glass slipper (which incidentally is a disgracefully dangerous piece of footwear. And don't tell me that *vair* means fur in the original French, because I know that, and I don't want to get into animal rights here, or we could be at it all day).

No sooner has she been complicit in undermining the self-esteem of uglier girls, including her stepsisters (who were possibly victims of depression owing to their hideous faces) than she flees home, and waits for her prince to come back and start discriminating again, with his unpardonable prejudice in favour of tiny feet. The sisters then hack off their toes and make themselves disabled – which obviously should not count against them under Article 1 – and are thus suffering, in non-compliance with Article 2, a discriminatory punishment on the basis of their 'expressed opinions and beliefs' that Cinderella is a scullion, not to mention their ugly faces.

Cinderella, in short, has sided with the oppressor, a prince whose only claim to lord it over womenfolk is his high birth.

Frankly, the whole thing stinks. Hampshire, be warned. You might do better with *Little Red Riding Hood*, as long as you change the ending so that the wolf goes to an animal sanctuary and her parents are arrested for letting her cross the forest alone and encouraging the grandmother to eat high-cholesterol foods.

Or you could, of course, ignore the wild old stories altogether and write your own. What do you mean, they might be dull?

Sing a song of citizenship

It was always the highlight of the primary school summer term. The May Day festival – generally, it must be said, delayed into June – included the usual dancing round poles and the presentation of the May Queen. It also generally involved the sly insertion of *John Ball*, a wonderful song by Sydney Carter, written in 1981 to commemorate the leaders of the Peasants' Revolt on its 600th anniversary.

'Who will be the lady
Who will be the lord
When we are ruled

By the love of another?' we sang, and swung into the chorus: 'Sing, John Ball!', in which the singer addresses the turbulent priest with the promise:

'I'll crow like a cock
I'll carol like a lark
For the light that is coming
In the morning!'

Disgraceful. Dangerous socialist propaganda. Who knows what John Ball's assertion: 'When Adam delved and Eve span, Who was then the gentleman?' planted in young minds? The school corridors reverberated to the sound of Carter's line 'Labour and spin for the love of one another'? How dare they! These, may I remind you, were the Thatcher years; no time for a stroppy little rural school to be echoing Ball's pre-Marxian letter, recorded in Froissart's *Chronicle*: 'Are we not all descended from the same parents, Adam and Eve? And what can they show, or what reasons give, why they should be more the masters than ourselves? Except, perhaps, in making us labour and work, for them to spend.' Dear oh dear. How could this have been allowed?

Well, it was wonderful. My children inform me that they never had the slightest idea of what was going on, and thought that it might have something to do with John Ball's Garage at Friston. Politics, capitalist or socialist, was a closed book, even thought

they knew all the song's words and enjoyed roaring out the sentiments.

But I reckon it was a citizenship curriculum by stealth, promoting co-operation, equality, 'All shall be ruled/By the love of one another', and a healthy scepticism about Lords and Ladies (believe me, in a rural area, this is still a useful service for education to perform).

John Ball is a wonderful song (available on CD, try Amazon) and very catchy. And humming it to myself again, I remember with surprise another village school in Suffolk, 30 years earlier, and the fact that my earliest political education did, in fact, come in songs.

We sang a lot, then: Mrs Brown could bang out a tune or two on the piano, and it was a cheap way of filling in the restless afternoons. And the songs we sang were, as often as not, about battle, rebellion, defiance, and general resistance to tyranny. In our piping voices we sang *The Song of the Western Men* ('And shall Trelawney die?'), *Rule Britannia*, and Bunyan's war-like invocation to be a pilgrim and brook no discouragement, even when beset around with dismal stories. On the religious side, we roared out *Fight the Good Fight and When a Knight Won his Spurs* and, in the secular corner, found various chronicles about Polly Oliver who dressed up to follow her sweetheart to the war, heroic maids defying barons to rescue their lovers, and the Farmer's Boy who won the hand of his master's daughter by diligent ploughing, sowing, reaping and mowing.

We liked the ones with a bit of defiance in them: the ballad of Mary Hamilton was my favourite, in which the Queen of Scotland's lady-in-waiting, made pregnant by 'the highest Stuart of all', is taken to the scaffold for infanticide but when offered mercy by the King retorts:

> 'Och, haud your tongue, my sovereign Lord!
> An ill death mat ye dee!
> If ye had wished to save my life
> You'd never ha' shamed me!'

You see? We're barking up the wrong tree with this dreary 'citizenship' curriculum and worksheets about local authority elections and disability rights panels. If you want children to get heated and passionate about all that stuff, first of all you've got to get the humanity and the fire into them.

Dig out the fierce old songs about right and wrong, bad barons, everyone being descended from Adam and Eve and chaps refusing to bow the head to tyrants and telling kings to hold their tongue. Revive the old forgotten songs, find the new ones to go with them (I am sure there are some red-hot rebel songs from the Caribbean, Africa and the Indian subcontinent). Bang the piano, make the windows rattle: citizenship through song.

They'll never forget it.

Careers advice . . . . what's it all actually *for?*

But can you bury a dead sheep?

The other night I ate my dinner on the mess-deck of the restored HMS Warrior at Portsmouth. We sat at bench tables suspended by iron bands from the deck head; over us were the hooks for the Victorian seafarers' hammocks, around us gun ports and workmanlike tackle. Where 600 men once lived, 240 members of the Hampshire Institute of Directors dined.

The restoration – mainly in Hartlepool – is a triumph of our time, carried out with beautiful precision from original drawings. Not an angle is wrong, not a millimetre of wood or metal out of its proper and useful place, not one element of decoration superfluous or ostentatious.

Something about these surroundings set us talking about craftsmanship, and the worrying decline in esteem it has suffered in this educational age. Next to me was the ebullient Graham Webb, who started out as a hairdresser (and rock drummer) and now runs an international salon empire and a host of committees. With roaring good-humour he likes to demolish the orthodoxy of graduate-worship, and the pious elevation of information skills and academicised management-theory.

Around him other employers keenly joined in. Where is the respect today for the 'craft' route to the top? Mr Webb reeled off a list of other ex-crimpers who now run companies. He hates to see anything advertised as suitable only for graduates (unless in a specialist field, like law) and holds the heretical view that there are plenty of other ways to get competent – not everything needs a diploma.

Over the following days I talked to other members of the 1999 bossclass and found a surprising number, off the record, ready to concede that university degrees are not all they are cracked up to be, and that if only their personnel department would be less anally-retentive about an 'all-graduate intake', they might get some interesting new faces in.

But even more enthusiastically; they talked about craft. 'I do like kids who can make things,' mused a marketing director sentimentally. 'Someone who can plumb a house or build a boat or take the back off a computer – they've got something, haven't they?' Suddenly I remembered my own husband, at the height of his farming career, arriving to do a show at LWT and gazing up at the great tower thinking: 'I am the only person in this building who buried a dead sheep before breakfast.' It imparted a glow of invisible, but useful, brio to his performance in the world of waffle and spin.

There is increasingly a received wisdom that we are entering the 'information economy' where nothing will matter except the ability to move information around on screens. This is compounding a situation that grew up during the years of expansion in higher education, when apprenticeships were sniffed at, and even technical colleges went on the defensive and started academicising their most practical courses with huge unwieldy modules of theory.

We have almost entirely lost the wisdom that the best way to learn something is Sitting Next To Nellie. Sometimes these days (when even the best plumbers and electricians are hard put to get apprentices, and school technology classes produce more neatly bound presentations than they do usable teapot-stands) it seems that the only practical skills which get any applause are those displayed by conceptual artists who saw up cows and pour plaster on their genitalia.

We should think again about the psychological (even spiritual) advantages of direct mastery over the material world. We should be more deferential to those who teach it, and challenge corporate employers to be open to the non-graduate with practical skills.

After all, whenever you go to one of those motivation seminars for business, who is on the platform, or leading the attempt to build a raft? Why, some round-the-world sailor or mountaineer or rugby captain who left school at 16. Row on row of HNDs, BTECs and MAs gaze at this hero, wistfully envious of that self-driven, gloriously uncertificated oomph and wondering how to get some.

OK, carried to extremes this line of thought would make us a nation of philistines. But you can always go back later and get a degree, can't you? All the more fun, so adult learners say.

Well, think about it. I am off now to exert my construction skills building a barricade of strawbales against an expected hail of brickbats.

Work ethic

There's a grand new book out by a chap called Bill Cullen: an Irish motor industry tycoon. It's called 'Its a long way from Penny Apples', because that's what his mother said to him when he was going into a multi-million pound deal. Cullen saw the film of Frank McCourt's 'Angela's Ashes' and promptly decided to tell his own version of a 1940's Irish childhood. Like McCourt, he was one of the huddled urban poor; he lost siblings to the ills of poverty and slept twelve to a room. Like McCourt he received charity from the St Vincent de Paul Society and cuffs from the Christian Brothers. Like McCourt he had a strong mother who held the family together through unimaginable privations.

But Cullen has a different take on it all. The community was strong. The holy Brothers were not so bad. The charity relief was very welcome, thank ye kindly. They weren't poor, he says: it was just they had no money. But there's always something to be done about that, so he sold penny apples with his Ma, and fish out of an old pram with his Granny Molly Darcy. She charged twopence a fish, threepence to people in fur coats, and told him he was an heir of Cuchullain in the land of saints and scholars, and never to forget it.

He set up his own business making paper flowers to sell outside the maternity hospital. He discovered a supply problem at the rosary factory, and boiled up cow horns to string beads at the kitchen table. He bought cheap plastic dolls and customized them, putting the hair in bunches and calling them 'Judy Garland dolls' and doubling the price. He queued in the rain for cinema tickets and resold them to the rich at a profit. It was all hard work, and there were humiliations when he came to look for real jobs (he had to borrow an address, since nobody would employ a lad from where Bill lived). But he survived and thrived, and is giving his royalties to a youth charity since he's too well off to need them himself.

There are two lessons here. The first is that unlike McCourt's, the Cullen father was teetotal. The darkness of Angela's Ashes is, to a great extent, not the darkness of mere poverty but of that overarching betrayal by the roaring drunken father. So moral number one: nothing is more important than good and faithful parents.

But the other moral is about business. Cullen blossomed in life and trade because his family taught him to be a trader from the age of four. The fish, flowers, dolls, cinema tickets and rosaries taught him that if you find your market and exploit it with a smile, you'll have money for the next meal and capital for the next trade. He was, in the modern jargon, empowered. He was not a victim. Even at the bottom of the social heap there was heat and activity and and the possibility of worming your way upward.

If you teach in a deprived area, you know children like Bill Cullen. Because the government is keen on entrepreneurial culture, you will be encouraged to teach them business 'skills' ranging from IT to 'communication'. You may set up a Young Enterprise company and get them to call each other Personnel Directors and Marketing Managers. Fine. But they won't feel the excitement in their bones, because it isn't real. They may raise money for charity, but not for themselves. And just about every single thing that Bill Cullen did in the 1940's would be illegal now. Fish out of a pram? Call the Environmental Health! Selling uninspected toys and passing them off with star names? It's a toss-up whether Trading Standards or the copyright lawyers hit you first. Ticket touting? Illegal. Child labour in school hours – impossible, disgraceful, unacceptable, 'inappropriate'.

Thus we have decided, as a society, that we are too refined to let children of the poor better themselves by their own efforts. They must remain powerless, not contribute to the family's pride and survival except by strictly limited activities like paper rounds, faintly tacky ones like catalogue modelling, or desperate ones like being a runner for the local crack dealer. A real business is beyond the reach of most children. We don't like the idea of them earning real money. It offends us.

Nobody wants a return to unrelieved poverty and child labour. Nobody wants children taken out of school to help put bread on the family table. But all the same, it is worth observing that we have, in fifty years, built an entirely new kind of society. And at the very bottom of the social pyramid, this may accidentally have made life, and hope, and self-confidence, a great deal more difficult. Interesting, huh?

SEPTEMBER 29 2000

Fuel for school

Did anybody else discover, during the Great Petrol Crisis, the joys of scrolling down the Government's list on the Internet of 'Britain's Essential Services'? There is material there for no end of earnest citizenship discussions with the lower sixth.

In case you missed it, here's the list of organisations for whose functioning, the Government ordered 'priority access to fuel'. At the top are the emergency services, then armed forces, health and social workers, telecommunications, the food industry and agriculture. Fine.

Then it goes on to coastguards, undertakers, nuclear, sewerage and water workers, prisons, and public transport. With that last provision, the definition of 'essential' broadens somewhat. If coastguards and undertakers are already speeding cheerfully around on priority petrol, if food is getting delivered to shops and social workers are available to make sure that the vulnerable get it, public transport is merely for ordinary people going about their business.

And ever wider goes the list: 'central and local government workers' are essential; well, it would be dreadful if tax inspectors had to bike to work or take the bus. 'Media workers' are also given a blanket blessing, because obviously if the *Sid Nerd Show* on Radio Gumboil failed to get on-air, or Graham Norton was stuck on the hard shoulder staring at a useless nozzle, there could be widespread panic (I should admit at this point that all BBC workers got a pretty stern e-mail telling them not to use any priority treatment for personal ends). But still on goes the list: 'Essential foreign diplomatic workers' must be given petrol, so they may trundle around to Chatham House to look up old mates from Stasi; and so must 'financial services staff'. Perish the thought that anybody should go without a stakeholder pension quotation.

Then, almost at the bottom of 'Britain's essential services' come 'special schools and colleges for the disabled'. Some panicking functionary must have suddenly thought: 'Oops! better make sure we don't have disabled schoolkids stranded without those funny low-loader minibuses they use. That would look bad! Even worse than if foreign diplomats had to use micro-scooters!'

So they bunged it in, and special schools heaved a sigh of communal relief. But the interesting thing is that nobody thought ordinary, common-or-garden schools were an essential service. Yet how can ordinary life carry on without them?

They guard and educate millions of children whose parents are coastguards, and undertakers, and telecommunicators, ambulance-persons, food deliverers and oil tanker drivers. If the kids aren't at school the parents might not be able to go to work.

Moreover, if kids miss work in an exam year, their own security and sense of control is every bit as much under threat as that of a financial services executive or a foreign diplomat whose BMW won't start.

I suppose school buses counted as public transport, but nobody seems to have thought that a rural school, whose teachers commute over dozens of busless square miles, should be given the slightest consideration. Nor was it deemed that a headteacher who manages 1,200 human lives on a day-to-day basis is as essential as any social worker, or that the delivery of knowledge is as useful as the delivery of bank statements or non-stop news bulletins.

Nope, sorry schools: you just didn't count. So many schools closed, or ran at half-throttle. Thousands of children lost teaching time, hundreds of families were disrupted. For all the rhetoric, for all the nagging, when it came to the crunch the needs of schools were invisible.

Still, one minority must have felt even more fragile. Imagine being a boarding school – not one of these cosy modern flexi-boarding outfits but the old-fashioned sort, founded to build the characters of empire-builders on some godforsaken moor. Imagine having charge of 600 children, assertiveness bred into their fee-paying genes, glaring at their plates in ill-tempered disappointment. Imagine facing a riot in the pavilion because the First XV bus has insufficient diesel to hammer off to St Gabbitas and bring home the cup. Imagine breaking the news that the GCSE theatre trip is cancelled in favour of Miss Muntjack's slides of the Acropolis.

It'd melt a heart of stone. Or, conversely, cheer you up just thinking about it.

Triumph of the teenager

The jolliest story of Christmas was the *Daily Telegraph's* account of the 17-year-old schoolboy, Adam Hughes, who went on a fortnight's work experience at a Liverpool printing firm. He spotted within hours that their mailshot marketing was years out of date and, within the fortnight, had put a new Internet strategy in place. The results, says the managing director were 'astounding . . . we received an American order for £70,000 to supply barcode tags in airports, and now we expect to make more than a million dollars from the system that Adam was solely responsible for'.

This story contains more good things than you could shake a stick at. First, the boy had the confidence to make his views known, rather than just giggling with his mates about the outdated old farts he worked for. Second, the company listened to the ideas of a work-experience kid rather than going 'Tcha!' and sending him off to stack cardboard boxes: no harm in a bit of hard work, lad; when you've been in printing 40 years we might listen to your computer fol-de-rols, meanwhile there's that warehouse to sweep . . .

Third, the employer had the grace and humility to stress that it was indeed a 17-year-old who turned his company round. He could easily have pretended that they had been 'looking for some time at cybermarketing in a dynamic context, and Adam assisted our ongoing rollout of Y2K technology'. But, being an honest Liverpool printer, he refrained from spouting bollocks and gave the lad a job offer.

Which brings us to the fourth good thing: Adam turned the job down to take an architecture degree. In other words, he knows what he knows, and intends to learn what he doesn't. Internet marketing is a good thing to know about but it is not everything.

He opted not to settle for being a nerdy, self-satisfied, hollow little dot.com millionaire with his picture in the papers. I shall inform my son and daughter (when they wake up) of this heartening tale. Not by way of reproof for having failed to make the fortunes of the flower shop and boatyard which hosted their own work-experience.

Rather, I hope they take it as a long overdue salute to that maligned creature, the British 17-year-old.

It is not much fun being 17. This generation has been tested to destruction year after year; the group now approaching A-levels sat the first infamous seven-year-old SATs, the ones that were remodelled without apology after a chaotic year of tick-boxes and bewilderment. They have lived through unparalleled public criticism. While they revised for GCSEs, commentators sneered how 'easy' the exams were. The same fate awaits their A-levels.

Outside school they are regarded with suspicion: the girls forever being insulted by store detectives in H&M who assume they are shoplifters, and the boys followed by police cars as they drive sedately along, proud of their test pass, taking their mother's car to the filling station. On top of it all, they are in UCAS hell.

With immense thought, they read prospectuses, fill in forms and try to stop their ears to fearsome rumours ('They won't look at you if you've tried Oxbridge, it's spite . . . private school kids don't stand a chance . . . no, they only want the public schoolboys, 'cos they think they won't drop out').

They have suppressed all natural self-doubt, modesty and sense of irony to produce embarrassing 'personal statements'. They have hoped that their head's recommendation will be eloquent enough to catch the eye of a jaundiced admissions tutor. A very few have actually been interviewed and had work read, at ancient universities which maintain the capacity and curiosity to look for individuals. Mostly, they wait humbly for a verdict from distant dons who have never met or read them. A conditional yes is good news, but still nerve-racking. A rejection is a brick wall: strangers have effectively said 'Judging by your personal statement and your GCSEs, we don't want you even with straight 'A's.' Sometimes they wait from September to March for this verdict.

Meanwhile, the quality press runs jeering stories about how universities are so 'desperate' for bums on seats that they'll let in any old rubbish. So they cheer themselves up by planning gap years, labour to earn a modest adventure, while contemplating Prince William being praised to the skies for spending two-and-a-half months kayaking and wiping down a lavatory. Poor old teenagers. Never mind. Soon they will burst on the world and reform it as Adam did, by being young and energetic and optimistic. Maybe their experiences will make them nicer to the next generation. We can only hope.

JULY 14 2000

Not in front of the men . . .

Hooray! Once again the award for controversialism in a head's end-of-term speech goes to an East Anglian challenger, John Arkell of Gresham's school, Norfolk.

Mr Arkell warned his girl pupils that they might not manage to meet Nicola Horlick's benchmark of combining five children and a high-flying career, and should 'think carefully about what they want to achieve finally out of life . . . I have noticed that a lot of girls want to concentrate on work and put off getting married and having children till rather too late'.

Uproar. Outrage. One prod from the *Daily Mail* and Ms Horlick said 'rubbish!', the head of policy at the Institute of Directors said 'pompous and pathetic', Anita Roddick said 'preposterous and antediluvian' and the Equal Opportunities Commission put up a spokesman to witter on about 'enabling women and men to balance work and other responsibilities'.

The school's parents, allegedly, divided between those who said it was a 'wise point' and 'thought-provoking' and those who accused the head of being 'anti-feminist, chauvinistic and undermining the female role'.

Well, I call that splendid. After all, normally, the most commonly heard phrases after a headtecher's prize-giving speech are 'Eaah . . . whaat? I wasn't asleep!', 'How long till tea?' and 'Just my luck! He went well past 16 minutes, and I had a 20-quid bet on 14 minutes 30 for him, and 12 minutes dead for the Lord Lieutenant'. Stirring a prize-giving audience from its summer torpor is a fine deed, and I salute Mr Arkell for having a go.

I was initially mystified as to why his remarks caused so much comment; I have said much the same thing myself in girls' schools. I have told them that it makes sense to think about what you really want, to give due weight to your human relationships, and to plan your career from the start with an eye on the possibility of being a bit flexible if a family comes along. That way, if the family doesn't materialise, you still have the flexibility, the open mind and the contingency fund anyway, and can use them to take a fabulous sabbatical, or do a few years' VSO, or start up your own business.

I have told girls that it's actually quite fun to stay cool, refuse to be pushed along male rails, use your head and – while you're young, single, hungry and rising in a trade – to glance around sometimes to see how senior family women manage their juggling act. I have also informed them that the real secret of combining family and career is never, ever to do any housework that is remotely avoidable, and be a low-maintenance dresser and groomer. I have told girls to get a life, not just a career – and indeed would tell boys exactly the same if any were to ask me.

So why did the head of Gresham's get pulverized in the Press? His speech seems quite mild. He stressed that girls' education matters, and should be taken seriously and he spoke approvingly of their professional potential.

After some brooding I have concluded that he got pilloried, not for saying and thinking these things, but for saying them at a co-ed school while being a bloke – worse, a bloke of 60.

It seems that, in the safety of a single-sex prizegiving, a woman can tell girls the terrible truths about womanhood with a nod, a wink and a conspiratorial sisterly grin. But maybe, now I think about it, even I wouldn't say these dangerous things in front of boys, in case they thought: 'Ha! Girlies! they *are* at a disadvantage after all – just as I always hoped!'

And maybe, if I were a man, I would not say any of it, lest the girls and women present rose up, threw rotten eggs at me and said 'preposterous!' to the *Daily Mail,* in order to keep up the pretence that it isn't really so.

That must be it: the business about women, work and family life is the Truth that Dare Not Speak its Name in Mixed Company.

Perhaps next year Mr Arkell should send the boys, fathers and journalists out for a bracing run round the playing fields in the Norfolk rain while he says it all again. The girls might listen. Girls, as he well knows, are not stupid.

Fake work

They'll be sitting round at school now, comparing notes on work experience and laughing themselves sick at the vagaries of the adult world. Good luck to them. Meanwhile we parents are mopping our brows with relief that it is all over.

At our school, work experience happens in the holiday before Year 11 and parents are supposed to find the 'placements'. Our generation, for whom the first experience of work meant baby-sitting, or wheeling an ice-cream cart along the front in a humiliating hat, finds itself anxious to do the right thing.

In the Sixties there were plenty of rubbishy jobs for teenagers and not much regulation. Money drove the deal: it was a question of supplementing your two-and-six pocket money in order to buy a Dansette record player, and nobody was interested in whether you were being 'prepared for the opportunities, responsibilities and experiences of adult life' (Education Reform Act 1988), or developing 'personal and social skills and erasure of stereotyping'.

As for an 'understanding of the functioning of industrial and commercial employers', we learnt a lot about scraping up the last saleable mouthful of raspberry ripple before washing out the freezer, and which householders would put up with a bit of mud on the sports page without shopping you to the boss. But nobody sat us down to explain flat management structures or workflow.

The first inkling I had of what work experience means to the stressed and guilty parent was when friends with older children kept ringing me up to swing them deals. 'Any chance of finding Maddy a billet at the BBC?' 'James is terribly keen on journalism, perhaps *The Times* would like him for a week?' I had one or two successes – a budding comic writer to BBC light entertainment, a sultry glam-ourpuss to *She* magazine – but most of the petitioners probably had to fall back on the usual middle-class ploy of dragging their off-spring along to work with them and foisting the surly brat on whichever department owed them a favour.

Most of the kids who go through this process report that their week is spent 'shadowing': wandering like a faintly embarrassed wraith behind some high-flyer, accepting the occasional nugget of mystifying information or improbably idealistic waffle about Banking's Role in Service to the Community.

Other parents take a more Machiavellian approach, and urge their children into the greasiest, dullest employment in order to make them come back saying 'Help! I must work hard, hit those A-levels, get a degree, or I could end up in a McJob'. Mind you, I suppose it is quite possible also that a week shadowing a stressed-out chief exec could make you wonder whether ambition is worth bothering with at all.

No sooner have you made a decision in principle than you come upon Appendix I of the leaflet, *Prohibited and Restricted Employment of Persons under 18.* It is wonderful reading, almost enough to convince you that Britain is still a robust industrial nation.

No luminising with radioactive materials, no crane or locomotive driving, blasting, chromium plating, lead processes, brass casting (for young women) or certain work in connection with self-acting mules. Absolutely no scalding out ships' boilers, worm pressure extruding, or contact with pie and tart-making machines.

Dazzled by this, our children begged to be allowed to stamp out radioactive jam tarts with a steam pressure machine, and descale the bilges of oil tankers. After such enticements, maundering round a tedious office with an IT manager somehow lacks pizazz.

So in the end we chucked the eldest into a boat yard, where he cleaned out the glue store and carried lumps of pig-iron and came home nightly looking like a DH Lawrence figure fresh up from t'pit. He left with mutual regret and congratulations, and now knows that manual work is not the worst thing in the world.

When the younger one's turn came she hastily enrolled herself in a flower shop, bunching up freesias and gerbera and delivering dazzling, false smiles to customers. I suppose she learned something about the industrial and commercial world and erasure of stereotyping. But the main thing is that it's over.

They're safe back in the wonderful makebelieve world of education. Next time we worry about their jobs it'll be for real.

Parlez-vous?

The general idea these days seems to be that you don't learn for the
sake of it; the main point of education is now financial profit and
loss, with narrow-eyed calculations being made daily on the precise
future value of every degree. This philosophy is bound to filter
down into the classroom soon ('Kevin! pay attention! it is a proven
fact that not colouring in the right boxes in the Roger Red-Hat
worksheets causes up to 14% lower lifetime earning power!').

So here's a useful development for number-crunching pedagogues. A little report last week alleged that a leading European
holiday park company is charging people up to £126 more if they
book in English, through a British website and giving a domicile
here. Germans, Dutch, and other Europeans are not surcharged. We
are. There was the usual chuntering of complaints about 'rip-off
Britain', but a company spokesman apparently said that it was justi-
fied. It is their attempt to recoup some of the cost of hiring multi-
lingual staff to deal with British visitors, both during the booking
process and when they actually turn up. British visitors, it appears,
do not speak foreign languages. Well, there's a surprise.

Myself, I punched the air, overcome with a sense of justice. Going
round Europe, whether by land or on the tall ships races in summer,
I hear young Danes and Dutch and Norwegians politely talking
German and French; Germans making spirited attempts on Spanish
and Italian, and even the French squaring their shoulders and doing
what they have to do in Dutch. Nearly all of them happily talk
English. But two places in front of them in the queue, there is always
a pink, perspiring Briton who will talk only English. Slowly, with a
slight raising of the voice as if to a senile dog. And hidden away in a
hundred Costas and holiday parks there are more of us, mewed up
in holiday ghettos because we daren't go out and face a frightening
world in which a muttered 'Habla Ingles?' is not sufficient to guarantee that your interlocutor will say 'Si'.

We are a disgrace to ourselves, the way we don't regard getting
even a smattering of the language as a courteous prelude to visiting

other people's territory. I include myself in this: my French is OK because I was at school there for a few years, and I can struggle through most transactions in German: indeed I once managed to flirt all evening with an Austrian postman, though it later turned out that he thought we were discussing Princess Diana. In Italy and Spain, however, I am rubbish: tongue-tied, confusing the two vocabularies, helpless and embarrassed. Italy is slightly the easier of the two because I have a smattering of Grand Opera, but there is a limit to how far you can get at the car-hire desk with 'Rittorna Vincitor!' and 'Addio – senza rancor!', and appeals to the Virgin of the Angels to have pity on you. In Spain I mostly point and shrug.

Years have passed while I regretted this hopelessness; I have done nothing about it. My father learned Portugese in two weeks when he was sent to work in Angola; he would have thought it disgraceful not even to try. But these days, with cheap flights and arrogant consumer choice, it is the norm. When did you last hear someone saying 'Oh no, I don't think we can go to Greece on holiday, we don't have time to learn any Greek'. When did you last feel a pang of guilt because you, relatively affluent and idle, are delegating the task of communicating to some poor Croatian waiter poring over a borrowed phrasebook on his rare evenings off?

But now here are these splendid holiday-park managers laying it on the line to us. 'If you wanna come and have a holiday here and you won't even try to speak to the maid or the pool attendant in the language of the land, welcome – but it'll cost you.' Even better if they go further, and agree to return the extra charge if you pass a short, simple language test on arrival. Then all you language teachers can tell the yawning louts in the back row that this isn't just about SATs and GCSEs: if they pay attention, they'll save enough for a whole crate of vin rouge and a damn good night in a strip club. If they don't, it's back to Pontins for another year.

JULY 8 2005

Right angle on salvation

Well, we will know by now how many schools and children obeyed Bob Geldof's instruction to bunk off and head for Edinburgh, in a rather unsettling echo of the Children's Crusade.

'I want,' he cried, waving his invisible banneret and sword, 'every school to decamp on July 5. I want the teachers to lead the kids to Edinburgh. I want to see all their buses, their blazers, their flags up there demanding that they tear down trade barriers to African farmers and write off the continent's international debt.'

But then he added rhetorically: 'What's more important – learning geometry or remembering these two days all your life?'

Er . . . let us not answer that straightaway. As a rule I am all in favour of children being whipped out of school from time to time for exciting and inspiring activities, but I do so wish that he had not chosen geometry. The phrase gave too much away: Geldof's age, his pop-starry, bunk-off-school mentality, his groovily ignorant We-don't-want-no-educashun generation. I wish the great man had said: 'What's more important, personal, social and health education classes or taking direct action for what you believe in?' or 'What's more important, getting home for your favourite television programme or trying to help Africa?'

But geometry? . . . oh dear. Wrong message.

A grasp of geometry, the root of all engineering practicality, might lead you on to do something far more useful for the developing world. Once your understanding has stretched beyond Pythagoras and the *pons asinorum*, you might go further. You might become an engineer, civil or mechanical, and an inventor. You might join a radical third-world aid movement like *Engineers Sans Frontières* and be a real star in the fight for humanity, not just yet another fun-loving demonstrator surfing a wave of self-righteousness and getting hammered on cans of McEwans in some Edinburgh gutter.

Take heart, you dear geek who remains behind in geometry class while the cool kids go north. It might well be you, not them, who in this century develops appropriate technologies and brings wells and irrigation, bridges and transport and healthcare to transform the lives of millions. Geometry is good, geometry is cool. So are maths, chemistry, physics and biology and all the handmaidens of practical progress. Politics is not the only thing that solves problems; nor is protest.

Kipling said it all in his poem about Martha and Mary, in which the Sons of Martha are toilers doomed for eternity to transport and illuminate and keep safe all the dreamers and politicians descended from the idle mystic Mary, who merely sat at Christ's feet and did no food preparation or washing-up at all. As a paid-up arts-graduate daughter of Mary, I think we hacks and Geldofs should salute the sons and daughters of Martha more often, not sneer at them. So do not pick on geometry teachers, Bob. Without them you would not even know what was going on in Africa, because you would never have been there. The wings would have fallen off the plane on the way. Oh, and without physicists you would not be on television, or have made any recordings. Perhaps it is time we hammered home this message in schools, as part of citizenship. It is all very well lecturing children on their freedoms and rights and telling them to vote and agitate, but perhaps we should urge on them more often their duty to become actually useful.

Perhaps instead of constantly saying that they should work hard to get qualifications and go to university and earn high salaries, which appeals solely to their self-interest, we should take another tack. Maybe we should routinely point out the actual uses of each subject to mankind as they learn it, starting the term with an inspirational lecture entitled Why Maths Changes the World or Geographers are Vital to the Future of our Species, or Chemistry – the Building Blocks of Everything, or even English – a Tool for Peace and Understanding.

Perhaps we should lay it out for them honestly: 'Look, you've all got to do maths/biology/geography – there will be wastage, we know that, we are aware that some of you will never take it further and joyfully forget everything we teach you. Fine.

'But the odds are that a few of you might get it. And on those few the future rests. Learning is a lottery – but the next Brunel or Einstein could be you.' If Bob Geldof can light fires by making the little bleeders feel important to the future of the world, perhaps subject teachers should ponder on how to do the same.

Times of transition

All things end

These past two weeks, whenever the sun shone and the air was hot and drowsy and I caught on the air the smell of warm grass, I was transported back to a piece of school: to the brief Elysian eternity that lay between A levels and the end of it all. The memory was intensified, I suppose, because my own children are getting to that stage. One: has left, the other will a year hence. But whatever is causing it, it is powerful: long days, long grass, relief at the lifting of long years of pressure to revise and remember. I can feel again now the high spirits, the extravagant hopes for the new life and the occasional sickening plunge of self-doubt: *hell, this is it, this is real, I'm not a schoolkid any more . . .*

On one of these last days of term three of us – and we are still in touch now – sat on a grassy bank overlooking the railway line at the bottom of town, sharing a bottle of cider and wondering where we would be in a year, ten years, thirty. We were boarders, but elsewhere on that blessed embankment sat girls and boys from the Grammar Schools in town, doing exactly the same as us. And, what is more, both they and we would be expected back for the end-of-term assembly and the final moments with our teachers and peers. The British system being what it is, there was no graduation – by the time any of us knew our A level results we would be scattered. But we all finished the school term.

That was how it was: and how the odd, dreamlike time of transition was granted. We each found our own way of passing it, although altruism was suggested. I spent hours down in the school basement confronting the bin-bags full of milk bottle tops we had collected 'for the Blind': the recycling charity had suddenly closed down, so until the school could find another one, it was stuck with a mountain of cheesy-smelling aluminium foil. It was starting to stink out the pottery room, that hot summer, so a couple of friends and I washed the bottletops. Our efforts were more or less disastrous – amusing though it is to pour hundreds of tinkling niffy bottletops into the craft-room sink and shoot hot water at them, it has little effect – but it kept us busy. Then I wandered off to join a favourite teacher who was struggling with costumes for the Junior play, and offered to read aloud to her; her tastes were eclectic and thus it was that Sister O'Leary and I got through the whole of George MacDonald's *Phantastes*, in the gap between the end of examinations and the beginning of real life.

All this came back to me, with the power of a long-forgotten riff from Manfred Mann. And today, among the 18-year-olds and even the 16-year-old leavers, there is evidence of the same kind of time being had: fêtes prepared, spirited attempts made to wade in and help down at the local playgroup. But mostly, it seems to be dull diaspora. Just as many schools – state and independent and even boarding – have taken to copping out of their responsibilities by declaring 'study leave' back in April and sending the examinees home unsupported, so they have rejected the old idea of hanging on to the very end of term. And every year we get the same news stories about insitutions so unconfident in the loyalty and sense of their leavers that they declare an early end-of-term and throw them out without warning, or simply inform parents that once the last exam has been sat, their child is no longer welcome on the premises.

I suppose it is tied up with the fact that 18 is legal adulthood; and I daresay there is something to be said for abolishing the cultures of suspicious supervision and old-school sentimentality. And good luck to the kids who use the time selling ice-creams or working on tills to save up money for university. And respect of a kind to the cheery hedonists who take off immediately with the only friends they care about, for a prolonged gap year debauch.

But when I smell the hot grass, or hum a bar or two of 'Doo wah diddy diddy' as I see the few remaining end-of-termers hugging and sniffing and spraying one another with fizz on the last day, the pang of nostalgia is strong There are not many points in a modern life when time stands still and nothing is urgent and one phase is over and another not begun. That interlude at the end of school was one of them: you were not adult and not a child, not busy but not bored, uncertain of your future but not scared. You floated free. It was good.

Prize day torment

'Good afternoon, boys and girls! And parents, ha ha! Congratulations to the prizewinners, though of course we must remember, mustn't we, that the race is not always to the swift? I was certainly no swot . . .'

In front of the prize-day speaker, the children slump glassy-eyed, longing for freedom, tormented by the July sun beyond the high windows of the hall. On the platform, staff and governors glare back at them, each wrapped in private memories and plans. Parents perch on hard chairs, burning with pride or resentment. The speaker falters, lost in the maze of scribbled notes, and tries to remember what it is that seemed so important to convey to the next generation. 'I'd like to end with a little story . . .'

Everyone relaxes. It's ending. Soon the most reliable member of 7Z3 will bound onstage with a presentation flower-basket and the head of school will read a vote of thanks bearing no relation whatsoever to the prizegiver's speech, which will intensify the general feeling of dislocation. Then everyone will go home and the head will thankfully retire from role-modelhood for two months, and indulge in a very large drink and a good swear.

I am a connoisseur of prizegiving ceremonies. I went to five schools and have had children at five more; I have been a prize-day speaker two dozen times before hardening my heart against even the nicest letters. I entirely sympathise with those who are hunting for speakers because, as a governor, I have helped.

It is a uniquely delicate problem: no budget, an audience ranging over seven decades, and an unstable *fin-de-siècle* culture in which some of the best known public names are more than likely to a) crack blue jokes b) cancel at short notice for detox reasons or c) be exposed by the Nolan Committee or the *News of the World* in that dangerous gap between printing the programme and the event.

No wonder Radio 4 people are in demand: they think we're safe. One rather grand school was so desperate years ago that it sent a helicopter for me, out of which I staggered feeling sick, to speak green-faced and refuse the teatime éclairs.

What my years of sampling have told me is that, despite the above caricature, the variation in tone between prize-days is astonishing. Some are lovely: it is possible to create an atmosphere of celebration of youthful achievement and happy community.

Girls' schools do it particularly well, with banks of flowers and jokes that everyone laughs at. I won't forget Dame Stella Rimington wowing St Felix with one-liners like: 'Frankly, nothing worth knowing can be taught.' A large shabby mixed comprehensive I once went to had such a fizz that the headmaster – in the middle of what is usually a hellishly dull annual report – pulled 36 silk handkerchieves out of his ear to make a point. Nobody had even known he was taking lessons in conjuring. It was, in fact, a serious and moving point, but gave me as speaker a good opportunity to offer to let the man saw me in half for his next trick.

Some are highly ceremonial. Done well, this is rather good; a certain amount of banner-draping and valediction poems at least raise it above the commonplace. Too many fall into the trap of sounding like the opening session of a particularly grim middle-management conference in a Midlands Forte Posthouse. Some do not even reach those heights. Parents and children fidget miserably while some retired Lord Lieutenant drones on about how he lost his pet ferret in 1912 and learned a valuable lesson about the dangers of socialism; or stare at their feet in embarrassment while a faded pop star tries to be hip, or a prominent local employer makes heavy-handed references to the low literacy standard among his last batch of recruits.

Some day, someone will invent something new. Meanwhile, handy hints for all. Parents – bring a cushion. Children – if the speech gets tedious try the game of finding a rhyming echo for every phrase ('I'd like to tell you a little story' – *I'm a very brittle Tory*, 'The secret of life is to persevere' – *Keep a rifle, live in fear*, etc). Staff – run a sweepstake on the length of the speech. This kept one staffroom I know very happy: from the floor you could watch their faces fall as the time on their ticket went past. Heads – don't book Gary Glitter. Good luck all. Soon be over.

A revisionist view

The house is immaculate. The grill-pan shines, and the filter on the tumble drier has never been freer of lint. The dog has had so many walks that she refuses to leave the basket. Clothes are even folded.

You guessed it: A-level revision is under way, and giving rise to furious displacement activity.

Yes, yes, I know: it does not take every teenager this way.

I have met the other kind, too. Some find it more helpful to their revision to spend their breaks messing up the grill pan with weird snacks, creating Tate Modern exhibits out of dead drinks cans, whingeing into mobile phones or lying around in angry torpor with Jerry Springer on daytime satellite, trying not to let themselves believe that if they fail their A-levels they too will end up with big hair and a shiny shellsuit, trying to validate their existence by yelling at Jerry that their trailer-trash partner done them wrong. I realise I am lucky that it is just grill-pan cleaning.

But I recognise the symptoms all too well, over the gulf of years. This wretched year-group, the most heavily examined and experimented-on generation in the history of British schooling, is doing what we all did. Revision is hateful: all that marking time and stepping backwards, stacking up of stale facts, losing impetus and excitement in the loathsome process of consolidation, yearning for the bloody exams to be over one way or another, and in the end hardly caring which. Jack Dee has a very funny comic routine about revision, starting with making out a revision timetable – 'several hours precision ruler-work there' – and then realising that the time you have spent drawing coloured lines and boxes means that you have lost the first half-day, and therefore must start again and redivide the work to allow for the delayed start.

It is a perennial misery, but I think it is probably even worse than usual for this lot, and not just because it is their third year running of major public exams. Increased anxiety about life and jobs is accompanied by a crumbling of trust in the examination boards. AS-level marking – notably maths, but other subjects too – did not

inspire confidence. One school I know had its entire history AS level group re-marked, and every single pupil went up at least one grade. What does that say about the examiners' first try? The recent Edexcel shambles, after the Scottish meltdown, has been disastrous for examinees' morale. Add to those the numerous anecdotal tales from several boards of mad grades (in both directions), slow re-marks and lost papers, and it is apparent to the most casually news-wise teenager that whatever result comes in there will be an element of luck in it.

So when you cannot stand the solitude and anxiety of revising any longer, you have a coke. Or switch on Jerry. Or clean the grill pan.

Even in my A-level term at boarding school, before the Fall, I got so restless and irritable that I smuggled large numbers of wild flowers from the convent grounds into my room, stole sugar from the dining room, and attempted to brew bluebell wine in a plastic, family-size shampoo bottle.

My friend Rosalind and I put a lot of scientific research into the recipe, but not quite enough to prevent the bottle exploding after five days and splattering the walls with purple dots. But the subsequent afternoon washing the walls down took my mind off the life of Marcus Porcius Cato and the Defenestration of Prague, and the lurking question of how much they mattered, with the sun shining outside.

So you flog on, and then come to the equally tricky decision about the last few hours before the exam itself. A couple of years ago there was some wacky research from Reading University cybernetics department, which tried to find out what worked best. Studying 200 students, the researchers found that those who watched *This Morning* for 30 minutes found their IQ level up by six points, whereas last-minute revision lowered it by six, making a potential full grade's difference. A BBC2 documentary gave you four points, and *Friends* one point. It then went a bit off the wall – classical music, orange juice and chatting to friends scored negative, peanuts positive, and beer worked both ways, depending on the individual. Professor Warwick, who dreamed this up, concluded that watching undemanding television just before an exam 'warms up the brain without stretching it too much'.

Goodness. I always thought that was what the first question was for. No wonder I got a D in Latin.

FEBRUARY 4 2005

Waiting for Magwitch

Rather agreeable, the Child Trust Fund. Who could not warm to the idea of £250 (£500, for the poorest) being popped in a savings account for every British baby?

Who could object to the invitation to parents, godparents, grannies and uncles to salt away up to £100 a month, to accumulate tax free during the years of infancy and schooling? What a tantalising portrait it suggests: a prudent nation of savers, popping the odd few pounds away in the toe of a virtual stocking, to launch the young person into adult life as a man or woman of substance!

One could slip away into a lovely daydream of prosperous sunlit uplands, of parents looking on fondly at sober students with shiny hair and gingham shirts, who frown with concentration as they sign their first cheques for university tuition, laptops, chemistry textbooks, a deposit on a modest studio flat close to work or some really high-quality spanners for that first toolbox. One's eyes mist over. Then they suddenly widen in horror.

Deep in my comfy daydream of a Britain where every 18-year-old has an invisible Magwitch to turn to for help in the transition years, I had omitted to read the small print. It is not just the bit about how we'll be encouraged to salt it away in the volatilities of the stock market, to be creamed off by fund managers with the brains of goldfish and the bonuses of Croesus. That's bad enough, but mercifully one can ignore the suited bastards and invest it as cash.

No, what really made me start hyperventilating was the stark revelation that when the dear baby reaches its 18th birthday, the money becomes fully and immediately available, in toto, to spend as that ex-baby wishes. The fund, if parents and well-wishers have done their thing, could be worth £45,000. Even if they haven't, it will be a good lump. And – ohmigawd – owing to the age of majority being 18, it will be entirely under the control of the holder, even if he or she is a complete dingbat still labouring under the influence of raging hormones and violent Teenage Attitude.

Withdrawals will be under no parental, educational, or governmental control whatsoever. The 18-year-old is legally adult. It's his – or her – money. A Chancellor's idealism and eighteen years of benign contributions will be handed over, without restriction. Aaaaghhhh. Look, do not write to me saying: 'In our school, the vast majority of young men and women are responsible and sensible, owing to our matchless standards of pastoral guidance and PSHE'. Do not send me aggrieved letters in tidy writing, saying: 'I am 18 and have always taken care of my money. How dare you insult my generation?'. I know you exist. I know there are lots of you. I take my hat off to every student from families of modest means who saves, scrimps, and works through the summer vacation to keep the debt down. I wish I could give each of you a trust fund of your own, right now. I think you're great. I look forward to you ruling the world.

But glance around you, young paragons, as you slowly sup your half-pint in the college bar. Chuck a beermat, and admit that it will bounce off at least one 18-year-old who should not be trusted with control of twenty quid, let alone twenty thou. In an age when even an Eton-educated royal prince fully 20 years old manages to be a copper-plated twit, one must be realistic about the variableness of human maturing. Think of the people you were at school with at 17, and consider what the modern world lays out to tempt them daily: the clothes, the cars, the bling, the Caribbean holidays, the booze, the boats, the wet-bikes, the snowboarding, the party drugs, the larks, the get-rich-quick investments, the tantalising notion of flouncing-out-of-home into a flat because your parents are so, like, moody. And now imagine those kids turning 18 and receiving a polite Government chit saying: 'Hi! – there's £45,000 in your account to do as you like with.' And now imagine being their parents, wringing your hands in disbelief as the money melts away, and knowing how sad and stupid they will feel a year later.

Doesn't bear thinking of, does it? But what's the alternative? Some parents, after all, are equally daft about money. And nor can one warm to the thought of having to submit your spending plans to some Child Trust Fund quango composed of failed local politicians, retired headmasters who hate everybody and bossy women in tweed who couldn't pass the exam to be magistrates.

I have no answer. Have you?

AUGUST 4 2000

A cure for heartache

Fifty years old, and still it is worryingly easy to get in touch with the inner adolescent. Bang on the old Bob Dylan, and key straight into that lovely, swampy, old self-pity. 'It ain't me babe . . .' Sniff a bit. Recapture that inner hollowness, that howling agony of rejection. Then slide into defiance: 'Come mothers and fathers throughout the land/ And don't criticise what you don't under-stand/ Your sons and your daughters are beyond your command . . ./ For the times they are a'changing . . .'

Music does it instantaneously. You don't even need to light a joss-stick: a few twangs of the old guitar and you're right back there, 17 going on 70, so mired in complex intensity that you entirely fail to notice that the adult world is beaming soppily at you and thinking: 'Ah, to be so young and fresh . . .'

Adolescence feels different from inside. Our children may laugh with us at Kevin and Perry when they shout 'It's so unfair! I hate you!' (in a better way than we never laughed with our own parents) but deep down teenagers inhabit a different reality, another country.

Remember how it was? You made conversation, you took in facts, but all the time you were elsewhere. Your own emotional reality was reflected in other things. It was in the music you chose, whether loud or maudlin; in the glimpse of a mountain-top from the bicker-ing back-seat of the family car; in a book, a poem, or, above all, in a face. Your truest reality, the Platonic archetype which made sense of the universe, was there in the first stranger you dared to love. And you loved not with low carnality but with the desire of the moth for the star and the night for the morrow.

When the love object failed to notice (he usually did) there were only Shelley and moonlight and Paul McCartney's 'Yesterday' to comfort you in the sphere of your sorrow.

Listening to Channel 4's sexually active teenagers on the recent *Generation Sex*, season it occurred to me that their dreary, knowing chorus of 'I'd give 'im one' and 'great shag' was only another kind of defence: a barrier of sexuality to protect them from the blinding terror of first love.

My teenage years were odd because I was a diplo-brat, moved on every three years and – from 13 – grounded in boarding-school during term-time. The effect, I suppose, was to ratchet up the intensity a few notches. One minute you are at school, in a menstrually synchronized hothouse; suddenly you are at home, in baking Johannesburg or boring Berne, wearing out records in your room and squabbling with your little brothers. The boredom of life fixes things in your mind; you brood about escape, about a future, about the current object of desire.

Later, in Hamburg, there was a shade more freedom: my brother and I clubbed in a cautious, decorous manner, dared each other to walk down Herbertstrasse where the whores sat in the window, and chatted up fresh young submariners (who generally wanted to talk about their Mum).

We lived over Dad's office. Once, a friend's friend left his stash of cannabis upstairs under the table when we had all been playing strip ping-pong, and we disposed of it secretively, terrified of what would happen if the newspapers found out that HM Consulate-General had been polluted by an illegal substance.

Then came the summer, and liberty in the far west of Ireland where, one afternoon, broken-hearted as usual, I was chatting to my friend Sheila as she boned bacon in the supermarket. The owner of the attached pub zipped through and shouted 'Libby, would you ever mind the bar?'. So I did, and found by accident the perfect cure for the sickness which had gripped me for so long.

You perform, socialise and flirt from the safety of your bar. You are efficient and everyone wants to catch your eye. Before opening time you have soothing, repetitive jobs like stacking tonic water on the shelves and (in my day) bottling up the Midleton whiskey with a cask and a siphon-tube, happily dizzy in the fruity fumes.

I worked there three summers running and, by the end of it, I was more or less grown-up. So, that's the answer: be a barmaid. You know it makes sense.

University blues

Puppets find new master

It is a strange moment, when your youngest child starts university, and it has little to do with the traditional 'empty nest' feeling of parental obsolescence. For one thing the family nest is far from empty during the vacations, so the innate maternal longing for a messy kitchen and sodden bathmat can be fulfilled for several months a year. For another thing, you can't feel entirely useless when you're still writing cheques.

No: my focus group of educationally keen parents all agree that the most startling thing about the start of the university years is the sudden loss of any power, control, responsibility, decision, or right of consultation whatsoever.

On one hand this is fabulously liberating. Every time I read about school standards, school trips, admissions battles, SATs, GCSEs, AS/A2 or UCAS forms my heart soars in a silent oratorio of gratitude that it is over, all over. Never again need I bother with any of it, except in a journalistic, citizenlike or auntly spirit, which of its nature lacks the raw emotional power of a family crisis.

On the other hand, once they are 18 the puppet strings are finally cut. It has been coming gradually for years: only a foolish parent tries to force a child into a particular GCSE option, still less A-level, and university ought to be a personal choice, guided by cautious, informative advice from the posse of surrounding adults.

But, nonetheless, until the end of school a parent gets reports every term, sits across a table from assorted teachers trying to understand what they are on about, and may even still belong to the PTA. If, like me, you have a taste for schools and teachers then you can wallow in it: be a governor, raise funds, chat to the staffroom, get to know your children's classmates and generally get happily involved in the whole extended educational family.

Then it stops dead. When I dropped off my eldest at college there was a wonderful moment at the welcoming address to parents. The Master, an eminent and jovial engineer, ran us through the history and habits of his college and then asked for questions.

Whatever calumnies are heaped on Oxford, I have to report that my mingling with the parents that day indicated that this college at least has a lot of first generation university students, and is by no means overwhelmed with the privately educated and the suave toff. A distinct confusion about the whole business was evident in some parents. Eventually from the back, a hesitant female voice said: 'How will we know how he's doing? Do we get, sort of, reports?'

The Master looked fondly at his interlocutor, plainly very glad to have been asked the question and given the chance to clear up this little misunderstanding for good and all.

'No,' he said. 'You don't. This is a new phase. Our contract is directly with the student'. There was an audible gasp. 'You can ask them how they're doing and I hope they tell you. The only time the college would normally contact you would be over a serious welfare matter. Otherwise . . . well, it's us and them.'

Well, I thought I knew all about universities, but until that moment it had never completely dawned that certain forms of communication, practised to perfection over 13 years at the school gate, had abruptly become obsolete. All those years of learning how to ask teachers the right question and interpret the answer were over.

One does not have nice little reassuring chats with an offspring's tutors about their progress, ability, health or happiness. It is Not Done. They are young adults, and if they are not ill or requiring police bail, their lives are now truly their own.

I am getting used to it now. But I suppose the moral is that if you have enjoyed your life as a parent, cheering on the educational side-lines, you'd better make sure that the lines of communication are friendly and frank enough for you to get the occasional bulletin about how it's going, direct from the young horse's mouth.

If you're on the home straight now with a sixth-former on your hands, cultivate the pose of an admiring fan rather than a nagging virago forever finding fault. If you don't, a sphinx-like silence may frustrate you this time next year. Which would be terrible.

For years and years we've main-lined on exam results and been drip-fed bulletins and cups of tea and prizegiving ceremonies by dutiful schools. Now we must go cold turkey, and face the information desert that lies beyond the final parents evening. Who would ever have thought it was possible to miss those . . .

Nobody likes a smart-arse

'Hello. I am an organised and motivated person, as evidenced by my captaincy of the school debating, judo and hockey teams, my vacation work running a youth TV station and the fact that I am head of school, head chorister and senior anti-bullying counsellor as well as leading the Sea Cadets.

'During my GCSE year I passed crumhorn and viol-da-Gamba at grade 6, and headed a neighbourhood campaign against new housing which successfully preserved a habitat for the silverweed moth.

'In my capacity as MD of our Young Enterprise company I have made a £250,000 profit for charity and been awarded the Alan Michael Sugar medal for crunchy management.

'I run, row, ballroom-dance and cycle for my county and have gained a Royal Geographical Society grant to head an expedition to the Falklands during my gap year researching penguin-droppings and soil fertility, although I hope this will also leave me time to spend six months teaching Su Doku techniques to autistic children in a leper colony in Uttar Pradesh. I would like to study at your university because . . .'

No point reading on, is there? You hate the candidate already, smug little bleeder. It's two in the morning, the applications are lying in a drift under the desk, and you are an exhausted, underpaid, overstretched university tutor. You basically try to keep loving your subject and your students, but find it uphill work as ever more get shoe-horned into your tattered lecture theatres. You want to teach bright, focused, energetic, and if possible entertainingly quirky young people, who will bring a new generation's intelligence to your field. You don't want whey-faced little swots who never go outdoors, or illiterate oafs with multiple Asbos, or idle lumps who watch *Big Brother Live*. You know why UCAS personal statements are necessary. Yet there is something about them which makes you want to rip and stamp and fling and howl. If you have to read about one more multi-skilled head girl with 18 starred GCSEs you will sink an axe in the vice-chancellor's door.

Imagining this scenario, I was dismayed to read – in a book about parents and the university years – that it is 'never too early' to get your GCSE child fettling up his or her CV to look better on the Ucas statement – get them off up the Himalayas, sharpish, was this author's advice. Anything to make them 'stand out'. She also claimed that most parents write their children's statements. I think she's wrong: ultra-pushy parents and teachers may do just that, but in my experience the only advice kids accepted was 'don't start out by saying you're a prefect, universities are full of clever difficult people who hated prefects'.

But by and large, a sensible adult just advises them to remember that university is a course of study and not a gold medal for general fabulousness, and lets them be themselves. Only rarely is a caveat necessary: one innocent kid from a militaristic institution was found to have written in the first line that he held the Parade Ground Cup for smartness and bearing. Since it was a leftish Midlands ex-poly he was going for, it was gently suggested that he might move that a bit lower down, beneath his burning enthusiasm for geography.

The whole idea of children that age having to lay out a boastful, artificially padded version of their lives is strangely depressing. Just as it is depressing when a school says 'he ought to play an instrument, it's very good on the CV', without first saying that it might bring joy, open up new pathways of sensitivity and confer skill. The same goes for other activities: if you are good at games, adventurous, musical, or enjoy taking responsibility, great. Do it for its own sake, and mention it on your UCAS form in a brief, modest line at the end. Obviously if your hobby is relevant, like scuba or beach-combing for a marine biology degree, you could put that in. A politics don will be glad that you lobbied the council; an English tutor might be pleased to note that you won a short story competition. On the other hand, if you list too many starring parts in school plays, he or she might start to suspect that your hidden intention is to join drama soc and be permanently unavailable for seminars owing to your rehearsal schedule. Think on.

And eschew this *braggadocio* piling-up of ski-grades, day skipper certificates, expensive expedition-holidays funded by your parents, and the fact that you have so many enamel lapel-badges on your blazer that you walk with a permanent list to starboard. Pushy parents, butt out. University officials are, ex officio, not stupid. They know which ones you write. It doesn't make them warm to your offspring.

Several degrees below par

You might think that a curmudgeonly old nostalgic like me would be sulking at the news that more institutions are going to be able to call themselves universities. I did groan at the first wave of name changes, not least because I knew a bit about the distinctiveness and sense of purpose of the old polytechnics (I once had a boyfriend who taught in one and talked about it endlessly). It did not seem to me that calling more courses by the honorific of 'university degrees' would contribute to that sense of purpose.

Now the horse has bolted. Universities are so diverse in size, purpose, quality and reputation that the word means nothing special, and guarantees nothing much: any more than the word 'hotel' or 'shop' or indeed 'school' indicates quality or type. Summerhill is a school, Eton is a school, likewise city academies, beacons, sinks, middling comps. Parents know that they have to ask more searching questions than just 'is it a school?'. The same with universities: so we might as well spread the term around until every 18-year-old thoroughly understands that any old 'uni' is not as good as any other.

Those in the trade may scoff and say that kids know this already: not so. Not every family has a wide circle of academic friends and reads the trade press. There are bright, capable kids even now being lured into low-value courses at low-regarded institutions, simply because for reasons of mealy-mouthed political correctness it is not made clear to them that some universities will teach them more intensively, expect higher standards and work them harder. Some sign up – especially at clearing – without understanding the difference between modules and final exam systems. They choose by location, by rumour, by glossy brochure, by artfully-named course. Sometimes they choose something which turns out to be exiguous, underplanned, underfunded and unchallenging.

It is a maddening waste of talent, and a confidence trick played on people who get into debt to pay for it. One extremely bright girl I know had an offer from Durham, but short of information and understanding, turned it down in favour of a new university closer to home. Now she finds that the sum total of teaching offered to her is two short lectures a week, with no tutorial or seminar sessions, no opportunity to argue and discuss. The tasks she has been set are in her view rather below sixth-form level. Flatmates think she's eccentric to care: they are merely enjoying being students, drinking and lying in and using the time to grow up slowly. She is so frustrated that she is considering doing an Open University course at the same time as her 'degree', and then waving the qualification when she graduates, saying 'That's all of my time and energy that you didn't want'.

We need a merciless, impartial *Which*-style report on university courses, not just the Push and Virgin guides to halls of residence, clubs, beer prices and the rest. When they go to open days – a luxury not all can afford – they need a list of searching questions; and though they might not feel like it, in the middle of A-levels, one of those questions should be 'How hard will you work me?'

And there's another matter, which affects even the most highly-rated universities of all. Teaching undergraduates is no longer respected. One plain-spoken correspondent to a national paper recently remarked that it was actually 'despised'. The research and assessment excercise has encouraged academics to concentrate their efforts on churning out papers, often of dubious value, to cut short seminar time, avoid tutorial activity, and delegate teaching to the most junior PhD students they can get away with using. Yet anybody who had a good university experience will tell you that the core and beating heart of it was the stimulating, often alarming relationship with a tutor, whether in a class or a smaller group. These figures loom like colossi, and become internalised voices which challenge you all your life.

'Support your statement. Your analysis rests on what, precisely . . .?' Sometimes it is kindness that we remember; sometimes it is pure, rabbit-in-the-headlights terror of being exposed for idleness, inadequate reading or sloppy thinking. Both approaches have their merits. But one of the interesting things is how many of these legendary tutors did not publish much – or at all. My own Dorothy Bednarowska once remarked that 'my students, such as they are, must be my monument'. They did not feel compelled to climb the greasy pole of public acclaim. They just taught.

Someone must found Carrut – the Campaign to Respect Real University Teaching. Carrut Awards may turn up in the most unexpected places, unsung minor universities. Sixth-formers should know where they are, and what they teach. In a choosy consumer society this vital and expensive choice should not be made with a blindfold.

Hurrah for the Hildabeestes

I'm not sorry about the Hildabeestes. There may be some exasper-
ated sighing over the undergraduates at St Hilda's College, Oxford,
who campaigned in lilac to keep the college single-sex. There may
be something incongruous in preserving female modesty by parad-
ing in T-shirts saying 'Let men in? Bollocks!' It is undeniably true
that thousands of students live happily in mixed halls, and that
the long stand-off at St Hilda's has pushed it down the academic
table.

But yes, on balance, I'm glad the refuseniks won. There has to be
some sanctuary for those who want a single-sex environment to
study in. I would actually approve if there was a men-only college
too, as long as it wasn't the richest. If we value diversity, we should
value St Hilda's.

For women's colleges had a special atmosphere. There was something in the air at my own – St Anne's, in the early 1970s. It was a
compound of cosiness and idealism, earnestness and high spirits: a
whiff of Margaret Rutherford and Joyce Grenfell, with darker, more
powerful undernotes of Pankhurst and Iris Murdoch. It grew out of
the history of women's education, and the bitter struggles of the
late Victorian and Edwardian eras. Women suffered insult, belittle-
ment, and obstruction in their battle to win entry to the higher
ranks of academe. A bishop preached in a sermon that bluestocking
women would become infertile, because blood needed in the womb
was diverted to the brain. When the Oxford Home Students began
attending lectures (they were not allowed to take degrees) there was
one occasion, not I think entirely legendary, when a don arriving for
a lecture where only women had turned up sniffed, and said 'Oh,
nobody here' and left.

The women soldiered on, underfunded and resolute: determined
to be doctors, scholars, teachers. Many gave up the chance of family
life because they dared not take their eye off the ball: one of the
most touching things for a woman of my generation, in a public job,
is to get generous letters from old, old ladies from forty years before

saying 'It's good that girls like you can have children and a profession. Good luck to you. We couldn't.' One old Girtonian had refused a proposal of marriage because her fiancé felt that if she continued her studies as an ophthalmologist his well-connected family would cut him off, so disgraceful was a working wife.

So the women's colleges and their dons always had a sense of their proud and stroppy history. Years ago, Lady Margaret Hall put on a play about its early days and unearthed a wonderful anthem beginning 'Joy, joy, joy, joy, the battle is won!/ No more despised and oppressed/ We shall argue and learn with the best!' The women who founded those colleges made them learned, rigorous, and questing, but also comfortable and warm. When I think of a women's college, I see worn but clean carpets, soft chairs, pale gold scuffed bookshelves and kind canny women with sharp eyes for an unhappy girl. They didn't have endowments or rolling acres or cellars full of port or Shakespeare Folios to flog when the chapel roof fell in: but they had spirit and dedication.

There is another reason not to discard all that history forever. Even though most women's colleges have bowed to economics and let the clumpy boys in, there are still families – notably Asian – who might impede their daughter's higher education if the only way she could get it was by living hugger-mugger with young men. We may snort, but it happens. In the recent TV soapumentary about St Hilda's, the most impressive undergraduate was the Indian medical student. In one of the most telling sequences, elderly women reminisced about curfews and the rule that young men could not drink tea in a room with both a bed and a girl in it. This, one of them pointed out, was not because the dons were prudes but because, without such rules, parents of that chaperoned age would not have let their girls study. Such parents are fewer now, and mainly Asian; but there has to be somewhere for their daughters.

And in all eras, the denizens of women's colleges have loved to roam beyond the walls and prowl the wider university in search of men. So that's another tradition that would have gone west if the Hildabeestes had not been stubborn. I suspect the citadel will fall eventually, but a stay of execution is welcome. Floreat St Hilda's.

P.S. Three years later, the citadel did fall . . .

SEPTEMBER 28 2001

University rage

The University of St Andrews was turned over, good and proper, the other week in a film called *Wills' World*. I watched with interest, because my father and all his siblings went there in the days when 'poverty walked in a scarlet cloak' and you took your own oatmeal. My cousin still owns, and wore in his own time there, the red cloak that my aunt had in 1928. Both my children had this ancient university on their UCAS lists. I have been there lately and found it a friendly, scholarly, pleasant place.

However, there is another side to any institution, and Channel 4 homed in on the circumstance that St Andrews is also fashionable among the English rich-but-dim. Having been refused permission to make an insider documentary, they got students to make 'video diaries' and edited them with mischief bordering on spite. Not, I suspect, that it took much editing. Video cameras all too readily bring out the inner prat, and nothing is so prattish as a high-spirited, sociable, only medium-bright child of the privileged classes who still feels adored.

The film majored on Hoorays, airhead Sloanes and the clumpingly public-school Kate Kennedy men's club. It was an act of vengeance, for nothing in nature is more savage than a TV producer denied entry. So they gave us a braying nincompoop with neither chin nor forehead who didn't even manage to make it to his art history exam, but subsequently spent 'a very successful summer on the European poker circuit'. There was a clever, but somewhat emotionally retarded young Scot, who tittered coyly over his love life and preened through a production of *Grease*. There was a pair of teenage kittens who shrieked, flicked their hair and explained how stressful it was 'doing coffee' all day long. All bragged that they had essays due but not even started, and how it was 'like, impossible' to stay in and revise. In stark contrast there was a girl from Newcastle – broke, first-generation university with proud, proud parents – who worked her socks off. She was shown looking sadly out of the window at a procession of rich boys in fancy drag and saying 'This is the kind of s**t you have to put up with, all the time . . .'

There was footage inside a debate, but it was brief, which leads one to suspect that the debate got serious. Permission having not been granted, there was no view inside libraries, tutorials, lectures, seminars or chapel. The result was a travesty.

It dramatizes yet again the near-impossible problem of how an educational institution should respond to a request from a documentary film crew. Summerhill, the free-school in Suffolk, let the cameras in a few years ago and was grievously traduced. Rugby once got filmed during an experimental exchange with a northern comprehensive, and I have never been able to hear its name since without sniggering.

If you are a school, at least you have the power of exclusion, bolstered by the rules on consent for the filming of minors. But universities are in a cleft stick. If you let them in they can trash you in the editing. I could make a damning film about any university in the country just by pointing the cameras at a small cadre of exhibitionists, boozers, sex addicts and skivers, and intercutting them with tutorials and lectures to make ironic points. Here is your philosophy student, scribbling notes about the concept of Good, and whoops! here he is again, drunk as a skunk, falling over the turntables in a night club while lunging for the bosom of a sweet young thing last seen pedalling along in a scholars' gown. And here is a shot of a door marked Student Counselling – cut to some disaffected teenage grump complaining about how his tutor made him feel like a fool for not reading any of the set books.

And here is a student actually working, but the camera pans round to the filthy mugs and spilt baked-bean plates, artfully arranged by the producer, and the half-naked girl on the bed (who is, if truth be told, sleeping off an all-night session with an essay on Zola).

That's if you co-operate. If you don't . . . look at what happened to St Andrews. You can threaten to chuck your students out if they film Prince William, but you can't stop legal adults making video tits of themselves. Nope: basically, there's nothing you can do.

Unless you offer the film department students a prize for the best exposé of the daily lives of Channel 4 executives, with bits of their own programmes intercut ironically with dinner-party braying and quotes from their mission statement. That might be good. Perhaps Jeremy Isaacs, founding father of C4, might help out.

NOVEMBER 29 2002

Topping up teenage misery

The thought had to come from somewhere, but I'm damned if I expected it to come from Whitehall and Charles Clarke. I had been going around muttering on the subject, unheeded by family and colleagues who have learned to ignore worried monologues: 'Top-up fees . . . bad thing anyway . . . but even worse if you means test them on individual parental incomes! Are 18-year-olds legal adults, or not? And what about the Helenas? Where's the justice?'

We shall come back to Helena in a moment. But what was exercising me was the apparently universal assumption that if and when they bring in realistically huge tuition fees for university students, the adult children of poorer parents would be let off, and those whose parents could afford more would pay the lot. It happens at the moment: the £1,050 fee is thoroughly means tested, as is the student loan. And given the class-hatred militancy of Margaret Hodge's cry: 'Why should the dustman pay for the doctor?' it seemed likely that the Government would carry on the principle.

Never mind that there are numerous good reasons why the dustman might want to pay for the education of doctors. For one thing, his own kid might fancy being one. For another thing, he might have a wheelie bin dropped on him, and be glad of surgeons qualified to remove the handle from his cranium.

But, as I say, it seemed unlikely that Charles Clarke would challenge the received wisdom that the affluent middle-class parent – whether or not he or she took a degree – must pay like a sugar daddy till their darlings are 23, and that only the working-class 18-year-old is truly a separate individual. But suddenly, government veered away from this insulting idea, and admitted that if 18-year-olds can be shot dead in Iraq or defiantly marry wildly unsuitable divorcees with peroxide hair, they are adults. Just because fortune put them in a middle-income family, they shouldn't be at their parents' mercy about whether they go to university, and what they study.

Which brings us to Helena (not quite her real name). Back in the days of student grants, she was, like me, on the minimum level, designed to be made up to a reasonable living allowance by 'parental contribution'. My parents faithfully paid the prescribed sum, and that was fine. I tended to live on potatoes for the last couple of weeks of term owing to the bookshop bill, but it was manageable.

Helena's parents, on the other hand, wouldn't pay a bean. They were sulking because she wouldn't study law, like her great bully of a father. They had meant her for a lawyer, planned her chambers place, and all but bought the wig. Helena thought otherwise and read music (today she is a distinguished musicologist) so her father wouldn't pay her a bean. He thought she'd crumble and switch her course, but instead she worked hours in a pub kitchen. Meanwhile, her peers from homes with lower incomes got the full grant. They didn't think it fair, and neither did she.

Of course, most parents who can help to pay will do so. The habit of supporting your children dies hard. But some will not. Some fall out with their children, others use their economic clout to dictate a son or daughter's direction, others despise university as a waste of time. Top-up fees, based crudely on parental income, would lead to a lot of misery. Mind you, the alternative of gaily charging everyone £5,000 a year is pretty awful too. Mr Clarke thinks students spend their money on cars, but the poorest do no such thing: they just make themselves ill with anxiety at the scale of their debt.

We are told that the alternative of a 'graduate tax' is unworkable because it would take too long to come through. Well, yes: but only if it wasn't retrospective. The fair answer is staring us in the face. There are tens of thousands of middle-aged graduates who were financially featherbedded through university decades ago, and who are now high earners.

They – we – could quite easily be asked to pay a few hundred a year, to repay the gift that we were offered by fellow citizens. It would not be just another income tax hike, because it would be ring-fenced for universities and charged to those who went there and subsequently prospered. Most of the Cabinet and Shadow Cabinet would pay, but John Major would not. In our family I would pay, but not my husband, who went to work at 18. Two of my brothers would pay, but not the eldest, who has been paying tax ever since A-levels. It would be fair. It would bridge the time gap and prevent the top-up fee. It is the obvious solution. All it needs is a bit of bottle.

OCTOBER 27 2000

Virgin on the ridiculous

I see that the Government initiative on sexual mores (Virgin on the ridiculous, or whatever it's called) endorses sexual inequality. Girls are being urged to keep their hand on their ha'penny; boys are just being told to use condoms. It would appear that national policy has capitulated to the perception that girls and boys just don't think the same way when it comes to sex. Biologists insist that young men can't help it: they're programmed to reproduce. Ancient instinct urges them to spread their seed like demented budgies, and love need not come into it. Whereas girls – well, we're sweet creatures, and we want to bond.

From time immemorial, therefore, wise women have taken wooing with a large pinch of salt. Whether it's ballads under the window or whistles from the scaffolding, we learn early that they may not *necessarily* mean the bit about eternal devotion, but they do definitely mean the bit about coming upstairs. So you decide: if this one's just a bit of fun, is it worth the hassle? Or, if you have fallen devotedly in love, is it wise to presume that he whose hand is creeping up your knee feels the same?

Well, well: growing up is a mass of such decisions. But sometimes the issue gets inordinately clouded. I mean, look at academics. They complicate everything, as usual. A young girl knows where she is with ordinary blokes, all the way from 'Cor, what a pair!' to 'Have some more madeira, m'dear'. They try it on, and you either giggle along à la Barbara Windsor, or shriek 'Ooh, you are awful!' like Dick Emery and give them a powerful shove.

But academics can't just come right out with 'Gettemoff!', like the simple working man, or ply you with champagne like Sir Jasper. They can't even stumble through protestations of honest love like the boy next door. Instead, they try to make you share their weird conviction that the experience will be educational, and confuse you into bed with monologues on the Sartrean Motiveless Act. The most famous enunciation of this theory of educational sex concerned a chief inspector of schools, who has had the phrase 'educative and experiential' following him around like a misshapen dog ever since. But the notion itself is pure redbrick, circa 1970, pure Bradbury.

I thought it might have died out by now. I thought that the duffle-coated lecherous young don might have become extinct in the age of assertive women with briefcases and thongs. But he still has a following. I know this from an extraordinary article in the *Sunday Times* by Howard Jacobson.

Apropos an American woman academic who allegedly offers sex to male students 'as a way of interesting them in the syllabus', he recalled his 1960s' university teaching career with the words: 'Sex with students? Not only a private satisfaction but damn near an educational necessity . . . most philosophers did it, a goodly number of geographers, not quite so many historians, but in English literature we all did it.'

Some subjects, he explained, 'encouraged, invited, maybe even demanded a greater intimacy . . . There's a sort of propriety about sleeping with your lecturer. It's something I believe you should go through as part of the education process.' He admits the pain caused, and that not everyone can end up as the professor's wife. He acknowledges the difficulty of marking an exam paper when you have been examining its writer the week before.

But, all the same, looking at the more sober profile of modern universities, Jacobson insists that the teaching is worse since lecturers learned to stay zipped up. 'We've gone cold, that's what's happened. We are no longer expectant. We were better teachers and better students when we slept with one another.'

Poor old sod, I thought. How they do like to live in their golden dreams. Just as well things have changed. But then I showed the article to a couple of current girl undergraduates and they set me right. 'Yup, you still get that line', said one. 'Licence my roving hands, because how can a virgin understand Donne?'

Her friend named two familiar culprits and said 'Jeez, you'd think they were offering you some sort of scholarship, not a shag . . . one told me that I would never develop as a writer without "connecting" with fine minds. But when it comes down to it, he's just a guy on the pull who wants to do all the talking himself and not spend any money.'

Lessons in failure

Last week, on a sweltering day, I led an expedition round the M25 with a carload of 17-year-olds.

I had been elected chauffeur for an Oxford college open-day, with strict instructions to make myself scarce as soon as we got there, and when it was over to meet them in the pub and not – repeat not – hover maternally round the Lodge.

These open days are becoming a fine art for many universities, from old stone to redbrick to concrete. Some, I am told, have the tone of pure sales pitches: choose us, we're cool. A few don't even demand booking, but desperately flypost the local town.

At the other end of the scale, more restrained institutions only let those in who already hold provisional offers ('What's that all about?' demanded my car-load. 'How'd you know whether to waste a UCAS line on them if they won't let you in to nose around?')

This one, though, was first-book, first-served, so none of them had offers. And the first thing they were told, with cheerful brio, was that most of them never would have.

There they were, the pride of their various schools, glistening with starred-As, bearing heavy hopes from teacher and parent. But the first thing they were offered was reality. The admissions tutor greeted them: 'Hello. Many of you sitting here have never failed at anything. But take it from me, you might well fail at this. Have a go, only don't be disheartened if you fail.'

They really liked that. A buzz of general approval filled the car as they told me about it. Later on, I discussed it with a 25-year-old doctor, who sagely said: 'Yup. They do well to warn them. That's the trouble with being a high achiever. It's all the worse when you trip up for the first time.'

Then he told me a cautionary tale. He had been head boy of his school and captain of chess and cricket. He had 12 A-star GCSEs, four A-levels, a place on Operation Raleigh and a scholarship from his first choice of medical school. He also played the cello for a spell in a youth orchestra, and the best parts in school plays. Then he started driving lessons in the September of his gap year, and failed the theory test twice and the practical test four times in succession. This everyday skill, mastered by every Neanderthal oik in a battered white van, every fluffy white-haired lady in the supermarket car park, appeared to be beyond him. He fell into bitter depression.

'Devastating. I couldn't believe it was happening. I nearly decided not to go to university because I never wanted to be tested again, on anything. I had no idea failing hurt so much. Why did nobody ever train me in how to fail? Even at my primary school I always won the egg and spoon.'

Well, there's a new curriculum challenge for you. A whole new key skill. Despite the strenuous efforts of the Department for Education and Skills to set so many tests that even seven-year-olds get anxious, there must be children out there who are so insouciantly able that they sail through their education without ever learning how to fail and then stick their world back together.

Clearly, the staff at the young doctor's school should have put their heads together and ensured that there was something at which this monster of perfection would be sure to make a complete fool of himself while others cantered past. The more baroque activities a school has, therefore, the better. I speak as the parent of a daughter who had to leave the school guard troop because she kept holding her gun upside down at the salute, and whose dramatic and academic successes are pleasingly offset by her fame at having let through 28 goals in one netball match, and failed to get into the National Youth Theatre after an audition in which she began giggling during her Sylvia Plath recitation.

So while more normal pupils are guided towards a sense of achievement, educators of the bright should be devising activities and tests to ensure that everyone has a fair chance of falling flat on their face. Set the gung-ho athletic boys to knitting, and the glitteringly academic girls to one of those hideous technology projects which end up in a puddle of solder and plastic on the floor.

Or get the cleverest 10 per cent to do one extra GCSE subject, at which they have a more than sporting chance of ignominy. Failure: it's what life's all about.

The wilder shores

Scooter panic

I see it's scooters this time. The baleful eyes that peer through staffroom blinds spot a new burden to blight the new year.

Following in the long and honourable tradition of conkers, Gameboys, skateboards, snakeboards, yo-yos, inline skates and text-message phones, those dear little aluminium mini-scooters are the new term's craze. The thin high rapid rattle of bearings is everywhere.

Indeed, we have already reached the stage of the ritual dance in which reporters speak wildly of 'speeds up to 30 mph' and find a worried headteacher to quote.

A primary head from Birkenhead frets 'We've got 500 children here. I don't know what we would do if they all turned up on scooters. We haven't got the storage. I know they fold up, but I don't think our coat hooks could take the strain'.

The finger of blame is being pointed at such yuppie miniscooter icons as Robbie Williams, Kylie Minogue and Jude Law; to whom I would add Angela Rippon (who turned up for her first day at her new ballet job riding one with all the frosty assurance of a duchess on a skateboard) and Pierre-Yves Gerbeau, who whizzes round-the Millennium Dome on teeny wheels, grinning.

The next stages of the dance are expected any minute, as the media rev up. Some 'leading heads' in search of a bit of publicity will ban the wee scooters, possibly using the word 'inappropriate'.

An upmarket tabloid will publish an attack on parents who are willing to spent £69 on a scooter when they could have used it for extra maths coaching. A health campaigning body in need of an image boost will announce portentously that the asymmetric kicking motion required for a scooter could cause permanent spinal imbalance. A junior minister will be wheeled out looking wholly ridiculous to underline government advice that scooterists should at all times wear helmets, face-guards, neck-braces, padded gloves, elbow, shin and knee pads and a corrective truss.

Teen magazines will be urged to publish a government safety-code, explaining that the safest enjoyment of your scooter may be

found by using it as a plant stand, or folding it up and hanging it on a coat hook permanently (provided the coat hook meets BS 900345), to prevent tragic incidents of scooters falling on to the headmaster's toe as he prowls past, causing him to take a year's gardening leave.

A canny scooter manufacturer will fuel the craze by offering free 'safety training' to the larger and more affluent-looking primary schools (this happened with the new wave of yo-yos, when manufacturers sent out free ones with 'safety' videos to teachers, so that in demonstrating how not to knock your teeth out with an up-and-over they actually conducted sales demonstrations in assembly).

School scootermania will grow and grow. Chris Woodhead will speak out, followed by Nick Tate on whether Winchester will permit scooters in the cloister, and a further clutter of posh heads murmuring, 'Well, of course, the paving at Gruntfuttocks goes back to 1482, hna hna hna, so I doubt very much that these scooters will be popular with our boys and girls – because, of course, we do have girls now in the sixth form'.

Meanwhile, the leading-edge children will have quietly got fed up with their scooters and traded them in with less hip friends to fund the next craze.

Why do we let them wind us up so very easily? Once, crazes large and small swept naturally through child communities – dressed-up Boglins, trick bicycles, conkers, 'electrobugs' made by cutting up your rubber and drawing tiny faces on the bits – and teachers clamped down on the worst excesses with confiscations, and parents groaned humorously at the school gate and the press paid no attention.

Each mania rose, and spread, and ebbed away, quietly leaving only a few real enthusiasts doing half-pipes or baking sixers in the oven. Somehow, between safety hysteria, consumer guilt and sense-of-humour failure, we have lost the knack of shrugging our shoulders and saying 'Kids!'.

But the good thing about the Dance of Dismay is that by the time we have worked ourself up to the crescendo ('Minister lashes out at "senseless and wicked" scooter cult as tragic little Liam faces lifetime denture hell') the kids will have moved on, and will all be riding unicycles or smuggling in water-bombs. They know how to have a good time.

APRIL 7 2000

Justice shines on Summerhill

O frabjous day! Summerhill defeated the Department for Education and Employment in two rounds and a submission, a famous victory.

Those of us who steamed with rage over the Office for Standards in Education's persecution of AS Neill's tiny, eccentric and radical 'free school', punched the air. Our glee intensified with each revelation of what actually happened at the tribunal.

The forces of conformity and control caved in, that's what happened. The first wavering came on the Monday, when the judge grew impatient with the first point of complaint: that the tiny school, regarding itself as a home, does not separately label male and female toilets. After some faffing by m'learned friends, the court annulled that one. By the end of Wednesday the other complaints followed it into oblivion; not, as the Government press release claims, 'withdrawn', but annulled. The overwhelming evidence of independent inspectors under Professor Ian Stronach vindicated both the school's philosophy and – to the surprise of many – its results. The court believed them. The DFEE had no case.

Whereon Summerhill said that, being a democratic community, it needed to debate its response to the climb-down. So the judge let them take over the court-room, and a 15-year-old girl sat in the chair and took the vote as if it was one of their usual polls on bedtime rules or what age kids are allowed to cycle to the Leiston sweetshop. Yee-ha!

The spin put out by the DFEE tried to imply some kind of moral victory: it hopes we will think that thanks to Auntie OFSTED, the school undertook to improve teaching standards and 'encourage' children to go to its optional classes. Summerhill did no such thing. It merely undertook to continue upholding the principles of AS Neill, as before. It is OFSTED which must change its ways: after nine inspections in a decade it must hold off for five years. Even so, the principal Zoe Readhead insisted on the right to have the next inspectors watched full-time by her lawyers, so little does she trust them to tell the truth. Having seen the latest OFSTED, she has a point. It was a masterpiece of smear.

What a victory, but what a waste of taxpayers' money. While maintained schools with far worse outcomes went short, you and I have paid hordes of inspectors to harass one very small independent which had the full support of its parents and children.

A very important and generally overlooked point was won at this tribunal. The DFEE complaint spoke of the school not reaching 'national expectations' and Geoffrey Robertson QC rightly picked up that phrase. How *dare* the state presume to dictate the detail and pace of every child's mental unfolding? Are we products, to be quality-controlled as units of state wealth? In court that concept was quashed. A landmark sentence acknowledged that the school's duty was not to the nation but the child.

Summerhill is extreme, but it remains a powerfully interesting experiment. Summerhill pupils generally seem happy and confident, and are actually rather keener on rules than most children because they make them. They may not all be high-flyers but a reasonable proportion go on to higher education: they are not blocked or deprived.

Yet the OFSTED report and the DFEE treatment breathed petulant hostility: a sinister determination to see off these cheeky rebels for no reason other than their different philosophy of what it is to be human. So they fussed about lavatories and swearing and 'idleness', and forced this ludicrous tribunal. Which they lost. But even so, if Summerhill were not so famous it would now be ruined. Despite a small guilt-offering from the Ministry, the school now has a legal bill of over £100,000. Is that justice? All that was ever required was a lighter touch, a humble attempt to understand a divergent educational philosophy, and a bit of respect for the judgment of parents. Too much to ask?

But never mind; right has been done. Even if the senatorial white-haired figures down at the Headmasters' Conference shudder at its name, they should be damn grateful to Summerhill. From Gordonstoun to Hill House, from convent cloisters to Quaker foundations, every independent school in the country with the slightest pretension to individuality is a bit safer today.

JUNE 21 2002

Our schools are no refuge

Sometimes the unthinkable just has to be thunk. Sometimes the unsayable must be blurted. Deep breath, close eyes, clench fists – here we go: 'What's so damn special about "mainstream" education anyway?'

I am baffled by the outcry over the Home Secretary's plan that asylum-seekers' children should have separate schools during their six or eight months in those god-forsaken rural bunkers he favours. The asylum centres themselves are massively controversial, but leave that aside for a moment. What puzzles me is why such diverse interests as Save the Children and MPs are outraged at the idea that the school-age newcomers, while their parents' cases are heard, should be 'denied' the right to be hurled into mainstream British state schools.

Why, exactly, do we assume that this is the best thing for them? Say you're 10 years old – how kind is it, really, to chuck you into an overpressed primary school struggling with the national curriculum, facing cuts in its classroom assistant budget, and neurotically anxious to force enough of the native population through its national tests to keep off special measures?

Or suppose you're 15, speak only a few words of English, and have lately been chased by gunmen, watched relatives die of malnutrition, and been ripped off by people-smugglers who made you spend five days bent double in a stinking container. Precisely how useful a gesture is it to pitchfork you into a busy first-year GCSE group, in the interests of some vague political correctness about 'inclusion' and 'socialisation'?

Of course, in a perfect world every school would be oozing with resources, abundant personal help and special-needs teaching and infinitely elastic space. But they aren't. Face it. So, failing that, where is the problem in letting Mr Blunkett pour Home Office resources into education (he'll have to, won't he? These asylum-seeker academies won't grow on trees). Why shouldn't we offer refugee children safe, sheltered schooling for a couple of terms in an

environment specifically designed to help them to learn English fast and have their existing educational level assessed?

It might actually be better. Why can't the objectors wait until these asylum-schools are created, and then make a fuss if they are not good enough? What is this blind, dotty faith some people have that every child, of every background and ability, is always best served in the maelstrom of a big comp? Even some British children find it all too much, and have to be removed by kind parents into small independent school classes or home education. Why assume that asylum-seeking children would prefer it to something designed for kids in their position – particularly as, I stress again, we are told it it will last hardly more than half a year?

I feel rather bristlingly aggressive about this, because several times in my own childhood, as a travelling diplo-brat offspring of HM Consul, I was thrown into new schools in new countries with new languages. I had a steady home, plenty of help, a secure passport and identity, and parents who understood the system. It was still tough.

There was the convent in Bangkok where I was the only pink-skinned child, and all the Thai girls pinched me as if I were a lucky white elephant. I had to sit on my own with a nice nun called

Mother Mary and do my letters before I could join in with the group, even for PE; where will these individual Mother Maries be found in the average staffroom, huh? Then there was France, where the alien culture dumped itself on me in great bewildering dollops of weirdness – white tunics for *Danse Eurythmique*, full-length pinafores, curtseying to statues, beer at lunchtime, marks for deportment and hostile glares from my classmates whenever the subject of Jeanne d'Arc and the *maudits Anglais* came up.

Again, I had private tuition two hours a day to teach me French, and it took all of six months before I could join in classes and trade insults with Veronique at the next desk. The 'socialisation' of which the protesters piously speak was enhanced by a few months of special treatment. Even from a far more secure position, I know exactly what it is like to go into a school and be different, foreign, weird, and out of step.

Life is complicated and frightening when you have to decode all the local jungle-drums while trying to absorb some hist, geog, maths and the rest. And even though some schools are brilliant at helping refugee children, I doubt they all are.

These poor brats might well be far better served by six months of special attention and consideration, out of the swing of the sea. If they're not well served, then we must holler. But until then, the hollering sounds to me like PC posturing and political opportunism.

There you are, I said it. If anyone asks, I'm abroad.

Put them in overalls

I found myself in a car the other day with a new acquaintance who, like me, served time in a French convent school some 40 years ago. This happy and rare coincidence always provides a great opportunity for reminiscent whooping and giggling about *Reverende Mère*, white gloves, *dictée*, learning *Fables de la Fontaine* by heart, and doing *danse eurythmique* in white tunics.

Fellow inmates are the only people who will ever believe that they actually used to serve beer to us at lunch, at nine years old: a litre bottle between a table of eight. And sometimes I even meet someone who, like me, used to get nul points on her report for '*maintien*' or deportment: '*Elisabeth se tient très mal*' wrote the Maitresse.

But on this occasion, as it happened, our conversation turned to the subject of the *tablier*, or overall, worn by all good little French bourgeoise schoolgirls – and smaller boys – at that period, and which endures in some Continental schools even today. It was universal. Until you were in the senior school you wore a full *tablier*, a sort of chic, good-quality cotton housecoat, in our case sky-blue with smart navy-and-white pinstripes at collar and cuffs.

It was buttoned and belted, covered everything from neck to knee, and was not at all uncomfortable. even in high summer, as you could just wear your blouse and skirt beneath it. The *tablier* was the front line of defence against ink, pen, paint, food spills, crumbs from our mid-morning baguette, dribble from the school rabbits, and muddy playground games like *ballon prisonnier*, with which we blew off steam in the walled garden at break.

We only took them off for gym (or eurythmic dancing) and for formal occasions like chapel, when we donned white gloves and veils to add to the sense of ceremony. Your mother had to wash your *tablier* once or twice a week, depending on your habits, but that was nowhere near as much of a nuisance as washing or cleaning school skirts and sweaters. When you became senior in the school, upward of 14 years old, it was replaced by a dark blue, thick cotton pinafore, a simple sleeveless over-the-head job with ties at the side.

Remembering these details, we wondered why on earth school-children don't wear *tabliers* here and now. Think of all the problems it would solve at a stroke. Schools which don't have uniform would have their pupils vaguely homogenised in school hours, with minimal opportunity for designer one-upmanship and bragging. Schools with uniform would find the children less tiresomely insistent on 'customising' it by turning up the skirt, leaving the shirt hanging out etc, because there would be no point once you got your working overall on.

Catwalk behaviour would move back to where it belongs, after school hours. Parents would be spared the awful task of maintaining school sweaters – which could therefore be made of less offensively cheap wool – and nobody would have to contemplate the depressingly shiny seats of budget skirts and trousers polished on hard seats all day.

The growing problem of pubescent girls decked out in bare-bellied slutwear with visible thongs would be neatly knocked on the head, because the *tablier* would cover all pierced navels and bum cleavages with workmanlike, practical sky-blue cotton.

And all this might be resisted rather less than you might think. The overall, after all, would be seen not as a horrid imposition of schooly values (like the ghastly grey A-line skirt) but as something practical, a reminder that the school day is long and varied and tough and grimy. The *tablier* provided, as I remember it, a sense that it was OK to work a bit messily or scruff around in the playground, because that was the way it was when you were a schoolchild.

Rather than limiting children, it freed them. It was, in fact, the opposite of a ridiculous note we once got back from the worst school we ever used, which said primly: 'We expect our pupils to dress and present themselves at all times as if for interview.'

Damn ridiculous: what, in that case, is left for interview? And why should a busy Year 9, scuttling from lab to drama with an armful of books, be expected to worry all the time about interview-standard neatness?

No, it is decided. When I am in charge of things, there will be *tabliers* issued at all schools. It might be nice if the teachers wore them too, in a contrasting colour. Heads and deputies, perhaps, could have epaulets. Or special belts. Oh go on, think about it. I'll let you off the white gloves, for now.

Go to school or your mum gets it

I am as banjaxed as anybody about the case of Patricia Amos, in jail for not getting her daughters to school much over the past two years. Estelle Morris reckons it 'sends a message', but the trouble is it sends so many that it is hard to disentangle them.

The first, most obvious, message is from the Education Secretary to the nation's parents. It goes: 'Come on then, if you think you're hard enough, make my day! Next thing, we're going to get you in the arrow-pattern pyjamas and matching ball and chain for taking your kids to Torremolinos in termtime, see if we don't! And shut up about the cost – we know it costs more to put a woman in prison than it would to arrange a home tutor for troubled girls, but this is *pour encourager les autres*, OK?'.

But there are other potential messages. One is from the magistrates to the Government: 'You passed this rubbish law two years ago, and it's time someone demonstrated the result. Single mother, sad sack, chuck her in jail, what good will it do? On the other hand, we're not that mean, so we made sure there's a 25-year-old sister to look after these kids. Suppose there hadn't been, huh?'

Then there is the gender-specific message to single mothers: 'Listen up! So these girls' fathers are out of the frame. That may well have a bearing, but we cannot be bothered to track the idle bastards down and make them share the blame, so we will lock up their only half-decent parent instead. Your fault for being so soft, woman. Should have put them into care years ago, then they could have bunked off school as much as they liked, or gone on the streets like all those other girls we pretend to look after.'

The messages from the family are equally odd. The big sister says: 'She used to get them dressed and send them – it isn't her fault that they came home again.' The girls say that their mother had been low since their Nan died and they did not want to leave her. Which is quite sweet, I suppose, but we are talking about two years. Which sends a message that this community is not very good at supporting families which have fallen into drifting depression.

But the really unnerving message, which I devoutly hope has got through to Estelle Morris, is that these girls plainly saw no point whatsoever in being at school. Kids, however kind to Mum, tend to do what they want. School, for the Amos girls, was not it. School was somewhere they were told to go. It was not, in their view, a dynamic centre of life, a community of friends and mentors, a stepping-stone to achievement, freedom and security. It was irrelevant.

Why was it irrelevant? Because their mother had five children by three men, the earliest in her teens, and the elder sister is also a youngish mother? Were the girls siding with Professor Tooley (of 'the mis-education of women' theory) by preparing for nothing but motherhood? Or were they just bored? It can happen even in a good school. So I browsed the school in question's OFSTED report to look for clues.

It has a dynamic head, is improving and oversubscribed, but inspectors found key stage 3 teaching faulty, communication with parents poor, and punctuality and attendance not impressive. But on the whole it is no different from hundreds of others. Not anarchic, not a sink, not failing.

But it did not grab these girls. They only went because they had to. Exams cannot have mattered in their scheme of things, nor what lies beyond. No play, no project, no concert, no outing, no promised fulfilment of a common end drew them through the school gates. They got dressed, set out, then thought 'what the hell!' and headed back home to Mum.

Their sister says they have grown up during these events and will go to school now: but still the message niggles. They may go physically, but in spirit? How can they be made to *want* to go?

I sense cynical jeers from staffrooms and authoritarian barks from the education right-wing. But still I worry. The School Exclusion Unit produced a report called *Truancy and School Exclusion* in 1998, and proposed 'tackling disaffection' with no imaginative approaches to the curriculum. I do not see much evidence of that.

And I do not see, either, much joy in a system where great swathes of the pupils are only in class because their parents will be locked up if they are not. There is a message in there. Someone decode it.

Blame the parents

I should have learned my lesson from the spectacle of the Prince of Wales ranting on last week about how we have all lost our souls while 'brutally vandalising' the moral and aesthetic heritage through teaching the wrong stuff in classrooms, and succumbing to a 'profound malaise, a deep disease, a disintegration . . .'

I should have said to myself: 'Let that be a warning to all recent over-fifties! Let your guard slip and you turn into a cantankerous old geezer grumbling about the modern world!'

I should have taken out a subscription to Curmudgeons Anonymous, so that whenever I am tempted to rant on about the mores of the age, I could phone a counsellor and be reminded of the many advances clocked up by the wicked western world since the good old days when single mothers were locked up in loonybins as 'moral imbeciles' and children currently afflicted only by key stage 2 were forced up chimneys by having fires lit under them.

I should have sworn an oath, as the Prince never does, to button my lip and refrain from mad, ranting generalisations. But alas, I haven't. Help! I feel it coming on, the potion is taking effect, I am turning into Prince Charles, quick, strap me down.

The fault lies entirely with the National Association of Head Teachers for assisting the education media with a story about a situation so horrific, so dumb, so demoralised that the only correct response is to call down fire and brimstone.

It is not even a story of physical abuse of children, but merely the almost casual revelation that schools are finding an increasing problem over the re-naming of pupils. The kids have their surnames changed every time their mother shacks up with a new man. Sue Sayles of NAHT reports with admirable calm that it is 'quite a common issue' and that it is not unusual for a child's surname to be changed two or three times in as many years. One primary teacher, with that endearing primary-teacher focus on tidiness, laments that 'there's no more room in the name box on their file because there have been so many crossing-out'.

The children, they report, get 'weepy' and confused and occasionally aggressive, and sometimes can't remember their current
name when asked. Boys in particular may get deeply upset at having
their father's identity forcibly removed. And so forth.

The schools, having neither the time nor the powers, can do very
little when informed by some self-righteous hag that Johnny is no
longer called after that treacherous bastard whose name she gave
him to expunge the one bestowed by his natural father, and that he
must from henceforth be called Smith, after the guy she met at salsa
night. So they just scratch out the last surname and Johnny Smith,
né Jones, formerly Wilkinson, has to get used to it.

It is not fashionable to condemn the lifestyles of others, but in this
case – knowing how much names mean to children, and how deep
identity goes when you are small – I think I must make an exception
and say that women who impose multiple surname-changes on their
children to suit their current romantic status are stupid, selfish cows
with less imagination and empathy than the average puddle of
slurry. But before I am tempted to ramble off into hellfire denunci-
ations, just note the other little moral of this story.

Who told us about this? Teachers. Who is at the sharp end, facing
up to the daily effects of social disintegration, self-indulgence and
the uncoolness of fidelity, self-sacrifice and family responsibility?

Teachers are. Who has to bandage the wounds of a decadent,
thoughtless, stupid society at its most vulnerable edges? Teachers.
Who is the last best hope of these lost children whose fathers drift
away to the next shag, and whose mothers have been pap-fed on
dreams of Brad Pitt and rubbish about self-reinvention?

Teachers, teachers, teachers are those children's hope. They are
supposed to provide not only learning but the stability, the courtesy,
the attention, the encouragement and the confidence without which
nobody can function. Especially when they are only seven.

Sometimes, teachers do precisely that. They save souls.

Sometimes, however, they try and fail, and are depressed and
defeated, and run for it. But it was not teachers who caused the
problem in the first place. School is not a magic pill for every social
ill. At the very best, it is a Band-Aid. Sometimes, the emotional
landscape out there must feel like the worst end of the casualty-tent
in the Crimea.

SEPTEMBER 9 2005

Empty nest? Grab a bottle!

Another new term: schools back, universities revving up, dons rolling up their sleeves and spitting on their hands or whatever they do.

So in media-land, features editors are looking glumly round the office for suckers to write the two hardy perennial articles of the season. These are How to Survive Freshers' Week, and Coping with Empty Nest Syndrome. Work experience kids are dispatched to the photo library to dig out a picture of a girl in a strappy top shrieking, and a Depressed Mum with a gin bottle.

Every year, the advice to both sides recurs, putting terror into the hearts of families. The Freshers'. Week article is my least favourite, usually being written by nostalgic twentysomethings deep in debt and short of a girlfriend, who need to reassure themselves that they were really wild, man, when they were 18. It paints a picture of kids, off the leash and far from home, plunging into non-stop compulsory debauchery, drunken corridor parties and random sex. 'Don't think of staying in! You'll meet tonz of new friends,' cries the writer, in one recent case adding the instruction: 'Grab a bottle and a handful of condoms and join the fun!'

The result of this terrifying instruction, in the case of one girl I heard of, was a weepy phone call home saying 'I don't like noisy parties, I hate discos, but if I don't go on this coach to the freshers' club night rave I'll never, never have any friends for three years!' Her parents spent ages persuading her that lurking in rooms all around her were kindred spirits, anxious for a quiet cup of coffee and a chat about home and hamster, or even (good grief!) about their course of study.

Others believe the hype, plunge into freshers' week with gusto, and end up making such tits of themselves that they spend the rest of their first term in embarrassed purdah, broke.

The second seasonal article, Coping with Empty Nest Syndrome, is designed to demoralise parents already reduced to jitters because the stuff on Freshers Week makes the start of higher education sound like the last 20 minutes of the Roman Empire, only without a separate vomitorium. Empty Nest symptoms, we are given to understand, chiefly afflict mothers and involve weepiness, marital discord, a sense of futility and a constant snivelling over the lost darling's bed, teddy, and discarded trainers.

Without our teenagers to prop us up, it explains, we will soon take to drinking sherry at 9am and bursting into tears of grief for vanished childhoods every time we pass a branch of Toys R Us. The cure apparently is to take up a new hobby or evening class, and spend 'quality time' with our husbands, who may seem disgustingly cheerful at having the house tidy but who are actually suffering as much as we are, so there.

Some of this is true – Jack Rosenthal wrote a wonderful TV play called *Eskimo Day*, about parents coming to terms with this phase, because someone once told him that when eskimos feel they are no longer of use to their offspring they go off and die in the snow, on purpose. However, just like Freshers' Week it is monstrously overplayed for the sake of dramatic headlines.

Perhaps this year we need a fresh, creative approach to telling people how to survive the autumn trauma of either being at university or having a child who is. Resisting the impulse to shout: 'Oh, pull yourself together – you're not clinging to a roof in the Mississippi Delta!,' I have a suggestion. Let the next article cunningly amalgamate the two sets of dire predictions, and start a trend for Freshers' Weeks For Parents. 'Yippee!', we begin. 'They've gone! We're free!' No need to make cups of cocoa and give them priority on the computer because they've got A levels!

No more being tied to the house clearing up their mess and setting a good example and making nutritious balanced meals! Party time has come, and this is Fresh-empty-nesters' week!

Neighbourhoods must organise raves, karaoke nites, pub-crawls, piss-ups and risqué new clubs and societies for liberated parents to join during termtime: Strip Poker Soc, Extreme Golf, Women's Karaoke. Go party! Grab a bottle and a handful of condoms (and, obviously, your reading glasses in case you get breathless dancing).

Make tonz of new friends! Forget to ring the kids just as they forget to ring you! Fill that empty nest with empty bottles and pizza boxes! Well, it would make a change.